For David Baksh

"If the production of thought, the dissemination of thought, the implementation of thought and the resulting wealth created by that thought, is all controlled by a tiny rich elite, then we no longer live in a democracy but in *The Prostitute State*"

Donnachadh McCarthy is an author, broadcaster and journalist on environmental issues. He was Deputy Chair of the Liberal Democrats during the two years leading up to the Iraq War and an elected member of its Federal Executive for seven years. He served as a councillor in Southwark, was a Parliamentary candidate in Peckham and was elected to be a London European Parliamentary candidate. He was twice short-listed to be the party's London Mayoral Candidate.

His home in Camberwell was London's first carbon negative house. He is currently not a member of any political party.

He was the on-screen eco-auditor for the hit BBC 2 TV series, "It's Not Easy Being Green", ITV's "How Green is Your House" and Sky's "Green Britain Week". He has appeared frequently on national TV and radio, including The Today Programme, Newsnight, BBC Breakfast News, Radio 5 Live, BBC World Service, CNN, Sky News, London Tonight etc

He is the author of two previous books "Easy Eco-auditing" and "Saving the Planet without Costing the Earth".

First edition published in the UK in October 2014 by:

3 Acorns Publications, 2 Coleman Road, Camberwell, London, England, SE5 7TG.

Further copies can be bought online from www.theprostitutestate.co.uk

Printed in the UK by Footprint Workers Co-op, 16 Back Sholebroke Avenue, Leeds, West Yorkshire, LS7 3HB UK.

Printed on Evercopy Paper made from 100% post-consumer waste paper, using a risograph process requiring no heat, water or solvents.

Cover printed on Cyclus Paper, also made from 100% post-consumer waste.

A catalogue record for this book is available from the British Library.
ISBN 978-0-9930428-0-5
An ebook version of this book is available from www.lulu.com
eISBN 978-1-291-99783-5

The Prostitute State

How Britain's Democracy Has Been Bought

By

Donnachadh McCarthy FRSA

3 Acorns Publications

Contents

Acknowledgements & Disclaimer

As with any book, it cannot be written without the generous help and support of numerous people. But firstly I would like to thank my friend David Baksh, who has been a rock of solid emotional support right through the entire project. I can never thank you enough David!

Thanks also to my long departed mother Noreen McCarthy, who helped fund the project in the most extraordinary way. Thanks Mammy – that was truly amazing! Thanks are also due to Joan Millbank, Ruth Bright, Simone Plaut, Pauline Davis, Linda Jack, Tristram Wyatt, Tamsin Cave, Satish Kumar, Oliver Tickell, Maddy Harland, Rubbish Rider, Jason and Ingo Tantra, London Faerie, Phil Chandler, Unlock Democracy, James Graham, Corporate Europe Observatory, The Alliance for Lobbying Transparency and Ethics Regulation (*ALTER-EU*), Clare Thomas and John Merivale.

I need to also thank all those who kindly helped crowd-source the publication of the book by pre-buying it and to all those who gave their support in one way or another over the last two years, including all my Facebook community.

Thanks also to Gareth Epps, Fiona Hall, Jenny Bentall, Ruwan Uduwerage-Perera and Lord Tony Greaves for agreeing to be interviewed for the book. Especial thanks are due to Matthew Hendrickson for his friendly proof-reading and website creation and to Greg Branson for generously providing free editing and helpful comments on the final manuscript. Thanks also to Suresh Ariaratnam for commenting on the original book proposal and to Júri Gabriel for that original crucial suggestion on the day that the idea for this book was born.

Thanks to Spinwatch for permission to use their bio-technology background on David Sainsbury, to Craig Murray for permission to use the extract from his article on Margaret Thatcher and to Simon Sweeney, University of York, for permission to reproduce his letter to The Guardian on EU achievements.

For clarity, the prostitution in the book title refers to the dictionary definition of selling services in a corrupt or unworthy manner for personal or financial gain and not to the alternative definition of honestly paying for sexual activities. I fully respect the human rights of adult consenting sex-workers (of all genders) and abhor any discrimination against them. Indeed, it is my belief that many of them provide a valuable and healing service to their clients.

Disclaimer: Where the text refers to corruption or tax avoidance, unless expressly stated, it is not alleging illegal behaviour in any way, by any named individual or organisation but rather means, corruption, in the sense that it is my belief that the behaviour is immoral for someone holding a position of authority.

Cover Credits: I would like to thank Robert Taylor (photography), The Flying Dutchman and Antonio Mori (venue and props), Spela Strukelj (graphics) and Goddess Cleo (model).

Extra copies of this book can be ordered online at: www.theprostitutestate.co.uk

Chapter 1

My Introduction to the Prostitute State

"Before the Federal Executive discusses Donnachadh's motion, I must inform you that if the executive passes this motion, I will tender my resignation as leader."

These were the first words I heard Paddy Ashdown utter, the then leader of the Liberal Democrats, at my first meeting of the party's Federal Executive after being elected to it in September 1996. I had proposed that Lord Holme, Ashdown's general-election campaign director, could not simultaneously be external-affairs director for Rio Tinto Zinc. Little did I realise that I had come face to face with the political lobbying cartel that I was to battle for the following seven years at the top of the party.

They were to teach me how the British political system invisibly works on behalf of rich vested interests rather than on behalf of the country at large. Instead of a democratic state we have *The Prostitute State*. It permeates nearly every aspect of our public life and is responsible for two of the most negative global developments of the last century.

The first is the climate and environmental crisis which is creating an unfolding global genocide and ecocide on an unprecedented scale.

The second is the destruction of social justice caused by a vast transfer of wealth and power to a small group of global corporate elites and billionaires, who have usurped our democracies.

Let's first however explain how this dramatic confrontation with Paddy Ashdown came about. Bizarrely, it started following an accident at the Royal Opera House in 1992, where I worked as a freelance dancer with the Royal Opera Ballet. My therapist, Linda Mutch, was going on a trip to the Amazon to visit the Yanomami Indians with some alternative health practitioners and offered me a place which I accepted.

In the Amazon I saw first-hand the devastation we are causing. Prior to the arrival of Europeans, there were more than six million indigenous people living there. There are now fewer than 200,000. This genocide continues to this day, as the Amazon tribes have their forests destroyed and their people killed by murderous ranchers and gold-diggers. Fourteen Peruvian tribal shamans were massacred in another terrible slaughter in late 2011.

Chapter 1

I spent about three weeks by myself in a Yanomami shabono as a guest of the tribe. Their hunter-gatherer lifestyle was almost untouched, having lived in harmony with the forest for over 20,000 years. In comparison, since the industrial revolution we have brought our entire planetary eco-system to the edge of destruction. The tribe lived in thatched wooden buildings around a central circle where the children played, overseen by the older children and adults. On my first morning in the shabono, I was woken by the family who slept in the hammocks beside mine. They wanted me to go with them into the forest. We reached a clearing where there was a dead sloth, killed by a hunter the previous day. The family skinned and cut up the animal and we brought it back to the village. Fascinatingly, their culture does not allow the hunter to eat the game he has killed. This simple device prevents greed from stripping the forest of its game and ensures plentiful meat for future generations.

In contrast, with our corporate supermarkets the only restraint is income. Instead of eating meat about every 10 days and fish once a week as the Yanomami do, many people now eat meat with every meal. This has contributed to global environmental and animal-welfare disasters and a human obesity epidemic. The UN reports that meat production is one of the largest sources of greenhouse gas emissions, at one-fifth of the total. Industrial rearing of cattle and pigs has led to vast swathes of the Amazon being bulldozed to grow soya beans to feed them.

I was only the fourth non-Yanomami person to stay with this tribe and was honoured to be invited to become a tribal member. I declined as I wished to return to London, but they held an honorary ceremony for me before I left, crowning me with a headdress of monkey-skin and feathers. They made clear however that they wanted no more outsiders to disturb them.

Upon my return to London, I resolved to help stop the environmental destruction threatening the Yanomami's very existence. Whilst I did join Survival International (a charity working for indigenous people's rights), I decided to concentrate on tackling our destructive consumer lifestyles. I felt despair for the Yanomami in the face of the bulldozers aimed at their forest homes. Dedicating myself solely to rainforest protection, I would endure the fate of Sisyphus, condemned for eternity to push a rock up a hill, only for it to roll down again. I wanted to tackle the consumer anti-society that was driving those bulldozers.

Following Mahatma Gandhi's maxim that we should be the change that we seek in the world, I felt the most important first step was to tackle my own consumerism. I had very little idea how to do this but decided that every time I went grocery-shopping I would buy at least one organic product. And so on my first week back, I bought a jar of organic ketchup. Since then I have gradually installed in my 1840s Victorian terraced home in Camberwell, solar-electric panels, solar hot water, rain harvester, wood burner, composting toilet, solid-wall insulation, triple glazing and LED lighting. I am a net exporter of electricity, use about a tenth of the average UK mains water consumption and produce about half a wheelie bin of non-recycled rubbish a year. I am learning to produce more food whilst also helping wildlife in the garden.

Soon after returning, I learnt that Southwark Council was planning to build on my local nature reserve and sell off whole sections of Burgess Park. I felt that I could not campaign to save the rainforest, if the last tiny bit of wildlife on my own doorstep was to be bulldozed.

With no knowledge about campaigning, I dived in. I had inherited a modest sum of money which paid for the time I took off from dancing to campaign. Local Liberal Democrats were supportive and I admired the anti-nuclear direct actions by Simon Hughes, the local Bermondsey MP. So I joined the party. Within a short time, with Ruth Bright and Alf Langley, I was selected as a candidate for the local elections in Faraday Ward, which covered the huge Aylesbury Estate, famous for its visit from Tony Blair immediately after he became Prime Minister. It had always elected only Labour councillors. But in May 1994, this overwhelmingly council-tenant electorate voted in three Lib-Dem councillors and we duly delivered on our promises. We blocked the building on the park, switched estate maintenance from poisonous pesticides to manual weeding, and our community politics work with the police and residents resulted in an extraordinary 50% reduction in local crime.

A few years after being elected, I received a letter from Survival which led to that dramatic confrontation with Paddy Ashdown. One of Survival's main tactics is to identify threats to indigenous tribes and then ask supporters to write to the relevant head of state. This letter asked us to write to the Indonesian dictator President Suharto. Rio Tinto Zinc (RTZ), one of the world's largest mining corporations, was proposing a vast open-cast mine in the forests of the Amungme people. They wanted to remove the entire top of the mountain where the Amungme believed they went when they died, akin to the Christian heaven.

Driving mining roads into rain forests is like banging stakes into their hearts – they kill them. It leads inexorably to the death or destitution of the indigenous people who live there. The mine represented a threat to the Amungme's very existence. As I read the leaflet, a bell rang in the back of my mind about RTZ. It was that the Lib Dem Peer Richard Holme was both an RTZ executive-director and their principal political lobbyist, and was also the chair of the party's general-election campaign, with Lord Rennard as his head of campaigns.

It would have been hypocritical to write only to Suharto, so I wrote instead to Paddy Ashdown objecting to Richard being the spokesperson for two conflicting organisations. RTZ was the world's largest private producer of uranium. It had repeated human-rights indictments from the UN and was condemned by numerous environmental groups due to its destructive mining operations.

Chapter 1

Meanwhile the party supposedly opposed nuclear power and stood for human rights and environmental protection. Sadly when the Liberal Democrats eventually got into power, their Environment Secretary Ed Davey became one of the most enthusiastic pro-nuclear ministers in the developed world.

Paddy's reply to my letter said that Lord Holme had assured him that RTZ's environmental performance was among the best in Europe! No reference was made to the plight of the Amungme. Furious, I contacted various non-governmental organisations (NGOs) for documented evidence against RTZ. I sent this with a covering letter to every member of the party's national ruling body, the Federal Executive (FE), calling for action on the scandal.

As I was not an FE member at the time I did not hear the discussion the package elicited. No one responded to my letter but I later learnt that rather than deal with the scandal, they instead requested officers to devise a media strategy, in case it arose during the general-election campaign! This should have acted as a warning light to me about the party's capture by *The Prostitute State*. But I did not know then that it even existed.

Having failed with the leader and Federal Executive, I took the campaign to the party's Federal Conference. The issue had become such a *cause célèbre* for radicals that they named their conference disco Rio Disco Zinc. Shortly after my arrival at conference, Simon Hughes MP asked to speak to me. He was then the party's charismatic environment spokesperson. Surely he would not oppose my objecting at conference to a nuclear lobbyist fronting our general-election campaign? But sadly he did, saying that raising the issue at conference might damage the party.

I replied that having failed privately to get the leader or the FE to take action, it was perfectly reasonable to raise the issue at conference. Simon's attempt to silence me was my first taste of how fear of the UK's media billionaires subverted the party's accountability procedures.

I duly raised the issue during the FE report to conference but was brushed off by then party president Robert Maclennan MP. No media picked up on the story despite the leadership's worries. However, on my way home I read an article in The Evening Standard quoting Richard Holme saying his position had been endorsed by conference. This outraged me and I promptly decided to stand for election to the Federal Executive on a platform opposing the party's links with RTZ.

Shortly after submitting my election address to Party HQ, I got a call from the party's chief executive saying that I would have to change it. He claimed that as it stated that the party should not be associated with RTZ, it meant the party could be sued by RTZ. I thought this was preposterous. It meant one could not oppose the party being associated even with organisations condemned by the UN. I refused to change it. Weeks later I received the mail-out containing the candidate election addresses and ballot papers. When I opened it, I found they had blanked out my opposition to the party's link with RTZ. But once I recovered from the shock of seeing such censorship, I started laughing.

I realised that the visibly crude censorship would make a lot of liberals angry and result in them voting for me. On my first attempt at standing for the FE, despite being almost totally unknown, I was duly elected and thus able to table at that very first meeting, a motion requesting that Lord Holme choose between his two roles. The FE is made up of fifteen elected Parliamentarians and Party Officials including the Leader and fifteen directly elected members. Usually a small minority of about five were radical liberals. In the run-up to that first meeting of the newly elected executive, I contacted all of them. Whilst appalled at what Richard Holme represented, none would second my motion as they felt it had no chance of winning.

My final hope was Lembit Opik. He kindly agreed to meet me for lunch on the day the FE met. I outlined how I felt the party's integrity was at stake. He undertook to think seriously about seconding the motion but gave no commitment. So I turned up at the meeting that evening, held in the wood-panelled boardroom at the party's then HQ in Cowley Street, without a single ally, despite having grass-roots support all around the country.

I walked into the boardroom as nervous as hell. The only seat remaining was at the opposite end of the table from where the Party President Robert Maclennan and leader Paddy Ashdown were sitting. The seat beside me to my horror was occupied by Lord Holme! I had never before attended a meeting remotely like this, filled with MPs, Lords and senior party-figures. But Robert chaired it fairly and when it came to my motion, he politely asked me to address it.

That was when Paddy interrupted proceedings and made his startling intervention. I thought to myself – *Oh my God, I have not even uttered a word and the leader is threatening resignation over my very first motion*! Robert indicated for me to proceed. Thankful not to have fainted, I continued. My motion was not a personal attack but simply dealt with the un-tenability of Richard's dual roles.

All of the interventions after I concluded were by the leadership's supporters. The radicals stayed silent and left me hanging out to dry. Maclennan proceeded to the vote, at which point he asked for a seconder. The room went deathly silent. Lembit Opik was sitting to my right, half-way along the board-table. I caught his eye and he stared back with the look of a rabbit caught in the headlamps. I held his gaze and silently asked if he had the courage to put his hand up. To my immense relief he started to raise his hand millimetre by millimetre, as if he was being tortured. But to his credit, raise it he did and the motion was formally placed before the meeting. The vote was 26:1 against with a few abstentions.

I had been trounced but had forced the leadership and FE to put on record their support for Richard's and hence the party's duplicity. I had done what I could but the corporate lobbyists had won their first battle with me and my supporters.

Chapter 1

Over the next seven years that I served on the Federal Executive, including the final two years as its Deputy Chair, I was to have many such battles over the party's soul.

My second major exposure to **The Prostitute State** was over Paddy Ashdown's attempts to secretly align the party with Tony Blair's New Labour party before and after the 1997 general election. It was this battle that taught me that in addition to Holme, there was an entire political-lobbying cartel around the leadership, whom we had been battling and not just Ashdown. Soon after I was elected to the FE, rumours were swirling that Paddy was secretly negotiating a pact with Tony Blair. It was referred to euphemistically as The Project. It had little support among the membership but the powerful group of professional political lobbyists around the leader were hell-bent on delivering it.

Many senior party figures, who I spoke to, were appalled at what was going on behind closed doors, outside the democratic structures of the party. The future of three-party politics was being endangered. To organise opposition to Paddy's project I helped set up a new party grouping called *new radicalism*. Its purpose was to act as a grass-roots members' think-tank, to formulate the philosophical and policy basis for the continuation of an independent liberal party. But crucially it was also to act as a rallying point should the leadership suddenly try to bounce the party into a pact with Blair.

We drafted a set of five principles for *"new radicalism"* that radical liberal members of the party could rally around. One of these was *"Politics by Example"* which called for the party to be run in line with its principles. I had realised that the party repeatedly failed to practice what it preached in how it ran itself. The party advocated an annual government environmental audit but did not carry out one on itself. It advocated recycling but did not use recycled paper. It advocated Freedom of Information but had a blanket secrecy-clause for its own Federal Executive. It advocated elections for the House of Lords but did not elect its own nominees to the Lords. It advocated clean government but Lib Dem Peers were allowed to sell services as political lobbyists. It advocated transparency in political donations but refused to declare its own donations. It advocated honesty in politics but ran deceitful by-election campaigns.

"New radicalism" sought to tackle this hypocrisy with quite a few successes at the party conference. Whilst none were of national importance, they represented opportunities for the party to boost its moral backbone, so that when it entered government, it would have the strength to uphold the party's principles. The lobbying and tax-haven elite in the party's upper echelons however regarded such proposals as *"troublemaking"*. Practicing what we preached was not on their agenda.

As part of our battle to stop the Ashdown/Blair deal, we drafted an amendment to the leadership's strategy motion for the 1998 Southport Lib Dem Party Conference. We sought to make clear our commitment to independence but did not want to threaten Ashdown's popular leadership. In other words we wanted a motion saying *"We like you Paddy but don't betray us by hooking up with Blair."*

Conrad Russell (son of Bertrand Russell and one of the party's most distinguished thinkers) became an invaluable personal ally and supporter. Working with his immense intellect was an intimidating privilege. His early death from smoking was a terrible loss to liberalism. As the conference came closer Ed Davey MP, Robert Maclennan MP and many others got involved. I was in the centre of a swirling draft negotiating storm. Our amendment was accepted for debate, along with an additional amendment by future Cambridge MP David Howarth.

The debate drew huge interest and the hall in Southport was packed. I moved the motion and it was summated by Conrad Russell. The atmosphere crackled, as delegates knew that an historic choice was being made. After a nail-biting two-hour debate, the conference chair Liz Barker called the vote. A sea of hands went up across the hall supporting both amendments. Our majority was in excess of 85%! The leadership had been overwhelmingly defeated. The message was clear we did not want to be hitched to New Labour.

Our successful *new radicalism* amendment stated:
"One of our important aims is to complete the task begun in May 1997, of the Liberal Democrats replacing the discredited, reactionary Conservative Party as the official Opposition, as a step to the strategic goal of a genuinely liberal and radical Liberal Democrat government.

Any expansion of the subjects covered by the Joint Cabinet Committee will only be carried out after a genuine consultation with the party and the express consent of the Parliamentary Party. We will seek to involve those from all other parties who support constitutional reform and a more liberal and democratic Europe in the current constitutional process."

David Howarth's crucial amendment detailed what that consultation should be. It required the parliamentary party, federal executive and conference to vote by a two-thirds majority or else all members had to be balloted. We had high hopes that we had succeeded in securing our independence whilst retaining our leader. But events were to prove us wrong on the second point. Paddy and his lobbyist co-conspirators, despite the vote, continued their secretive negotiations with Blair.

Then on the 11th of November 1998, just two months after Southport, Paddy gambled on destroying the Southport agreement by pressing what we called the unilateral nuclear button. Late that afternoon I got an urgent message from the

Chapter 1

new radicalism activist Gareth Epps to listen to the 6pm news. There were Ashdown and Blair issuing their "Joint Statement" committing both parties to work in parallel in joint-cabinet committees across the entire spectrum of government, despite Blair already having a large majority in the Commons and against the expressed democratic wishes of the Lib Dem Conference. If it went ahead, the only opposition to the right-wing Blairism in Parliament would be the even more right-wing Tories. The lobbyists around Paddy had got what they wanted – direct access to government ministers. On TV Paddy looked embarrassingly like an old public-school teacher with a crush on the handsome new head-boy.

Well, if Paddy had pressed his nuclear button, we also had a button to press. One that the leadership had never before had to deal with and that was *new radicalism's* nationwide e-mail network. As soon as the TV news was over, we immediately messaged all our members. Within hours we had set up a new campaign group to lead the opposition to the Blair/Ashdown pact. It was called the Campaign for Liberal Democracy. An agreed statement for the press was immediately issued, opposing Ashdown's betrayal of the democratically approved party strategy.

We then started collecting signatures to trigger an emergency conference. Within ten days we already had 120 of the 200 elected conference-delegate signatures required. This gave us a very strong hand going into the fraught Federal Executive meeting that followed the Joint Statement, where Ashdown had to get a two-thirds majority to back his trashing of the Southport Motion. Ashdown however had planned to bypass the Federal Executive, Parliamentary Party and Conference opposition by going directly to an immediate *"back me or sack me"* all-member ballot. This was Ashdown's best hope of destroying party opposition to the Joint Statement. There was one problem. He had to get the FE to authorise it.

It would be challenging for us to explain why such a referendum was potentially undemocratic. Paddy knew it would not be a referendum on the Joint Statement but on his leadership. We therefore decided not to contest the referendum but instead chose the slogan *"No Referendum without Debate"*. This meant that Paddy would not get his ballot until after an emergency conference had debated his proposal.

So, when called to speak in the FE debate, I simply said if the leadership insisted on the *"back me or sack me"* referendum, then I could guarantee by the end of the week, we would have the two hundred signatures required for an emergency conference. Paddy would face the humiliation of an awful destructive public row in front of the nation's media. In light of the 85% support for the Southport Motion and the activists' outrage across the country after the Joint Statement, he would almost definitely be trounced.

One of Paddy's main allies, the lobbyist Tim Clement Jones, then asked: if the leadership promised not to hold the shotgun referendum, would we promise not to call an emergency conference prior to the autumn conference. My response was immediate. *"That's a deal!"* It was an extraordinary moment. The release of tension was enormous. Organised party members had taken on the might of Ashdown, Blair and the lobbyists and succeeded. But it was also the moment that sealed Paddy's fate as leader.

Ashdown's failure at the FE gave manoeuvring space to the Parliamentary Party. Nearly every single member of his parliamentary team refused to join. Ashdown's Project was dead. Just two months later Ashdown's leadership was finished. On the 20th January 1999 at 5.15 pm Ashdown announced his decision to stand down as leader. True to form, he had told Tony Blair of his decision before he told his own party colleagues.

On the evening of Paddy's resignation Nick Sutton, then editor of The Today programme on Radio 4, spent an hour in my living room urging me to go on-air and state the real reason for Paddy's resignation was that his grand Project was dead. I refused but paid tribute to Ashdown's achievements as leader. Despite his duplicity, I actually liked Paddy and was sad to see him go. To this day, Ashdown has never explained why having rescued the Liberal Democrats from oblivion and spoken passionately about transparency, bottom-up politics and ending the two party system, he then almost from the very beginning of his leadership, according to his diaries, bizarrely negotiated behind his party's back, trying to destroy in classic top-down fashion, the very three-party system he had sought to create. But what is important in this story is that despite their enormous advantages, the corporate lobbying state can occasionally be beaten by organised democratic action.

During the battle over The Project, it had become clear that the power base around Ashdown was largely composed of wealthy political lobbyists. Paddy, being an ex-marine, diplomat and secret-service member (MI6), was not himself an ex-lobbyist. But those he appointed to his inner circle included Lord McNally, a lobbyist and later Vice-President of the notorious lobbying firm Weber Shandwycks. McNally continuously broke the voluntary code banning the hire of parliamentarians as lobbyists. As mentioned, Richard Holme was head lobbyist for Rio Tinto Zinc. Ashdown's two deputy directors for the general election were Tim Clement Jones who worked for the international lobbying conglomerate DLA Piper and Dick Newby, director of lobbying firm Matrix. It also included Tim Razzall who was a director of various tax-haven registered companies. Nearly all of Paddy's corporate lobbying circle was appointed to the Lords as Lib Dem peers, giving them unrestricted access to parliament. This added to their commercial value as lobbyists.

Corporate lobbyists do not view democratic parties as the public views them. They see party membership as a legitimate route to access power. If that means doing sweetheart deals with the Murdoch-endorsed Blair or the equally Murdoch-endorsed Cameron, then so be it. Having senior members of the Liberal Democrats on joint-cabinet committees with government ministers meant they would have direct access to the corridors of power, which is gold for the professional lobbyist. I am not saying there was a deliberate conspiracy to achieve such access for their corporate clients but *de facto* that is what The Project, if successful, would have delivered. What we were really battling in our efforts to save the party from being tied to the Blair Project, was yet again *The Prostitute State.*

I realised that our huge but successful effort to defeat The Project, would have to be repeated again and again as long as the lobbying cabal retained their grip on the party's leadership. I therefore embarked on two campaigns to curb the political lobbyists' power over the leadership. The first was to put an end to the leader's unilateral power to appoint members of the House of Lords. This was being used to appoint lobbyists, tax-haven directors, party donors and corporate directors to parliament. The second campaign was to ban Liberal Democrat members of the House of Lords from selling their services as corporate political lobbyists. I had no idea what a powerful landmine I was stepping on with this. Its explosion would eventually lead to the establishment demanding my resignation as Deputy Chair of the Party.

We began as usual by drafting a conference motion on political lobbying. Being able to use our *new radicalism* electronic network to negotiate the text of motions and to tell people what was happening at Federal Executive level, meant we were reclaiming some party democracy back from the lobbyists. A measure of how successful we were was the viciousness of the bile poured over us by lobbyists such as Lord McNally in "Liberal Democrat News" and at the FE. At one stage Charles Kennedy angrily threatened to close the party's entire electronic messaging system down, after I referred to his key lieutenant Lord Clement Jones as *"Lord Cayman Islands"* in honour of his selling lobbying services to the infamous tax haven!

Our conference motion on lobbying stated:
"Regulation of Parliamentary Lobbying
Conference notes the public unease about the influence of unaccountable parliamentary lobbyists on the present and previous governments.
Conference recognises, however the value of constructive professional lobbying and the work done by voluntary organisations and individuals to influence and inform people in power.
Conference believes that to reduce the possibility of corruption and the exertion of undue influence and to ensure the full transparency of parliamentary procedures, the roles of parliamentarian and professional lobbyist must be kept strictly separate.

Conference therefore believes that:

- *No parliamentarian or their employees at Westminster or European level should be an employee of, receive any financial reward from or hold a financial stake in any of the duly registered professional parliamentary lobbying companies (i.e. ones that offer their parliamentary lobbying services for hire to paying commercial and other clients).*
- *A statutory register of such professional lobbying firms should be set up and supervised by the Commissioner on Parliamentary Standards. Furthermore Conference welcomes the voluntary ethical code of conduct adopted by the Association of Professional Political Consultants (APPC). Conference notes however that some professional parliamentary lobbying firms are failing to join APPC or to observe or support the voluntary code of conduct. This commercially undermines the position of ethically conducted firms.*
- *Conference therefore calls for a statutory Code of Conduct to be drawn up which should be supervised by the Commissioner.*
- *Conference requests that all Liberal Democrat Peers should abide by the terms of this motion within two years."*

The establishment threw a huge effort into blocking this motion, repeatedly persuading the Conference Committee to vote against its selection for debate. With each rejection, the motion's support among the wider party membership grew larger. A number of the Conference Committee members were actually political lobbyists or peers and so had a direct conflict of interest. Indeed *new radicalism* was told that a member said he was voting against the motion being debated because it would affect his lobbying career! We unsuccessfully appealed to the Federal Appeals Panel requesting that they outlaw political lobbyists on the conference committee voting on regulation of lobbying issues, due to the inherent conflict of interest.

In 1998, following yet more lobbying scandals in the House of Lords, Lord Neill was appointed by the government to investigate. The Lib Dem leadership brazenly issued a press release stating that the inquiry was *"long overdue"*, whilst at the same time continuing their strenuous efforts to suppress the debate within their own party. The refusal to allow debate at that year's Spring Conference meant that even if accepted for the Autumn Conference, it would be too late for its conclusions to be submitted to Neill, as the closing date was prior to the conference. This meant that the party's submission would be left to the leadership and their lobbyists. We wrote to Lord Neill, asking if he would accept a late submission following the vote at conference.

Neill replied that he would be willing to do so. However, even Lord Neill's acceptance of a late submission failed to budge the conference committee. The leadership again won by a couple of votes and the members were thus denied any democratic influence on the leadership's submission on lobbying to Neill. The corporate lobbyists had again triumphed.

The scale of the leadership's efforts to block the motion was revelatory of the depth of its capture by the corporate lobby. Remember in public they were calling for the cleaning up of British politics. The chief whip, Paul Tyler, told the conference committee that it was unconstitutional (not in relation to the party's own constitution but the so-called unwritten constitution of the United Kingdom), as it would restrict the rights of MPs and so should not be debated. According to Tyler, the motion also contravened the Code of Conduct for Members of Parliament! To me this demonstrated that liberalism is absolutely right. Everyone can have their values perverted and therefore institutional checks and balances are needed to hold everyone even liberals accountable.

Unwilling to give in to such bullying, in July 2000 I wrote to Elizabeth Filkin, the Parliamentary Commissioner for Standards, asking whether our proposal to stop parliamentarians being political lobbyists would be contrary to the British Constitution (sic) by potentially restricting the rights of parliamentarians. Filkin replied within a week stating "*I cannot see that the propositions in the motion could, in themselves, restrict the rights of Members of Parliament. It would be entirely for Members of Parliament to decide by vote whether any such changes proposed to them should be implemented.*" To my pleasant surprise, the Commissioner for Parliamentary Standards was actually working in the wider interests of democracy rather that the narrow interests of the lobbying establishment.

But the political establishment could not stomach such an independent Commissioner. The fatal flaw in the Nolan legislation (typical of so many of the fake accountability procedures put in place by the UK's establishment) is that the Parliamentary Commissioner is appointed by the very MPs whose ethics they supervise. The parliamentary committee responsible, including Lib Dem MP Archy Kirkwood (one of Paddy's inner circle) refused to re-appoint Elizabeth Filkin when her first four-year contract was up. They appointed the safe establishment figure Sir Philip Mawer instead. The highlight of Mawer's two terms in office was a ruling on two train tickets mis-used by David Blunkett MP. The entire parliamentary expenses scandal continued under his nose.

Filkin's ruling, unsurprisingly, made no difference to the Lib Dem establishment's determination to prevent the debate on lobbying. However the dam eventually broke. By the record thirteenth submission, it was the most widely endorsed motion in the history of the party. Crucially the balance of power on the committee had shifted by one in our favour and the debate was finally allowed at the 2001 Spring Conference.

At conference the leadership of both the Parliamentary Parties, in the Commons and in the Lords, opposed our motion. But we pulled off a coup when Diana Wallis MEP, who was to become Deputy President of the European Parliament, agreed to speak on our behalf. It was a heated debate. In opening it, I focused on the principles of transparency, accountability and the separation of powers. Political lobbying has an important role in democracy, but it must be free from even the perception of corruption. Ethically you cannot simultaneously be a legislator and a paid lobbyist.

After her speech, I thanked Wallis for her courage in speaking out. Her reply was illuminating. *"I was more than happy to speak. I am fed up of those bastards coming to my office trying to bully me."* She was referring to the Lib Dem Lords who were professional lobbyists. This brought home to me how crucial tackling lobbying was. As we were speaking, the chair moved to the vote. There was no need for a card vote - we had won by a clear majority! The Liberal Democrats were now committed to a statutory register for political lobbyists, a ban on lobbying by all parliamentarians and more importantly were going to phase out lobbying by Liberal Democrat legislators within two years, without waiting for legislation. Or so I thought.....

Despite the vote, the leadership remained determined to protect the corporate lobbyists. At the FE meeting following conference, its chair Lord Dholakia announced the setting up of a committee to *"consider"* the motion. As he said *"consider"* rather than *"implement"*, I realised immediately that they were trying to destroy the motion. All of the proposed committee's membership were members of the Lords and were appointed by a member of the Lords and it was chaired by Baroness Harris, also a member of the Lords - the very people affected by the motion. There were to be no supporters of the motion on the committee.

Time passed with no report from this "committee". Finally, following repeated demands at party conferences, they were forced to report to the FE. And unsurprisingly, their lordships announced that the motion was *"un-implementable"*. A heated debate ensued. The process had taken so long that there was by now a new leader, Charles Kennedy, whose inner circle was again dominated by political lobbyists.

I asked did we want to clean up politics or were we willing to damage the party's soul for the sake of lobbyists? Amazingly, the FE overrode Kennedy and upheld the motion and deadline for Liberal Democrat peers. So with both the party conference and FE endorsing the motion, it would finally be implemented. Or would it......?

I am afraid not. The corporate state is grindingly persistent. The leadership played one last card. At the following FE, which I missed as I was working in

Chapter 1

Finland, they tabled legal advice from Lord Goodhart that the motion contravened the rights of Lib Dem peers under the European Convention on Human Rights! I was absolutely gutted that such a supposedly distinguished liberal constitutional lawyer as Lord Goodhart could twist the Convention on Human Rights into justifying the practice of parliamentarians selling their services as corporate lobbyists.

I had described the advice by Lord Goodhart as being *"spurious"*. Commissioning legal advice from someone who as a peer was affected by the motion and whose colleagues were impacted financially was a clear conflict of interest. He should have recused himself. Kennedy's response was to say my claim of spuriousness was *"legally actionable"*. Yes, he tried that old bullying tactic of legal sabre-rattling in order to get his way.

Despite not having any funds to defend myself against Kennedy's threat, I refused to withdraw my criticism of Lord Goodhart's advice. But they tabled the advice anyway. In my absence, the FE caved in and agreed not to implement the conference decision on lobbying. Years of work trying to tackle corporate lobbying corruption in the party was swept away, using Goodhart's *"advice"*. The subsequent FE report to the next Federal Conference made no mention of its refusal to implement the conference motion on lobbying and Lib Dem peers continued their lucrative corporate lobbying. I felt I had a duty to let conference know. I therefore took the rostrum and outlined the FE's suppression of the conference decision.

The Party President Lord Dholakia then took the rostrum and, instead of explaining why he was refusing to implement conference's democratic instructions, attacked me for raising the issue, claiming I had no right to do this as I was covered by the *"collective responsibility"* of the FE. He then in an unprecedented action, called publicly from the platform at conference for my resignation, despite my being Deputy Chair of the party.

Something inside me snapped.

The fact that such enormous democratic effort over so many years, by so many Lib Dem members, should result in absolutely no action being taken, made me realise that it would take decades to cure the party's endemic corruption from the inside. The three examples outlined above are just a sliver of the culture of **The Prostitute State** that I as a party officer experienced at the heart of the Lib Dems; a heart riddled with corporate political lobbyists.

Over a decade of trying to democratically reform the party from within but being repeatedly subverted by lobbyists, finally boiled over and in anger, I stood up and announced rather melodramatically from the floor *"Right Mr President, it is outrageous that you are refusing to tackle the corruption that lies at the heart of the party and it is also clear that it is becoming impossible to clean it up. So you get what you are asking for. I am quitting."* With that, I stormed out of the conference hall.

There was a stunned silence. Many of my supporters, to be honest, thought I had been really stupid. I had destroyed in one moment of anger much of the political capital and momentum I had built up with my colleagues and *new radicalism* over the previous 12 years. But the years of bullying, frustration and constant legal threats had taken their toll. I was burnt out.

These battles demonstrate the power that lobbying has over our body politic and what that means in day-to-day terms, from the real life experiences of just one political activist. Let me assure you that if it is strong in the Liberal Democrats, it is pretty much overwhelming in the other major parties.

Seven years later, the Occupy Movement's heroic 2011 protest outside St Paul's Cathedral, forced me to re-evaluate my personal experiences of the corruption in the Liberal Democrats and to develop them into the wider political thesis of *The Prostitute State.*

You will see, as it unfolds in chapter after chapter that it is in reality a state that is phenomenally different from the one we are told we live in. Whilst largely invisible to the ordinary citizen, it controls almost every aspect of our democracy and the world around us. Like Lilliputians in Gulliver's Travels, we are like little people running around under a glass cake-stand, thinking we are players in a free democracy, when in reality the corporate billionaires are outside looking in and pulling our strings, as their gluttony grabs more and more of our common wealth and power and destroys our planet's core essential ecosystems in the process. Tackling *The Prostitute State* is the most crucial task facing humanity right now.

Chapter 2

The Four Pillars

The main reason I got involved in party politics was to help tackle the ecological crises facing the planet. I was convinced that if the Liberal Democrats could be a living example of how we wanted to govern the country in a liberal, democratic, transparent and ecologically sustainable way, then it would power ahead and become a party of government that could deliver on its promises. I spent about twelve years working for this vision.

The Lib Dem record in the coalition government under Nick Clegg sadly proved the truth of my prediction that having lacked the discipline of running even just their own party according to their values, meant they would frequently lack the strength to stand up for what they believed in, when they got into government. Their failure to cleanse themselves of internal corruption when in opposition, meant they brought it with them, just like Blair did, right into the heart of government.

Their refusal to tackle lobbying made me realise that it would take a lifetime for *new radicalism* to turn the party into an effective tool to tackle our ecological crises. But the world's ice caps are melting *now*. The rain forests are being bulldozed *now*. Indigenous people are being slaughtered and their livelihoods destroyed *now*.

The Lords lobbying saga made me realise that no matter whom we elect, the corporate lobbyists nearly always win. With no time left to change the system, I thought I should try and work with it. After leaving the party, I decided to try to harness that corporate culture by helping consumer power to change what lobbyists were lobbying for. I turned to journalism, media, writing books and eco-consultancy to help teach people and organisations how to change their buying habits and green their organisations. By greening their purchasing, they would be giving money to greener corporations, who would then lobby the government to save the planet, rather than funding lobbyists whose employers were destroying it.

A positive example of this is that because enough customers switched their domestic electricity supply to green-electricity companies like Good Energy and Ecotricity, those companies were then able to fund staff to lobby the Department of Energy for policies like solar-panel and renewable-heat feed-in tariffs. The Feed-in tariff successfully brought the cost of solar power down by over 50% in its first two years of operation, due to the large number of installations that it generated, making it more affordable for less well-off home-owners.

If you buy your electricity or gas from the Big Six energy suppliers, you are funding their nuclear and fossil fuel lobbyists. Consumer power, channelled through the lobbyists of greener companies, is often far more powerful than voting. Destructive corporations such as Shell, BP, EdF, Tesco and Monsanto only have huge political power because WE buy from them and so fund their lobbyists and destructive investments.

My first book *Saving the Planet without Costing the Earth* was on how to live a green lifestyle and was based on my personal experiences in greening my own lifestyle and my local campaigns to green my community. I launched an ecological consultancy, *3 Acorns Eco-Audits*, which assisted schools, charities, businesses and even a corporate pharmaceutical-company headquarters to green their organisations.

I wrote a second book *Easy Eco-auditing* on how to carry out an eco-audit of a business or home, which has been used successfully by people from California to South Africa as a basis for their own eco-auditing businesses. I did countless TV, radio and newspaper interviews on a whole range of eco-issues and had a regular eco-column in The Independent. I was the eco-auditor for the BBC2 series, It's Not Easy Being Green, Sky's Green Britain Week and ITV's How Green is Your Home. Thousands of people have come to see my carbon-negative Victorian retro-eco house during London's Open House Weekends to learn how to green their own homes and lives. I helped create the award-winning eco-auditing initiative launched by the Corporation of London's City Bridge Trust, which is greening charities across London and a similar scheme for the Specialist Schools and Academies Trust for secondary schools. The City Bridge project was crucial in encouraging some major funders to ask for evidence of good ecological behaviour from the charities that they fund and getting the Charity Commission to formally clarify that greening a charity did not contradict their charitable purposes.

It was a rewarding time. I felt I was helping to make a difference, in a way I that I was unable to in politics. My work was helping to reduce wasteful consumption and creating customers for green electricity companies, recycled paper manufacturers, insulation installers and recycling companies *et cetera*.

The wider ecological movement had been achieving some notable victories. Billions were being invested in renewable energy, recycling levels were soaring and animal welfare conditions were being improved even for battery hens. A number of extinct native species had been successfully re-introduced into the UK and the rate of destruction of the Amazon rainforest slowed temporarily.

However, the 2011 Occupy Movement's protest, at St Paul's Cathedral in the City of London, made me suddenly stop and take stock seriously about whether the path that I had pursued with others in the years since I left the Liberal Democrats in tackling our ecological crises was actually working?

Despite all that the movement was doing, the destruction of our ecosystems by global corporations was still progressing relentlessly. It is crucial that we understand the depth of this destruction so that we comprehend the urgency for us to tackle *The Prostitute State's* corruption of our democracy.

Over a third of Peru's Andean glaciers, whose melt-waters irrigate the crops on its coastal plains, have already melted. Scientists predict that they could all be gone by 2050, creating a huge food problem for Peru's exploding population of over 40 million people.

Rising temperatures have meant that areas of the Kenyan highlands which never had endemic malaria have now succumbed, with the resulting rise in human misery and deaths.

The Himalayan glaciers are disappearing at a terrifying rate. Hundreds of millions of people depend on the melt-waters from the 54,000 glaciers that feed the huge river basins of China and South East Asia, including the Indus, Ganges, Brahmaputra and Yellow River. In 2011, the International Centre for Integrated Mountain Development reported that the rate of loss of snow and ice had doubled over the past thirty years from the glaciers that they studied regularly. Even Mount Everest's glaciers are now losing ice.

22% of the Bhutanese and 21% per cent of the Nepalese glacier masses have gone already.

In England the effects are also already being felt. The 2014 catastrophic floods were a wake-up call to many. And nature itself is in trouble. Take just the fact that more than half of the country's horse-chestnut trees have been blighted by the leaf-miner moth. According to scientists warming temperatures have allowed the moth to get established in the UK. The deformation of these magnificent trees by ugly brown-pocked blight is a visible sign of rising global temperatures in Britain.

Over the last few years there has been a plethora of negative official reports from across the planet, warning that we are in the middle of a catastrophic destruction of our natural ecosystems, including:

- In September 2012, the US government's National Snow and Ice Data Centre (NSIDC) reported that the Summer Arctic Sea Ice Cover annual minimum of 3.42 million square kilometres had smashed all records. This was 36% lower than the average minimum for 1979-2000.

  But even more shocking satellite measurements indicated that **by 2012 we had lost 75% of the Arctic Summer Ice Volume since 1979. 50% of the Arctic Summer Ice Volume has been lost just since 2006.**

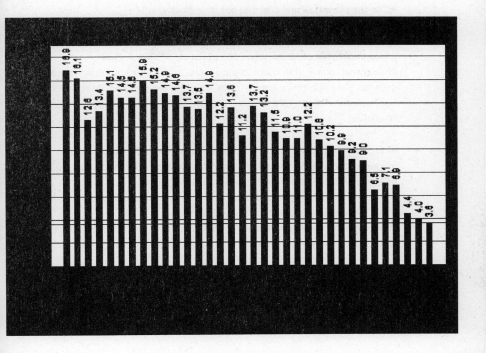

This volume graph published in September 2012 is the most terrifying thing I have ever read. It demonstrates the genocidal destruction *The Prostitute State* is wreaking on our planet. The newly open dark waters of the Arctic Ocean are now absorbing enormous amounts of heat, warming the planet even more, instead of the previous white ice which was reflecting it back into space. Then NASA in March 2014 made the chilling announcement that the melting of the Western Antarctic Ice-Sheets was now unstoppable, leading to an expected 1.2 meter rise in sea levels over the next 200 years.

The equivalent of two **TRILLION** tonnes of methane gas is beginning to be released, from the melting permafrost in the wastelands of Siberia and Canada and from under the Arctic Ocean where it was stored as methane salts. Methane is twenty-three times more powerful as a climate-change gas than carbon-dioxide. This means that a rise in global temperatures of 6C is now potentially unstoppable.

Chapter 2

And a 6C rise in global temperatures is "incompatible with life as we know it" on the planet, as one scientist put it succinctly.

- In 2010 the science journal Nature reported that *the amount of phytoplankton in our oceans has decreased by 40% since 1950.*
Phytoplankton are the microscopic plants upon which all fish ultimately depend. They are the source of 50% of global oxygen and have absorbed huge amounts of the CO2 released into the atmosphere since the industrial revolution.

- In October 2010 the journal Science reported that total populations of wild mammal, bird, reptile, amphibian and fish species had declined by an average of 30% in the past 40 years. Stop and think about that:
Since I was a twelve year old, human beings have destroyed nearly a third of all wild animal populations on our planet.
If we continue destroying nature at this rate, there will essentially be none left in ninety-three years' time.

- The World Resources Institute reported in 2011 that over 95% of the world's coral reefs, which feed and protect hundreds of millions of people in island and developing countries, are under threat of extinction by 2050.
40% of the world's coral reefs have already been lost.

- Hopes of preventing a global temperature rise of more than 1.5 degrees Celsius, the potential threshold for a runaway climate crisis, were termed "*a nice Utopia*" by IEA chief economist Fatih Birol.
The IEA reported that in 2011 a record 31.6 Giga-tonnes of carbon dioxide were emitted by human activities, which was a rise of 2.6 Gt on 2009. Remember a Giga-tonne is 1,000,000,000 (one thousand million) tonnes!
Professor Lord Stern of the LSE, author of the 2006 Stern UK Treasury Report into the economics of climate change, warned that "*These figures would mean a 50% chance of a rise in the global average temperature of 4C by 2100.*"
Annual greenhouse gas emissions are up over 40% since the 1997 Kyoto Protocol was signed, with developing nations now responsible for more than 53% of global emissions.

- 1.1 billion people in 2010 lacked access to safe drinking water. Groundwater and ancient fossil aquifers are drying up under Beijing, Delhi, Bangkok and other mega-cities, as well as in Yemen, Saudi-Arabia, Libya and Tunisia.

Many of the world's greatest rivers are now often empty when they reach the oceans.

These include the Ganges, Colorado, Yellow River, Rio Grande, Indus, Jordan, Nile, and Yangtze. In the former Soviet Union, the Aral Sea has shrunk to a tenth of its former size, leaving behind a salt-encrusted wasteland.

- **By 2010, nearly sixty per cent of our planet's rainforests had been destroyed.**

  Over fifty per cent were lost in the last 50 years alone. Nearly all of the remaining forests, with the exception of a few protected parks, may be gone by 2050, as we have been devouring them at a rate of 6.1 million hectares every year during the last decade. 200,000 acres of rainforest are burnt each and every day across the planet. One fifth of the Amazon rain forest has already been lost.

- The International Union for the Conservation of Nature's annual report in 2008 stated:

  Nearly 40 percent of the world's 44,838 species of animals, fish, birds and plants catalogued are "threatened with extinction".

  The Earth is undergoing the first wave of mass extinctions since the dinosaurs died out 65 million years ago. The IUCN estimates that this human-caused species loss is now between 100 and 1000 times the natural background rate of species extinction. Much of this is due to the bulldozing of our rainforests, which contain up to 50% of our planet's remaining species.

- In 2010 the Food and Agriculture Organisation reported the worst levels for global fish stocks since records began.

  One third of fisheries were over-exploited (i.e. fished at a rate beyond the ability of stocks to replenish themselves).

  The percentage of global fisheries that are over or fully exploited now stands at a shocking 85%.

- **In 2010 the Natural Resources Institute stated that the world's oceans were now 30% more acidic than prior to the industrial revolution.**

  Increased oceanic acidity is caused by the absorption of CO_2 released from the burning of fossil fuels. It eats the shells of crabs, oysters, clams and the nearly microscopic organisms known as krill and pteropods. This acidity could be 200% higher by 2100. Without shells, most of these animals would die. And as krill and pteropods are a major food source for juvenile salmon, herring, pollock, cod, mackerel and other fish, it threatens almost the entire oceanic food chain. Fish-protein is a crucial source of protein for between 500 million and 1 billion people around the world.

The above list demonstrates the shocking depth of the ecological crises facing our planet. As can be seen the climate crisis is only one of many.

If two more generations were to continue at our rate of destruction, there would be simply almost nothing left to destroy.

As I mentioned, the Occupy St Paul's protest forced me to stop and think. I had to painfully admit that my chosen personal approach of helping individuals, families, schools, charities and businesses to adopt more eco-friendly lifestyles, whilst essential, was by itself never going to work in time to tackle the catastrophes created by *The Prostitute State*. Having already realised that party politics by itself was not going to solve our ecological crises, I now had to admit also that simply greening one's own and others' lives was also too slow to deal with the tsunami of destruction. Unless we deal urgently with the concentration of environmentally destructive corporate power that lies behind the lobbying cartel that drove me out of the Liberal Democrats, our individual ecological and political efforts will be in vain.

The Occupy Movement had a second major theme summarised in their slogan *"We are the 99%"*. They claimed that a tiny 1% of the world's population were not only making huge fortunes on the back of trashing the planet but were also in the process of hijacking our common wealth. I decided to check the figures behind what sounded like Marxist propaganda.

A small amount of research from reliable mainstream sources quickly revealed the truth. There has been an enormous concentration of wealth and power in a small corporate elite over the last three decades. The age of the robber-barons is upon us once more. The following few paragraphs has a lot of figures and percentages. But do bear with them to get the underlying message about what is happening to wealth. They demonstrate starkly the second major impact that *The Prostitute State* is having on our societies – its decimation of social justice.

In the United Kingdom, the Department for Work and Pensions in 2010 produced the *"Households Below Average Income Report"*. It reveals how the poor are getting poorer and the richest ten per cent are getting richer.

The poorest tenth of the UK population now earns a tiny 1.3% of the country's total income. In contrast, the richest tenth are paid 31% (compared with 28% in 2000).

The income of the richest tenth is more than the combined income of half the entire population. According to the report the income of the poorest 10% of people *fell* by 12%, whilst the incomes of the richest 10% *rose* by a whopping 37%, between the years 2000 and 2010. Indeed the Duke of Westminster's family, which according to a March 2014 Oxfam report is the richest family in the UK, owns more wealth (£7.9 billion) than the bottom 10% of the entire UK population.

Together the top 5 richest families in the UK (total £28.1 billion) own more than the bottom 20%, i.e. 12.6 million people whose wealth averages £2, 230 each.

So much for the trickle-down effect of Reagan/Thatcher/Blairite economics! Who realised that when Reagan and Thatcher advocated trickle-down economics, they really meant a flood upwards of wealth leaving just a trickle for the poorest in our society. In the UK, between 1997 when Tony Blair was elected and 2010 when New Labour were thrown out of office, corporate chief-executive pay soared from forty times the average salary of their workers to one hundred and twenty times. The average pay for CEOs of Britain's top hundred companies jumped over a quarter to £4.5 million in the year 2010 alone, despite the recession. Their pay rise in just one year was the equivalent of thirty-six average salaries.

The OECD in December 2011 stated that the income gap between the top and bottom 10% in the UK was rising faster than in any other wealthy nation, with the UK heading towards the massive gap of the US. The UK gap of 12:1 is double the income gap in countries such as Germany, Denmark or Sweden, where the gap is 6:1. In an extraordinary warning about the stability risks for societies with such gross distortions of wealth, the OECD report said *"Youths who see no future for themselves feel increasingly disenfranchised. They have now been joined by protesters who believe they are bearing the brunt of a crisis for which they have no responsibility, while people on higher incomes appeared to have been spared."*

But it is not only financial wealth that is concentrated in a few hands in the UK. Land distribution is worse than it is even in Brazil, with a miniscule 0.4% of the UK population owning 66% of the country, making it the second most unequal land distribution in the world! The land remains almost exclusively in the hands of the old aristocracy and new oligarchs. The Occupy Movement was right after all! The government's own statistics confirm that the rich in the UK have been grabbing an ever larger share of the cake, with the poorest 10% left with a few measly crumbs. I could no longer keep my head stuck in the sand.

The figures for the distribution of wealth in the United States are even more extreme, as evidenced by the Wolff Report from the US Levy Economics Institute in March 2010. The top 1% of Americans own 36% of their country's wealth, up substantially from 20% in 1979. Meanwhile the poorest 40% of the US population owns a miniscule 0.3% of all US wealth, according to the 2010 Norton and Ariely Report. The large numbers of Americans who lost their homes in the recent great recession has meant those with no saleable assets has risen from 18% to 24% of the population. The lower 80% (i.e. the vast majority of the US population) now own only 15% of total US wealth compared to 19% in 1983. The drops trickling down from the rich people's table are getting continuously smaller.

If you strip out people's homes from these figures, the top 1% has a staggering 43% of all US financial wealth and the top 20% has 94% of it, leaving just 6% for the remaining 80% of the population! The almost total control of the US's economic assets by the richest 1% is breath-taking. They own 62% of all stocks, 60% of all financial securities and 30% of all real estate other than residential properties. The top 10% have nearly 90% of stocks, bonds, trust funds and business equity and over 77% of non-home real estate. In essence, as financial wealth is what counts as far as the control of income-producing assets, it would be fair to say *the top 10% actually own the United States of America.*

There are now over three million US millionaires and over four hundred and forty billionaires, far more than any other country in the world, including Bill Gates with a net worth of $59bn, Warren Buffett ($39bn) and Lawrence Ellison ($33bn). Between 1970 and 2006, the average wage of American corporate chief executives rose from thirty times the average worker's wage in 1970 to almost THREE HUNDRED times in 2006.

To cap all this research off, Oxfam produced a stunning report on global wealth inequality in January 2014 which reported that:
The world's wealthiest 85 people owned more than £1 trillion, which was more than half of the entire world's population (3.5 billion people) put together.
The world's top richest 1% owns £60.88 Trillion or 46% of the planet's total wealth and is sixty-five times the combined wealth of the poorest half of the globe's population.

These facts about how much of our common wealth is being monopolised by the ultra-rich, made me wonder how much of our markets were being similarly captured. The figures were again shocking. Almost every aspect of our economy has been captured by a tiny handful of corporate billionaires. Small businesses are being extinguished at an alarming rate and even the middle-sized and larger national-based businesses are disappearing, with the remaining monoliths gobbling up entire global markets. Monolithic oligarchies suffocate a competitive free market.

The following examples provide a snap-shot of some UK and international market shares in 2011 to demonstrate the point:

Groceries

In 2011 the Big Four UK supermarkets controlled 76.5% of the entire UK grocery market. Tesco alone took £3 in every £10 spent on groceries by UK citizens and employed nearly half a million people. Market shares were: Tesco 30%, Asda 17.5%, Sainsbury's 16.7%, Morrison's 12.3%.

Many of the 900,000 Big Four Supermarket employees' low wages have to be subsidised by state benefits, as they do not pay a living wage to their poorer workers. The Fair Pay Network reported that only one in seven workers for these corporations were paid more than the minimum living wage.

The average supermarket worker's hourly pay was £6.73 in 2012, despite the four supermarket corporations making in excess of £6 billion profits annually. The Greater London Authority stated that even with state benefits such employees would find it difficult to feed and clothe their families or even heat their homes. In a reverse Robin Hood operation *The Prostitute State* has created a massive direct transfer of billions of pounds from taxpayers, to subsidise the wealth of the enormously rich families that largely own these supermarket behemoths and their CEOs. These are the Sainsburys, Morrisons, Waltons and Buffetts. The American Walton family, who own the US Walmart retail giant, the owners of ASDA, are the richest family in the world and are worth $150 billion. Warren Buffett is the largest shareholder in Tesco. The pay package for Philip Clarke (CEO of Tesco's) was about £7 million.

In addition, an article I wrote for the Guardian in 2009, revealed another estimated £2.5 billion subsidy is provided annually to these supermarket corporations by local council-tax payers, to pay for the disposal of the packaging waste they create. The government has estimated that over 50% of all household waste comes from just the big four supermarket corporations. In some district councils up to 40% of local council tax is spent on collecting and disposing of household waste. With services for the poor, disabled and elderly being slashed across the board by local councils, this council-tax subsidy to rich corporate supermarket owners is nothing short of a disgrace.

The largely billionaire-owned UK newspapers have no interest in exposing the massive state subsidies to their fellow billionaires, who keep their papers floating with their advertising budgets. Instead they constantly headline on minor benefit fraud by the poor, the miniscule costs for so-called NHS tourism or the costs for housing fleeing refugees rather than the massive corporate welfare rip-off by the rich. Divide and rule being the ever successful strategy of oligarchies.

Not content with their monopoly on our grocery market, the Big Four have been grabbing other significant chunks of our economy, expanding into petrol (Tesco is the largest petrol retailer in the UK), banking, hardware, books, insurance and even coffee shops. They have decimated the small independent shops which gave Britain's high streets their unique character. Over 25,000 small shops have closed in the last twelve years, according to the Portas Report into High Street Retail published in 2011. Britain is no longer a nation of shopkeepers, but a nation of shops owned by four supermarket oligarchies.

Banking

In 2012 four banks controlled over 71% of retail banking accounts in the UK. Market shares were: Lloyds TSB controlling a whopping 30.2%, Barclays 15.8%, RBS 14.6%, and HSBC 10.7%.

The fact that the banking market was so concentrated meant that in the 2007 financial crisis they were just too big to fail and the government was forced to bail them out with over £1.2 TRILLION of support and guarantees. The taxpayer in 2013 was still nourishing losses of about 40% on the banking shares that they had to buy. The banking crisis was estimated to have cost about 13% of the country's total GDP, creating a disaster for workers across Britain with jobs lost, wages frozen and government services cut due to the collapse in government revenues. And whilst the poor guy who stole bottled water in the 2011 riots went to jail, the robber-barons from the big banks made off with huge multi-million-pound severance bonuses.

Milk and butter

Robert Wiseman Dairies (bought by Müller in 2012) and Dairy Crest control 60% of UK milk sales between them. Unilever and Arla dominate sales of butter and spread with 30% of the market each, followed by Dairy Crest at 19%, giving them 79% of the market.

Bread

Just 3 companies supply over 80% of the 9 million loaves of bread we consume in the United Kingdom every day, two of which (Associated British Foods and Premier Foods) are trans-national corporations and the third is Warburton's. If you add the Big Four in-store supermarket bakeries you get to 97% of the market, leaving less than 3% of the bread we eat being produced by small independent or craft bakers.

Domestic Energy Market

Over 99% of the UK domestic energy market is supplied by just six companies supplying both gas and electricity. The top three gas corporations supply 73% per cent of the market. British Gas still maintains a near monopoly with 43%. Market shares are: BG 43%, SSE 17%, and E.ON 13%. The top three electricity suppliers grab 62 % of the total market. Market shares are: British Gas 25%, SSE 20% and E.ON 17%.

Petrol Sales

Six companies in 2011 controlled 71% of the UK petrol market. The list includes three of the Big Four supermarket corporations. Tesco alone has 15.1% of the market. Market shares were: Tesco 15.1%, BP 15%, Shell 12.5%, Esso (ExxonMobil) 10.5%, Morrison's 9% and Sainsbury's 9%.

UK Tobacco Market

Three international corporations have 72% of the UK tobacco market with Imperial Tobacco at 34% and Japan Tobacco International at 31%. These two have elbowed nearly all other players out of the market with the US giant Philip Morris (world's number 1) being reduced to a modest 7% third place.

UK Branded Coffee Shops

Even the humble coffee shop is now part of the corporate domain. Just 3 corporations control 54% of all UK branded chain coffee shops, with Costa Coffee having 30%, Starbucks 14% and Caffè Nero 10%. One reason for Starbucks' ability to close competing local coffee shops is their ability to shift profits around their international network to jurisdictions with no or low corporation taxes. In October 2012 a Reuter's investigation revealed that over fourteen years, Starbucks UK paid less than 1% corporation tax on its £3 billion sales and had paid nothing at all since 2009, declaring losses to the tax authorities for the last five years.

Yet Starbucks was simultaneously telling investors that the UK business was profitable and they were pleased with its performance. Reuters revealed that the beans for UK stores are bought by a Swiss subsidiary and roasted by a Dutch subsidiary. Meanwhile local independent UK coffee shops are paying taxes on their profits, giving Starbucks an up to 20% competitive tax advantage.

More worryingly from the point of view of the sovereignty of the democratic nation-state, a similar rapid concentration of market power is also taking place globally, giving enormous financial and crucially from the point of view of *The Prostitute State,* political power to this small number of corporations and billionaires.

Global Corporate Accountancy/Auditing Market

There are now only 4 firms dominating almost 100% of the world's corporate auditing market. KPMG, Deloitte & Touche, PricewaterhouseCoopers and Ernst & Young shared a global market valued at over $100 billion in 2012. This is an especially dangerous oligopoly as they are now the only companies perceived as big enough to financially audit international corporations. It was they who had repeatedly signed off the accounts of all the global banks, including Lehman Brothers, whose demise led to the 2008 global financial crash.

Chapter 2

They have yet to receive any serious punishment for their failures, which led to the almost unparalleled destruction of individual wealth and which workers and taxpayers across the world are paying for in lost jobs and vicious cutbacks in government social programmes, in countries ranging from Greece and Ireland to the US and UK.

Global Proprietary Seed Market

Even the world's crucial seed market is increasingly monopolised by a small group of global chemical corporations specialising in genetic engineering. The US giant Monsanto now towers over all its competitors worldwide with an astonishing 23% of all proprietary seeds sold globally. The American chemical giant DuPont comes second with 15%. Syngenta of Switzerland has 9% and Groupe Limagrain has 6%. Between them the top five seed sellers control 53% of all proprietary plant-seeds sold on the planet and they are aggressively pursuing the remaining independent seed suppliers. This enormous market clout has enabled them to overwhelm government regulators even in the US, where they successfully persuaded the US federal authorities that foods that were artificially genetically modified should not be labelled as such.

Steel market

The global steel market is increasingly concentrated with Acelor Mittal now controlling 10% of the entire world's steel production. The top fifteen steel corporations already control over a third of the planet's steel production.

Cruise Liners

Whilst not a crucial industry even markets such as this are dominated by a tiny group of corporate owners. Two mega-corporations, the US owned Carnival Corporation (owner of the Costa Concordia which went down off the coast of Italy in January 2012 with 32 deaths) and the Royal Caribbean Group based in the UK, own a staggering 79% of the global cruise liner market. Carnival dominates the global market with a 54% market share. These two are followed by NCL at 8% and MSC at 5%, giving the top four corporations 92% of the world market.

Coffee Market

The global coffee market was worth $70 billion in 2011. Global Market shares were: Nestlé (23%); Kraft (12.9%); Douwe Egberts (6% percent). Nestlé controls over 50% of the world's instant coffee market, selling over $17 billion dollars' worth every year. Kraft is owned by tobacco giant Philip Morris. About 10% of coffee profits go to the growers, 10% to exporters, 55% to shippers and roasters and 25% to the retailers. In the early 1990s, people in the coffee-producing countries earned about 40 cents on every dollar spent on coffee. Now they only earn about 8 to 13 cents. This is mainly due to lower prices paid to farmers, despite higher prices being paid by consumers. Corporate power enables the rich to grab an increasing percentage of global wealth leaving millions poorer in their wake. Food markets are increasingly popular with financial speculators, as soaring populations and climate disasters put pressure on food prices.

Grain / Zinc/ Copper

Glencore is an Anglo–Swiss multi-national commodity trading and mining company with its HQ in Switzerland but registered in the tax haven of Jersey. It controls almost 10% of all internationally traded grains. In 2010 it had global commodity market shares that included 60% for zinc and 50% for copper. Its CEO Ivan Glasenberg owned 15% of the corporation in 2011 and was worth $7.3 billion.

Comments made by the head of Glencore's food division Chris Mahoney in July 2012 following disastrous harvests across the globe, including Russia, Ukraine, US, Australia and Europe, described market conditions following the global food-price rise of 6% in July alone as being *"good for Glencore"*. His boss Ivan Glasenberg described market conditions as being *"a time when industry fundamentals are the most positive they have been for some time."* These chilling comments graphically reveal how the global corporate elite often regards the rest of humanity as merely a profit opportunity, even when the resulting food-price inflation drives millions of the world's poor, many of whom already spend over 75% of their income on food, deeper into malnutrition or even starvation. They profit handsomely from food-price inflation created by global crop failures, some of which scientists believe are already a result of the climate crises.

But it is not just the grabbing of global monopolies that causes real concern. It is also the implications of how the size of these corporations dwarfs the GDP (Gross Domestic Product) of entire nations. For example the value of the top ten corporations on the FT Global 500 list is the same as the entire GDP of the UK ($2.4 trillion), which was the seventh largest economy in the world in 2011. The value of Exxon Mobil, the world's largest corporation in 2011, exceeded the GDP of 156 countries. Only 27 countries had a GDP greater than it, according to the figures supplied by the International Monetary Fund.

According to UNCTAD, Trans National Corporations (TNC's) already controlled 35% of global GDP in 2010. *The Prostitute State* is destroying our democratically regulated free-market economies, replacing them with global monopolistic oligarchies. As their wealth and power inexorably increases, it is essential that we ask what place, if any, would democracy retain in a world where 100% of GDP was controlled by such corporations?

What is not readily apparent in the above breakdown of corporate market shares is what proportion of global wealth is held by the richest billionaires. The

Chapter 2

2011 Forbes list of the world's billionaires lists the three richest people as being Carlos Slim Helu ($74 billion), Bill Gates ($ 56 billion) and Warren Buffett ($50 billion). The value of the top ten individuals combined comes to an astonishing $406 billion or almost the same as the world's largest corporation at $417 billion (Exxon Mobil). Mr Helu's wealth was greater than the GDP of the 119 poorest countries in the world. He was richer than the entire GDP of countries including Syria, Jordan, Bolivia, Ethiopia, Croatia etc.   The ancient classical Athenian oligarchs look like puny amateurs when compared to this new global oligarchy. Just as ruthless political power was exercised by those oligarchs in ancient Greece, it is crucial to understand the enormous unaccountable political power such staggering wealth grants today to this new global elite.

My negative experiences of corporate lobbyists within the Liberal Democrats and the political battles resulting from them, were not merely personal political differences with senior party figures who happened to be lobbyists but were symptoms of a deep malaise in our wider democracy. As I researched the corruption of our democracy, I realised that there were other pillars of *The Prostitute State* in addition to *The Corrupted Political System*. I had seen first-hand the impact that the tabloid media had on the Lib Dems' campaigns department and the MPs that it had helped get elected, when the party's core values and policies were repeatedly ditched to avoid tabloid attacks.

A tiny number of voters in the one hundred or so swing constituencies decide the outcome of UK elections. Many of these voters are regular tabloid-readers. This gives enormous power to the billionaire-owned media over the election of our MPs under the profoundly distorting and voter disempowering first-past-the-post system. The tabloids have warped the campaign departments of both the Liberal Democrat and Labour parties to such an extent that they have essentially become consumer-facing focus-group consultancies. Campaigning on genuinely held political convictions no longer seems acceptable. This led me to the conclusion that *The Prostituted Media* is the second pillar of *The Prostitute State*.

Another recurring theme during my time on the Lib Dem Federal Executive was my run-ins with people who were up to their eyes in tax-haven involvements. The party treasurer was almost invariably the leader's nominee and during my time there was nearly always either a director of a tax-haven based company or a paid professional lobbyist for a tax haven. I thought this was just an accident of personalities within the party, until I looked at the other two parties and realised that their treasurers and major donors were likewise closely involved with the notorious tax havens that have proliferated on the UK's offshore territories since the Second World War.

I realised that the ultra-rich who were able to use to the offshore tax haven system to maximise their wealth, were controlling our political party leaderships by funding them. This nicely helps protect the taxation systems that facilitate the transfer of their wealth into offshore accounts, which not only avoids their ethical share of taxation but also gives them a competitive advantage over decent tax-paying nationally-based companies, many of which have been put out of business or taken over by offshore owners. This is the dirty truth behind the massive anti-competitive concentration of market power outlined above. After all, why would party leaders energetically target this offshore scandal as a priority when they know it would alienate their major financial donors? This led to the conclusion that *The Thieving Tax Havens* were the third pillar of **The Prostitute State**.

A letter from a couple of academics in The Guardian that I read shortly after I had begun researching this book led to the realisation that *The Perverted Academia* was the fourth pillar of **The Prostitute State.** They were criticising another letter that had appeared in the paper from a professor praising the consequences of the collapse of the Soviet Union on health services. They pointed out that this professor had been a major beneficiary of the private health firms that had benefitted from the collapse. Such examples are endemic in a system where the ultra-rich and their corporations are increasingly taking over our schools, universities and think tanks, perverting their ability to be the wellsprings of independent expert knowledge, research and creativity that are so crucial to the fair and successful running of a modern democracy.

Many western countries including the US and UK, are not the liberal democracies that we are led to believe we are living in. You cannot have a true open and fair society if the political classes that make the decisions, the media that shapes the debate that leads to those decisions, the academia that informs that debate and the tax system that harnesses the wealth of those decisions are all dominated and controlled by a tiny group of people at the richest end of society, whose narrow short-term vested interests often clash with the needs of wider society and the natural environment. Ironically, in the longer term, their interests are also best served by social and environmental justice if only they realised it.

The following chapters lay out in detail how the four main pillars of **The Prostitute State** operate. If we are to cure our democracies of this malignancy, we need to be able to identify it when we see it in operation. The aim is to open your eyes to seeing the world in a new way. So that no matter what you are doing, whether it is academic research, watching the news or even grocery shopping, you will be able to become aware of how it surreptitiously tries to manipulate us and hijack our rightful share of freedom, health and prosperity. For with awareness comes power.

Chapter 3

The Lobbying Gutter

My experiences in the Liberal Democrats convinced me that political lobbying is one of the most powerful unaccountable forces perverting our democratic government. It ensures that the ultra-rich regularly get their way. With an astonishing estimated £2 billion being spent by the UK's political lobbying industry every year, the resources available to this army of lobbyists overwhelm our political defences. They can afford a massive array of tactics, many invisible to the public and are rarely exposed by the billionaire-owned media who are often complicit in their campaigns.

Lobbyists manipulate government policy, public opinion and scientific discourse. Manipulation of government policy is often achieved through the purchase of currently-serving politicians' time, contacts and influence by employing them on lucrative retainers as "consultant advisers" or offering them lavishly paid company directorships. Retired politicians, regulators and senior civil servants are snapped up by the professional political-lobbying firms or the lobbying departments of large corporations, on salaries that dwarf those in the public sector. Lobbyists will also provide free secretarial support and sponsorship to politicians and even actually draft legislation for All Party Parliamentary Groups of MPs sympathetic to their cause.

Among the methods used to manipulate public opinion are the treating of journalists to all-expenses-paid "fact-finding" trips, biased paid-for advertorial in the press, expensive advertising campaigns and pseudo "grassroots" campaigns which are created by the lobbying PR companies. Science is manipulated through the hiring of scientists willing to give the corporate line or through the sponsorship of "scientific" research that just happens to support the corporation's legislative needs, which sows doubt about environmental facts injurious to a corporation's existing market or PR-driven attacks on the credentials of legitimate scientists who produce independent research.

For as long as there have been human governments, there have been people seeking to influence it, as this quote from a US newspaper columnist in 1869 demonstrates:

"...winding in and out through the long, devious basement passage, crawling through the corridors, trailing its slimy length from gallery to committee room, at

last it lies stretched at full length on the floor of Congress - this dazzling reptile, this huge, scaly serpent of the lobby."

But what is new is the enormous amount of money available to the industry. The resources available to UK political parties are measured in the low millions of pounds but those available to influence and manipulate them are measured in the billions. It has been estimated that for each of the UK's 646 MPs there are twenty-two full time professional political lobbyists. The £2 billion spent annually on lobbying government is the equivalent of over £3,100,000 per MP.

Whilst the concept of lobbying is reasonably well known, what is not generally known is how far lobbying has penetrated and hijacked the political parties themselves. For example, most people are perplexed at how the nuclear industry managed to persuade the UK Labour government to build another fleet of hugely expensive experimental nuclear-power stations on land prone to flooding from rising sea levels. They managed this despite the Three Mile Island, Chernobyl and Fukushima nuclear catastrophes, the requirement for decades of massive taxpayer subsidies, the failure to find safe waste-disposal sites capable of protecting radioactive waste for over 100,000 years and the fact that the insurance companies refuse point blank to provide accident insurance.

The simple answer is that millions of pounds have been poured year after year into a massive political lobbying campaign by the industry. They bought a whole swathe of senior ex-politicians to work as nuclear lobbyists, spent a fortune on trying to manipulate public opinion through media and advertising and even funded school trips to their nuclear plants. As they managed to persuade a Labour government to abandon their election manifesto commitment to oppose new nuclear power stations, it is crucial to understand how deeply the nuclear lobby is embedded in the Labour party and so ensured no matter what Labour party members or the public wanted, that the Labour government served the nuclear industry.

Just consider for example the following list of Labour Party politicians:

- Former Energy Minister Brian Wilson became a non-executive director of Amec Nuclear, a client of BNFL, a nuclear operator.
- Former Energy Minister Helen Liddell was hired to provide "strategic advice" by the nuclear corporation British Energy.
- Former Secretary of State John Hutton, who as Business Secretary published the government White Paper announcing government plans to build new nuclear stations, was appointed Chair of the Nuclear Industry Association in 2011. He also joined the advisory board of U.S. nuclear corporation Hyperion Power Generation in July 2010.

Chapter 3

- Colin Byrne, the Labour Party's former chief press officer, headed up lobbying giant Weber Shandwick's UK arm, which BNFL hired to lobby for new nuclear plants.
- Gordon Brown's brother, Andrew, is nuclear giant EdF's head of media relations in the UK.
- Yvette Cooper was the Planning Minister who introduced fast-track planning for nuclear power stations. Her father was chair of nuclear lobbyists The Nuclear Industry Association and is director of the Nuclear Decommissioning Authority.
- Alan Donnelly, former leader of the Labour MEPs, runs the lobbying company Sovereign Strategy, which represented US nuclear engineering giant Fluor. His website promised "pathways to the decision makers in national governments".
- Former Labour Minister Jack Cunningham was legislative chair of the Transatlantic Nuclear Energy Forum, an organisation founded by lobbyist Alan Donnelly to foster "strong relationships" between nuclear power companies and governments.
- The Tory Peer Lady Maitland was a paid member of Sovereign Strategy's board.
- Donnelly funded Labour leadership contender David Miliband's constituency office refurbishment.
- David Sainsbury, Labour Minister for Science from 1998 to 2006 told the House of Lords that he regarded nuclear power as a form of renewable energy.
- Ed Miliband's barrister wife Justine Thornton advised EdF Energy on its Development Consent Order for a new nuclear plant at Hinkley Point.

This wholesale hiring of senior Labour Party figures by the nuclear lobby has successfully achieved its aims over the last ten years:

- It reversed Labour's commitment to rule out new nuclear power stations.
- They got the Labour government to commit to building 10 new nuclear power stations by 2020.
- They persuaded Labour ministers to introduce a fast-track planning process for new nuclear plants without lengthy inquiries.
- Whilst governments across the world were abandoning nuclear power after the Fukushima disaster, the nuclear lobby persuaded the new Tory/Lib Dem coalition to abandon their manifesto commitments to provide no public subsidy for new nuclear, by guaranteeing a price for its electricity that was

nearly double existing electricity prices and which would provide multi-billion pound annual subsidies for nuclear power.

- They persuaded the Tory/Lib Dem government to make the taxpayer liable for nuclear disaster costs after the private insurers refused to do so, as just one catastrophic accident would bankrupt most global insurance companies.

To understand the comparative power of political lobbying versus voting at elections, you need to realise that the final two aims above were achieved despite the Lib Dems having for decades supposedly opposed nuclear power and the Tories having opposed nuclear subsidies in the 2010 general election. I was never convinced by the Lib Dem leadership's opposition to nuclear power after it successfully, in the late nineties, squashed the adoption in policy papers of the phrase *"a renewable energy economy"* that I had proposed to replace *"a low-carbon economy"* which they favoured. The latter of course allowed the switch to a pro-nuclear policy once the Lib Dems were in government.

Ed Davey MP stood for election opposing nuclear energy, but as Lib Dem Secretary of State for Energy and Climate Change, he became nuclear power's chief cheerleader, announcing that the government's entire industrial strategy was now based on new nuclear. The UK government is already spending the equivalent of 93% of the Department of Energy and Climate Change's entire annual budget on nuclear subsidies! This was achieved despite polls indicating overwhelming support by the public for renewable energy over nuclear power. His brother, Henry Davey, works for the global law firm Herbert Smith Freehills which has advised EdF on its purchase of nuclear plants and the development application for a new nuclear plant at Hinkley Point.

But whilst most nuclear lobbying by bought political operatives remains invisible, the "Cash for Influence" scandal in March 2010 exposed the depth of general lobbying corruption at the top of the Labour party. Three former Labour ministers were the subjects of a sting operation by Channel 4. They were caught on camera offering lobbying services in return for cash. One of them was Patricia Hewitt, who after ceasing to be Health Minister and still serving as an MP became a "special adviser" to Alliance Boots and the private-equity company Cinven, which paid £1.4 billion for Bupa's UK hospitals.

It is no wonder that, despite overwhelming public opposition, our National Health Service is being privatised lock, stock and barrel, when even former Labour Health Ministers and MPs are selling their political services to private health corporations. Ms Hewitt was videoed by Dispatches brazenly claiming she was paid £3,000 a day and was helping a client obtain a key seat on a Government advisory group, thus helping to capture it for the corporate state.

Chapter 3

The second former Labour Minister caught in the sting was Stephen Byers, who had been Secretary of State for Trade and Industry and Secretary of State for Transport. He was filmed infamously describing himself as a *"cab for hire"* and offering his lobbying services for £5,000 per day. Byers claimed to have influenced outcomes for National Express and Tesco through his relationships with Lord Adonis, Transport Secretary and Lord Mandelson, Business Secretary, although he later denied this.

The third serving Labour MP caught in the sting was former Defence Secretary Geoff Hoon, already infamous for being the ultra-loyal Blairite Minister for Defence during the disastrous illegal invasion of Iraq in 2003. Hoon beautifully summed up how ex-ministers prostitute themselves by telling the undercover reporter *"One of the challenges I think I'm really looking forward to is translating my knowledge and contacts about the international scene into something that bluntly, makes money."*

Despite the Dispatches scandal, Hoon continued to prostitute his political services. Following his retirement in 2010, he set up the political consultancy Taylor Hoon Strategy. Its website shamelessly sought to capitalise on the privatisation of government services stating: *"To reduce spending, [Western governments] will be looking to the private sector to provide solutions involving cost savings through efficient restructuring and outsourcing. We can advise the private sector how to take advantage of this opportunity."* Again, what hope has the electorate of protecting public assets, when former ministers profit from their sell-off? Such actions by third world politicians rightly generate outrage in our media but ours never get the condemnation they deserve in the UK.

Another scandalous practice is former ministers being employed by the corporations whose lucrative state contracts passed through their departments whilst serving as Ministers. In May 2011 The Financial Times reported that Geoff Hoon was appointed to be AgustaWestland's executive senior vice-president for international business, responsible for the sale of helicopters. The Daily Mail reported that AgustaWestland had been named as the preferred bidder for the MoD's £1.7 billion Future Lynx new helicopter project in 2005 when Hoon was Defence Secretary. No other firms were invited to bid, despite claims that other manufacturers could have provided an alternative more cheaply and quickly. The Ministry of Defence's then permanent secretary, Kevin Tebbit, also joined AgustaWestland's Italian parent, Finmeccanica, barely a year after the deal was agreed.

All three ministers were censured by Parliament but none were expelled from the Labour Party. The scandal revealed how deep a grip the lobbying system has on some Labour politicians and how their ethics-free approach was beautifully summarised in Byer's *"cabs for hire"* and Hoon's blatant admission of converting of his government contacts into something *"that frankly makes money"*. But this scandal is only a tiny example of Labour's capture by corporate lobbyists, as demonstrated by the fact that the Advisory Committee on Business Appointments reported in 2012 that an astonishing twenty-four former Labour senior and junior ministers had gone into lobbying in the previous three years.

If you would like a taste of just how overwhelming a hold *The Prostitute State* also has on the Liberal Democrats, consider this non-exhaustive list of senior Lib Dems:

- Nick Clegg, Lib Dem leader and Deputy Prime Minister, worked as an oil/gas lobbyist when he ceased being an MEP in 2004 prior to election as an MP.
- Willie Rennie MSP, Leader of the Scottish Liberal Democrats, worked as a consultant for the lobbying firm McEwan Purvis.
- Lord Tim Clement Jones, Lib Dem leader Nick Clegg's general election Party Treasurer worked for lobbying giant DLA Piper.
- Neil Sherlock, head of government relations in Deputy Prime Minister Nick Clegg's private office, worked as a senior lobbyist for KPMG.
- Jonathan Oates, Nick Clegg's Chief of Staff, was a Director for lobbying giant Bell Pottinger.
- Lord Dick Newby, Lib Dem leader Paddy Ashdown's head of private office, was a political lobbyist.
- James Gurling, member of Lib Dem FE and Lib Dem leader Charles Kennedy's former brother-in-law, is a political lobbyist with Hanover.
- Mark Oaten, Lib Dem leader Charles Kennedy's Private Parliamentary Secretary, was a lobbyist prior to being an MP and became a lobbyist for the European fur industry after he left parliament in disgrace.
- Lord Tom McNally, Minister for Justice, was Vice President of one of the world's largest lobbying corporations Shandwicks.
- Nick Clegg's wife Miriam Clegg works for the international lobbying firm Dechert.
- Chris Huhne's partner Carina Trimingham sought work as a lobbyist whilst he was the Secretary of State.
- The partner of David Laws MP (Lib Dem Minister of State Cabinet Office and one of Nick Clegg's closest advisers) James Lundie works for lobbying firm Edelman.
- Chris Fox, Lib Dem chief executive, resigned after just 3 years to become lead lobbyist for international engineering corporation GKN.
- Ming Campbell MP, former leader of the Liberal Democrats, worked for the lobbying firm Westminster Associates *whilst* an MP in the early 1990's.

- Paul Keetch, former Lib Dem MP for Herefordshire, set up the lobbying company Wellington Street Partners. Keetch was Lib Dem Defence Spokesperson under Kennedy.

- Neil Stockley, Head of Policy for the Liberal Democrats, became a lobbyist for Bell Pottinger. The Bell Pottinger Website shamelessly boasted about Stockley being *"the most respected Liberal Democrat political lobbyist"*.

- Jeremy Browne MP, ex Lib Dem Minister of State for the Home Office, worked for Edelman, the world's largest independently owned public-relations corporation.

- Olly Grender OBE, former Lib Dem Communications Director, now works for lobbying company PMLR.

- Craig Harrow, Vice President of the Liberal Democrats, works for lobbyists MHP communications.

- Stephen Lotina, who served as the Liberal Democrats' Senior Adviser on Public Services and Health, now works for Bell Pottinger.

- Lord Alan Watson was appointed to the Lords by Paddy Ashdown whilst working for lobbyist Burson-Marsteller, notorious for its 1990's tobacco lobbying campaigns.

- Neil Weston, former Liberal Democrat Press Officer, is lead lobbyist for the British Air Transport Association (BATA).

- Mark Pack works for political lobbying corporation MHP Communications. Whilst an active corporate lobbyist he edited the party membership's main online communication tool Lib Dem Voice.

- Andy Mayer, former director of Liberal Future (a right-wing Lib Dem think-tank) is now a lobbyist for the GM foods and chemical corporation BASF

- Ed Fordham, former Head of the Lib Dem Office of the Local Government Association, lobbied for RBS.

During the 2010 UK general election Nick Clegg's official Lib Dem CV stated that: *"The travelling life of an MEP was difficult to reconcile with a young family and in 2004 I stood down as an MEP. I lectured part-time at Sheffield and Cambridge Universities before being elected as Member of Parliament for Sheffield Hallam in 2005."* However Channel 4 News reported that Clegg's CV failed to include the fact that in 2004, the Lib Dem leader spent almost a year working for the European lobbying firm GPlus.

In a GPlus press release Clegg is quoted as saying: *"It's especially exciting to be joining GPlus at a time when Brussels is moving more and more to the centre of business concerns. With the EU taking in ten more countries and adopting a new Constitution, organisations need more than ever intelligent professional help in engaging with the EU institutions."* The firm said it helps clients who want to *"shape policy thinking"* and have their *"voice heard in Brussels or in the European capitals"*. When he was asked, Clegg admitted that he earned far more as a lobbyist than as a part-time lecturer. Clegg's lobbying clients included the car-hire firm Hertz and the multinational oil and gas company BG. Prior to being elected an MEP, Clegg also worked for the political lobbying firm GJW.

KPMG lobbyist Neil Sherlock has long been part of the Lib Dem lobbying clique who jump from one leader's inner circle to the next, always maintaining enormous power compared to non-lobbyist members. In 2011 Clegg appointed him to be his head of government relations. The Telegraph reported in 2011 that Sherlock's government salary was estimated to be over £100,000. In September 2012 he was still listed on the KPMG website as being their partner in charge of public and regulatory affairs, a role Sherlock had held for nearly a decade.

This decade was the one in which the leading Big Four accountancy firms contributed hugely to the global financial meltdown. They lobbied for the abolition of various accountancy regulations and failed to identify or report on the systemic threat to the global economy posed by the out-of-control banking corporations and the derivatives market. They are also major advisers to the global multi-trillion-dollar tax-haven industry. Clegg appointed Sherlock's wife Kathryn Parminter, who is a Lib Dem donor, to the House of Lords. Sherlock was a regular donor to Clegg's private office, prior to Clegg becoming leader of the Lib Dems.

Whilst I had a strong interest in party policy, I was initially naive about the role of lobbyists in it. However I soon experienced first-hand how they pervert the party's internal policy-making processes, whilst I was serving on the Genetically Modified Foods policy group. Recognising the threat GM foods posed to the future of organic crops, *new radicalism* had successfully submitted a conference policy motion calling for the party to oppose GM food crops. The establishment blocked the conference vote by referring it to the policy committee, which unsurprisingly did nothing about it. We submitted a similar motion to conference a second time and again they blocked the vote but were forced to set up a policy working group on it. I successfully applied to sit on the working party, which had a significant proportion of pro-GM advocates on it and I led the opposition.

My position on open field-trials of GM crops was that they would release GM contamination, irreversibly corrupting neighbouring crops and the wider environment. The pro-GM lobby claimed "insulation zones" of a few meters surrounding the GM crops would protect neighbouring farmers. When I pointed out that pollinators travelled for miles and the wind likewise disperses pollen for considerable distances, they argued that I had no proof this would happen to GM pollen! I had thus come up against the classic tobacco-industry lobbying tactic of always sowing scientific doubt, no matter how preposterous the scientific case being proposed may be. However I prevailed and the working-group report opposed open-air field-trials and GM food crops.

Chapter 3

I then accidentally encountered the lobbyists plying their secretive trade. When a policy group produces its report, it is sent to the Federal Policy Committee for consideration and amendment, prior to being submitted to conference for final approval. Normally members of the working party do not attend this meeting. However, as I had spent nearly four years working to get the policy adopted, even though I had no right to speak, I attended the meeting. Also present, although not a member, was Peter Price, a former Lib Dem MEP who was now a paid GM industry lobbyist. He works for CJA Associates. Among their major clients are the Chemical Industries Association and Solvay SA (a multi-billion pound chemicals corporation). They also work for FORATOM the EU pro-nuclear-power campaign. To my astonishment he was given speaking rights at the meeting to address the GM paper, something I had no idea was even possible. Price proceeded to trash the paper and urged the committee not to adopt it. Thankfully he was not successful.

The paper was then submitted to conference and I moved the motion. It was third time lucky as we won by a comfortable margin. However, winning democratically at conference does not mean the leadership adopts it as policy, as I learnt so often to my despair. What matters is whether the policy gets into the general-election manifesto and this is crucially where the leadership can invisibly veto policies adopted by conference that the lobbying insiders want blocked.

Our hard-fought-for anti-GM policy providing vital protection for Britain's organic farmers and public health never made it into Charles Kennedy's manifesto. I have no idea how many behind-the-scenes meetings internal party GM lobbyists had with the leadership but I did not like what I saw of their modus operandi. It was an eye-opener to see how corporate lobbyists operated within the party. They were also able to directly affect policy-making through their access to being actual members of the federal conference and federal policy-making committees.

I was at an RSA Lecture in 2011 when a lobbyist told the meeting that the lobbying practices at the major party conferences were so corrupt that his company refused to attend them. In the Lib Dems, parallel to the main party conference there is de-facto another net-working conference to which the corporate lobbyists have almost exclusive access. This includes cocktail parties for the party elite funded by corporations like Bloomberg's, leadership receptions for exhibitors funded by McDonald's and a host of cosy dinners and sit-down breakfasts for MPs and Ministers funded by various corporate lobbyists. These are hidden away from the media spotlight and parliamentary regulations on lobbying, in various private dining-rooms.

Exhibition spaces at the party conferences are flooded with corporate lobbying stands. These push out nearly all but the best-funded party members' interest groups and most of civic society, who cannot afford the eye-watering exhibition space costs. Likewise, the Lib Dem conference fringe meetings which used to be a valuable forum for legitimate democratic debates are now subverted by the private-equity funded think-tank CentreForum, which lavishly funds over 30 fringe meetings and receptions at the party's Autumn Conference, drowning out the interests of party members.

Whilst Labour and the Lib Dems are seriously infected with lobbyists, the Tories take it to an extreme. Historically, being the party of the land-owning classes, it was the natural home for the new industrial millionaires in the 19th and 20th centuries and the private equity billionaires in the 21st century. Political lobbying complements the pre-existing Tory old boys' networks that continue to dominate Britain. Eighteen of the twenty two members of the 2012 UK coalition government's cabinet were former public or grammar school boys (and girls). If you employ these public schoolboys as lobbyists, it is very likely they will personally know some of these ministers from their school days.

At the 2010 Tory Party conference, the seven thousand lobbyists present, vastly outnumbered the four thousand actual conference representatives!

Numerous scandals have exposed how deeply enmeshed the Tories are in the corporate lobbying system. For over two decades the Tory peer Lord Tim Bell, founder of one of Britain's most notorious international lobbying corporations Bell Pottinger, has been the *éminence grise* of the lobbying elites. Bell Pottinger offers *"consumer, corporate and financial, healthcare, technology, industrial, public affairs, public sector, corporate social responsibility [!], internal communication, crisis and issues management services"*. Bell first established his lobbying credentials as Margaret Thatcher's advertising guru for the 1979 general election. At the time he worked for Saatchi & Saatchi, whose brilliant PR campaigns, including the slogan *"Labour Isn't Working"*, played a crucial role in Thatcher's first general election victory. Knighted by Thatcher in 1990, Bell was appointed a life peer in 1998. Bell Pottinger's clients include a who's who from an international gallery of dictatorships and arms manufacturers, including the governments of Belarus, Bahrain and Sri Lanka, arms manufacturer EADS and Asma Assad (the Syrian dictator's wife).

Bell helped the UK arms manufacturer BAE get the Blair government to drop the Serious Fraud Office (SFO) bribery investigation into the multi-billion pound Saudi Arabian Al Yamamah arms deal, which was signed during Thatcher's Prime Ministership. In 2006 The Guardian reported that *"veteran fixer Tim Bell"* and the Defence Exports Services Organisation had set up a chorus claiming that the investigation endangered the Saudi arms contract, for seventy-two Typhoon aircraft, thus threatening 100,000 jobs. But a University of York study indicated that 5,000 jobs were threatened. The Guardian reported how the classic lobbying PR campaign included an article in The Sunday Times (Nov 19th), a report in the Financial Times (Nov 28th) that BAE were saying that the investigation was damaging, questions in parliament accusing the investigation of *"gumming up"* the negotiations (Nov 30th), Telegraph reports that Saudi Arabia had given the UK government ten days to halt the investigation (Dec 1st), with more MPs stating the investigation was putting jobs at risk (Dec 3rd) and then the National Defence Industries Council saying *"it was going to write"* to the government (Dec 4th).

The SFO had managed to persuade the Swiss banking authorities to release a file on the payments from BAE to various Saudi destinations. But then on December 14th Blair's attorney-general Lord Goldsmith ordered the SFO to block collection of the precious Swiss banking file and closed down the investigation on the grounds of *"national security"*. This drove a coach and horses through the international OECD Anti-Bribery Convention which Britain had signed and set a terrible example for other nations. But this was a master-class on how **The Prostitute State** gets what it wants.

Bell employs senior operatives from all the major UK political parties to ensure his lobbying companies are effective no matter whom we elect. A key Tory recruit was Tim Collins, the former Tory MP for Westmoreland, who was appointed managing director of Bell Pottinger Public Affairs in 2009. There is almost no-one in the Tory government that Collins is not on first-name terms with. He was Press Secretary to Tory Prime Minister John Major, was a member of the Number 10 Downing Street Policy Unit and speechwriter to leading Tories including Margaret Thatcher, Michael Howard, Chris Patten and Norman Fowler. He was Shadow Transport Secretary under Iain Duncan Smith and Shadow Education Secretary under Michael Howard.

In a filmed interview sting in November 2011, by undercover Bureau of Investigative Journalism (BIJ) journalists pretending to be seeking lobbying services on behalf of the Uzbekistan dictatorship and its cotton industry, Tim Collins revealed a plethora of mechanisms used to advance their clients' interests, whether third world dictatorships or first world arms manufacturers, infamously saying *"We've got all sorts of dark arts"*.

Collins listed those that they could employ on behalf of the Uzbeks but would not put them in writing as they could be *"embarrassing"*. Among the *"services"* mentioned on tape were:

- Establishing regime-friendly third-party blogs posing as being independent
- Manipulating the regime's Google search-rankings so that negative stories would be buried
- Ensuring regime videos and positive stories would be highlighted in internet search engines

- Provide a team to *"sort out"* any negative entries on their Wikipedia pages
- Organising lunch with senior leader writers from papers such as The Times
- Getting MPs they knew to attack any media that criticised the regime
- Personally contact various members of David Cameron's team inside the Prime Minister's office
- Facilitation of a state visit to the UK for regime leaders
- Arrange joint events with influential government-aligned think-tanks such as The Policy Exchange
- Briefing sympathetic academics so that information would appear to be from *"independent"* sources

They stated that such a multi-faceted campaign for the dictatorship would run to about £100,000 per month. They did in passing mention the need for the Uzbek dictatorship (notorious for its forced child-labour record) to carry out human-rights improvements. However Collins added that it did not need to be very fast or as he callously said *"As long as you can see that each year is a little better than before, that's fine."* Some lobbyists do not really care whether Uzbek kids continue in forced labour or not, as long as they get their nice fat cheques.

His following words revealed the ice-cold world such lobbyists inhabit, as they slither around and undermine our democracy: *"Britain has this sort of moral ethic it thinks it can impose upon the world still, because of our colonial background and the Commonwealth. We forget that 100 years ago we had kids working in cotton mills here."* Tim Collins also spoke about his access to the Prime Minister's office: *"I've been working with people like Steve Hilton, David Cameron, and George Osborne for twenty years plus. There is not a problem getting the messages through."* He added that he had been Edward Llewellyn's (Cameron's Head of Staff) boss in Conservative Central Office and had worked with Mr Cameron and Mr Osborne in the Conservative Research Department.

The revelation of how Collins used these channels for clients caused outrage when The Independent reported it. It starkly demonstrated the ability of rich corporate clients to get our elected government to do their bidding. Collins said on tape that on the day before a state visit to China by the UK Prime Minister in June 2011: *"We were rung up at 2.30 on a Friday afternoon, by one of our clients, Dyson. He said 'We've got a huge issue. A lot of our products are being ripped off in China.' On the Saturday David Cameron raised it with the Chinese Prime Minister."* Collins added that, *"He [Cameron] was doing it because we asked him to do it,"* and because *"the issue was in the wider national interest".*

Lord Bell's response when the scandal broke was not to apologise but to use his lawyers, Carter Ruck, to legally attack the BIJ. He said: *"The conduct of the Bureau of Investigative Journalism does not remotely constitute responsible*

Chapter 3

journalism. It is an attempt by unethical deception to manufacture a story where none exists." Bell thus employed his own company's dark arts by attacking the messenger rather than dealing with the disgraceful allegations. When Bell complained to the Press Complaints Commission, it thankfully held that there was a *'broad public interest in exploring the relationship between lobbying and politics'*. Despite the outcry, Collins continued to ply his trade for Bell Pottinger.

Examining specific examples of how *the Prostitute State* uses lobbying is a useful way to get to understand it. Take for example the BBC news story on Heathrow Airport published in August 2012. The headline was *"Heathrow Capacity Harms Economy Say MPs"* and the story said that MPs had produced a report stating efforts should be made *"to ensure the UK retains and grows hub capacity"* at Heathrow or at a new purpose-built airport. Heathrow is already one of the world's three busiest airports, but is disastrously situated in the middle of London's residential suburbs, with up to 3 flights every minute at peak hours, making life hell for the millions who live underneath. It is estimated that 50% of people affected by noise pollution in the whole of Europe live under Heathrow's flight paths.

But the key question was who lay behind the report, which was written like a normal BBC news story. I discovered that this group of MPs was not an official Parliamentary Select Committee but was the All Party Aviation Group. In other words, it was a self-selecting group of pro-aviation-industry MPs and so any report from them would be inherently biased. Parliamentary regulations require that such ad-hoc industry groups of MPs declare their sponsors, so I looked them up. Sure enough, I found that MHP Communications (a lobbying company) provides the secretariat *"free of charge"* for this group. Such sponsorships usually enabled lobbying companies to get their hands on invaluable parliamentary passes that gave them access to parliament, where they could lobby MPs not on the aviation group. Sharp-eyed readers will recognise the lobbying company as the one that Mark Pack, the former co-editor of Lib Dem Voice, worked for.

I checked the MHP website and found that transport lobbying is one of their specialities and saw the usual political apparatchiks among their key staff. These included Paul Beaverstock, who formerly worked as Strategic Director of Communications for the Conservative Party. Also on their list was Sir Brian Bender. It is worth copying his CV as posted on MHP's website as it demonstrates the prostitution of his senior-civil-service experience:

"Sir Brian Bender retired from the civil service in 2009, having been a Permanent Secretary (the most senior civil servant in a UK government department) for nearly 10 years. His last post was leading the Department for Business, and before that the Department for Trade & Industry and the Department for Environment, Food and Rural Affairs (leading the process of creating that Department in 2001). In his

career Sir Brian has overseen a range of policy areas including energy, climate change, science and innovation and better regulation. Brian has considerable EU experience, having served twice in the UK Representation in Brussels. He was also Head of the European Secretariat of the Cabinet Office 1994-98."

These are very attractive political operatives available for hire by the aviation industry, which wants to overcome the democratic opposition of millions of London voters who do not want 220,000 more flights using Heathrow every year. They can get behind closed doors with senior civil servants and government ministers. MHP's website even boasts how it has been successful in getting a tax break for one of its corporate clients in the UK Budget! Yes - if you have the money, the political lobbying system can even get you Budget tax breaks.

Other invisible facts behind this seemingly unbiased BBC news story are also shocking. On the parliamentary register of interests for the All Party Aviation Group is the statement that *"A Fair Tax on Flying Campaign is providing administrative assistance and advice to support an inquiry held by the group"*. This sounds like a grassroots environmental group campaigning for more environmentally-friendly taxes on flying. After all, aviation is wrongly exempt from VAT on fuel. But the group was nothing of the sort.

"A Fair Tax on Flying Campaign" is actually a classic astroturf lobbying front for the aviation industry and is funded by the following: British Airways, Virgin Atlantic, Monarch Airways, British Airports Authority, Bristol Airport, BMI Airways, Gatwick Airport, Lastminute.com, Leeds Bradford Airport, London City Airport, Luton Airport, Manchester Airport Group, Newcastle Airport, Co-operative Travel (so much for their "ethical and environmental" branding) , Thomas Cook etc.

Possibly unknown to the BBC, this was not a news story but a carefully placed propaganda story on behalf of the Heathrow Airport expansion lobby. It was one small part of the multi-million-pound lobbying operation by the Heathrow Campaign that successfully got the anti-third-runway Tory Transport Secretary Justine Greening MP fired in September 2012. The BBC should not regurgitate such press releases without a professional journalistic investigation into their origins. Thousands of such manipulative actions are carried out behind the scenes every day by these lobbyists, in an attempt to shape public-opinion to their corporate paymasters' financial advantage.

Having seen the huge web of political lobbying lying behind just one BBC news story, examining the record of one individual professional political lobbyist can also help us to get a better understanding of how they operate as a group in our political establishment. Let us take the Lib Dem lobbyist Edward Lord. Lord is a former Tory National Executive member who joined the Liberal Democrats in 2003, as the Tories were taking a lurch to the right on human rights under Michael

Howard. Many economically right-wing Tories (some of whom were gay) but who were in favour of human rights, joined the Liberal Democrats in during this period. Their contacts and old-boy networks were a boon to the internal party coup being undertaken at the time by the right-wing Liberal Future/Orange Bookers, led by former lobbyist and one of Charles Kennedy's closest advisers, Mark Oaten and the former JP Morgan banker David Laws.

Lord almost immediately after joining the party, was appointed as a Deputy Treasurer by the lobbyist Lord Clement Jones who was then Party Treasurer. I met Lord a number of times whilst I was Deputy Chair and found him to be a pleasant individual, committed to liberal human rights. In January 2011, he was elected to the Party's Finance Committee. Parallel to his Liberal Democrat activities, Lord pursues a political career within the Corporation of London.

The Corporation of London led by the Lord Mayor of London confusingly acts as the "local authority" only for the business and financial centre of London, colloquially called The Square Mile. Unlike every other local council in the democratic world, it is elected primarily by the senior executives of the financial institutions located within it. One of its main functions is to act as the lobbying organisation for London's finance industry. It is not to be confused with the publicly-elected Greater London Assembly and Mayor of London who are responsible for London as a whole.

The Corporation even has its own separate City of London Police Force. This bizarrely meant that the police force who evicted the Occupy London protesters from outside St Paul's in 2011, were in effect controlled by the very financial institutions who had caused the disastrous financial crash that the protesters were protesting against!

Lord was first elected to the City of London Court of Common Council for the Ward of Coleman Street in February 2001. By 2012, he was chair of the City's Licensing Committee and has served as a member of the Policy and Resources, Finance, Police, Port and the Health & Environmental Services Committees. He is a Liveryman of the Fletchers' Company and the Broderers' Company and a Freeman of the Leathersellers' Company and Spectacle Makers' Company. He became a Freeman of the City of London in January 2000. Lord is also either a member or honorary member of various Masonic Lodges including:

- Honour & Generosity Lodge 165
- Phoenix Lodge 173
- Farringdon Without Lodge 1745 (also Royal Arch Chapter)
- Corium Lodge 4041
- City of London Installed Masters Lodge 8220
- Metropolitan Grand Stewards Lodge 9812

- Grafton Lodge of Mark Master Masons Lodge 415.

Lord's position in the Corporation of London gives him access to the higher echelons of the UK's national local-government infrastructure, despite it not being a primarily publicly-elected body. He was appointed to the Improvement Board of the Local Government Association (LGA) in 2004 and is Non-Executive Chair of Local Partnerships. As Chair of Local Partnerships, he was also a member of the Local Government Group's National Executive. He served in 2010 on the Member Task Group on local government investment. In 2011, Lord became chair of Capital Ambition, the regional improvement and efficiency partnership for Greater London and joined the Leaders' Committee of London Councils.

But there is a third string to Edward Lord's astonishing range of accumulated roles in local government and the Lib Dems. He also runs his own lobbying firm Edward Lord Consultants. Lord was filmed in secret in December 2011 doing a pitch for lobbying business with another prominent Lib Dem, Mark Pursey. Pursey was head of the Lib Dems' National Media Intelligence Unit during Nick Clegg's 2010 general election campaign. Pursey's BTP Consultants appear to specialise in promoting third-world regimes including the governments of Azerbaijan, Ivory Coast and Rwanda.

The filmed meeting was between Lord and Pursey and journalists from the BIJ, again posing as clients from the authoritarian Uzbekistan government. Pursey explained how he could neutralise negative entries about the dictatorship on their government's Wikipedia page. These include references to the dictatorship's human-rights abuses reported by Amnesty International, Human Rights Watch, the US and the EU. He outlined how he had undermined UN criticisms of the Rwandan Government, by attacking and undermining those making the criticisms as *"being unreasonable people"*. In other words his lobbying approach on behalf of clients was to attack and undermine the messengers rather than deal with the criticism. This is a classic lobbying tactic. A 2009 report from the Commonwealth Human Rights Initiative said that Rwanda's *'excellent public relations machinery'* had succeeded in hiding *'the exclusionary and repressive nature of the regime'*. Not exactly an enviable recommendation for a senior Liberal Democrat, a party whose founding principles include a fundamental respect for human rights!

On the tape Lord boasts about how he could assist with a state visit by Islam Karimov, the dictatorial president of Uzbekistan. The online footage at the Bureau's website requires no interpretation. It disgustingly records these senior Lib Dem lobbyists saying they were prepared to doctor Wikipedia pages, attack critics of dictatorships and facilitate State Visits for an authoritarian dictatorship. No action was taken by the party against either Lord or Pursey following the revelations.

Chapter 3

By law, Lord has to make a submission every year to the Corporation of London's Register of Members Interests, due to its unique status as a local authority. This mainly consists of a phenomenally long list of establishment events that Edward Lord was invited to at which he received free hospitality, an extract from which is included as an addendum at the end of this chapter. It gives an amazing insight into *The Prostitute State,* showing how party-political involvement by lobbyists can open doors right across the establishment for their clients. VIPs at the events he attended include the top echelons of the think-tank, corporate, media and political worlds. Having access for their paid lobbyists to such high-level meetings, right up to and including meetings with the UK's Deputy Prime Minister, could be incredibly useful for authoritarian regimes such as Uzbekistan.

How many people attending such events and talking to such British politicians would have any idea that they could be speaking to lobbyists for authoritarian regimes? The list does not record whether Lord used these events to promote his clients' interests. Neither does it list the many Masonic events/meetings that he would have attended arising from his membership of eight different Masonic lodges or if he used such meetings for lobbying activities or used the contacts gained.

Lord is a fairly typical example of the lobbying classes. The fact he got caught on camera plying his trade and whose hospitality unusually has to be legally reported provides us with a rare and enlightening glimpse under the surface of the lobbying system.

As David Cameron rightly said in February 2010, prior to being elected British Prime Minister, political lobbying is the great scandal that had yet to explode. But Cameron in office did nothing to truly tackle the scandal; indeed as we will see, in many ways in office he personified it. But if we are to reclaim the democratic state to serve the interests of all of the nation's citizens, these scandals must be detonated fully and the soiled political lobbying stables thoroughly cleaned out.

Addendum

The following is an extract from the meetings listed for Edward Lord's Corporation of London Register of Members Interests entry in August 2012.

Event	Host	Year
Dinner	James Gurling, Hanover Communications	2008
Directors' Box Tickets and Dinner, West Ham v Portsmouth	Mulalley & Co. Limited	2008
Africa Day Reception	African Union Heads of Mission	2008

Event	Host	Year
Reception	Ambassador of the Federal Democratic Republic of Ethiopia	2008
Beacon Councils Reception	The Secretary of State for Communities & Local Government	2008
Reception	ITV plc	2008
Dinner for World Bank PPPI Conference Delegates	Asian Development Bank	2008
Lunch	Richard Olsen, Orion Land & Leisure	2009 2009
National Day Reception	Ambassador of Kuwait	2009
Skinners' Company Luncheon	Deputy Robin Sherlock	2009
Independence Day Reception	Ambassador of Israel	2009
Lord's Grand Stand Box ticket	Deutsche Bank	2009
Dinner	High Commissioner for Australia	2009
National Day Reception	Ambassador of Portugal	2009
Reception and Lecture	Institute of Economic Affairs	2009
Diplomatic Reception	Ambassador of Morocco	2009
Private Dinner	Manchester Airport Group	2009
Reception	The Telegraph Group	2009
Reception	Tobacco Industry Association	2009
Reception	Ambassador of Germany	2009
Ronnie Scott's - Parliamentary Jazz Group	BP plc.	2010
Dinner	Policy Exchange	2010
Private View and Reception 'Baku with Love'	The Ambassador of Azerbaijan	2010
Chairman's Reception	Local Government Association	2010
Private Briefing Dinner with Chief Executive	British Council	2010
Dinner (at which I was the guest of honour)	Buro Four	2010
Reception	Institute of Economic Affairs	2010
Bakers' Company Livery Dinner	Her Honour Judge Zoe Smith	2010
Afternoon Tea	Ambassador of Macedonia	2010
Luncheon (at which I was guest of honour)	The D Group	2010
Election Night Party	Institute of Economic Affairs	2010
Lunch	C Elliott, Barclays Private Equity	2010
Dinner	Viscount Hubert de Marcy	2010
Dinner	M Gerrard, CEO, Partnerships UK plc	2010
Reception and Lecture	Institute of Economic Affairs	2010

Chapter 3

Event	Host	Year
VIP tickets and hospitality	Smithfield Nocturne	2010
Reception and Concert	High Commissioner Malta	2010
Dinner	Mark Greenburgh, Head of Local Government, Wragge & Co.	2010
Wembley Gold Tickets and Champagne Reception England v Bulgaria	Wembley Stadium	2010
Gala Dinner	The Tax Payers' Alliance	2010
Reception	Tim Hames and Neil Sherlock	2010
Reception	The Rt Hon Nick Clegg MP and Bloomberg	2010
Reception	The New Statesman	2010
Reception	Guardian Media Group	2010
Reception	Tobacco Manufacturers Association	2010
Dinner	Hanover Communications	2010
Dinner	Crown Group (UK) Limited	2010
Reception following the Quit Rents Ceremony	The Queen's Remembrancer	2010
Reception	Sir John Cass's Foundation and Coutts & Co.	2010
Roundtable Dinner - as chairman	Jacobs Engineering Group Inc.	2010
250th Anniversary Dinner	Board of Deputies of British Jews	2010
Court Dinner	The Broderers' Company	2010
Directors' Box Tickets and Hospitality	Dagenham & Redbridge FC	2011
Launch Reception	China Daily UK	2011
Republic Day Reception	High Commissioner of India	2011
Reception at 10 Downing Street	The Deputy Prime Minister	2011
Chinese New Year Reception	Hong Kong Economic & Trade Office	2011
Reception	Tim Farron MP, President of the Liberal Democrats	2011
Reception	Helen Boaden, Director, BBC News	2011
National Day Reception	Ambassador of Poland	2011
Lunch	Four Communications	2011
Court Dinner	The Fuellers' Company	2011
General Court Lunch	The Ironmongers' Company	2011

Event	Host	Year
Reception for the LGBT Community at 10 Downing Street	The Prime Minister	2011
Lord's Taverners Eve of Test Match Dinner	Macquarie	2011
Reception and Lecture	John Adam Society / PWC	2011
Installation Supper, Wax Chandlers' Company	Dr Jonathan Munday JP	2011
Lunch	Policy Exchange	2011
Dinner London 2012 Olympic Mission	LOCOG	2011
Directors' Box Ticket and Hospitality: QPR v Rochdale, Carling Cup Round Two	Queens Park Rangers Football Club Limited	2011
Lunch	Heathcroft Communications Limited	2011
Dinner with Managing Director of Government of Alberta UK Office	Hanover Communications	2011
Lunch	The Deputy Prime Minister and Leader of the Liberal Democrats	2011
Dinner	BAA Airports Limited	2011
Dinner	Bell Pottinger Public Affairs Limited	2011
Reception	Canary Wharf Group plc	2011
Dinner with Cllr Peter John (Leader, London Borough of Southwark)	Hanover Communications	2011
Lunch with Sir Andrew Cahn KCMG (Vice-Chairman, Nomura), Michael Fallon MP (Treasury Select Committee), and Kamal Ahmad (Business Editor, Sunday Telegraph)	Hanover Communications	2011
Directors' Box Ticket and Board Room Hospitality: AFC Bournemouth v Rochdale	AFC Bournemouth Limited	2011
Reception	Stonewall and Coutts & Co.	2011
4 day Conference including accommodation	British American Project	2011
Reception	Ambassadors of Bosnia and Slovenia	2011
Lunch	Peter Bingle, Chairman, Bell Pottinger Public Affairs	2012
Dinner	Webber Shandwick	2012
Reception	Hong Kong Economic & Trade Office	2012
Lecture and Reception	The World Traders' Company	2012
VIP ticket to Track Cycling World Cup	LOCOG	2012
Dinner with representative of the property industry and Leader of Wandsworth council	Bell Pottinger Public Affairs Limited	2012
Reception for IOC	HM Government	2012

Chapter 4

Pimps in Chief

If you want to know what direction a political party is likely to head in, examine the vested interests of those who ran and funded a winning leader's campaign to be elected party leader and which media organisations backed that campaign. Those people will generally become that leader's closest political advisers. Corporate lobbyists have the time, money, media contacts and office resources to assist their chosen leadership candidate to win, thus enabling them to be at the heart of the new leadership. With these resources they can usually easily defeat any popular grass-roots candidates. The Lib Dem leaders Ashdown, Kennedy and Clegg were all backed by a right-wing corporate lobbying clique that has successfully kept their grip on the party's leadership since its foundation.

Lobbyists can use their professional media contacts to crown their chosen candidate, years in advance of a leadership election, as the obvious "leader in waiting". Clegg, like Blair was a classic example of this. Numerous stories appeared in the media for years prior to his election that Clegg was a future leader of the party, even though he was a Lib Dem MEP in Brussels and not yet even an MP. This process generally favours candidates from the small right-wings of the Labour and Lib Dem parties and Boris Johnson, Rupert Murdoch's darling, is already being crowned as the potential next leader of the Tories before a vote has been cast.

The lobbyists' focus on leadership-capture rather than party democratic policy-making is cleverly very effective in policy terms. An academic study reported in the Guardian, revealed the scientific basis for this. It had polled the three major party memberships, asking which was more important: loyalty to the leadership or the leader's actual policy agenda.

Liberalism's philosophy of personal empowerment requires people to always hold those in power to account. I was horrified that 70% of the Lib Dem membership was prepared to grant the leader a policy blank-cheque. This underscored how significant were our *new radicalism* victories at party conference. The study implied that the leadership had a natural majority of 70% in any vote. To win, we had to win ALL of the voters who were not part of the leadership loyalty vote and nearly 30% of the leadership loyalists. Thus having control of the leadership gives a massive advantage in setting party policy.

And as we saw in the first Chapter, another key advantage of controlling the leadership is that even when the party votes against the lobbyists' interests, they can simply use the leadership to block implementation of those votes. The lobbyists' hold over the leadership also gives them enormous influence over the crucial general election manifestoes. This also applies even more importantly to drafting legislation if the party is in government. No matter what policy successes the party membership has won democratically over the lobbyists at conference, it is only what appears in the general-election manifesto or legislation that matters.

The figures in the study for preference for loyalty to the leadership versus the leadership's policies were much higher in the Labour Party, which was just over 80% and even higher in the Tory party at nearly 90%. So capture the leaderships and you capture the parties. A vivid demonstration of this was the abandonment of the long-held opposition to nuclear-power and fossil-fuels by the Liberal Democrat Conference in 2013, when it endorsed both nuclear-power and gas-fracking when urged to do so by the leadership. Game, set and match to the embedded nuclear and fossil-gas lobbyists in the leadership.

Many pillars of *The Prostitute State* converge within party leaderships. It is here that the billionaire owned media, the tax-haven cliques, corporate funded think-tanks and the hired lobbyists merge and ensure that the political parties and hence our governments carry out their wishes. The billionaire-press never encourages public participation in political parties. Instead they *ad-nauseum* demonise the volunteers who help run our political parties as "*militant activists*". The term "*party activist*" is now sadly one of abuse and party memberships are in free-fall.

Over four and a quarter million people were members of political parties in the 1950's. The Tories had three million, Labour one million and the Liberal Party a quarter of a million. By 2013 the total had fallen to 365,000. The Tories had 134,000, Labour 88,000 and the Lib Dems 43,000. This means that the operations of all the major parties in each constituency, including the selection of their candidates, are now often run by fewer than 20 active volunteers on average per party, as generally only one member is ten is actually active. Our human tree of democracy has lost the vast majority of its human roots and is now almost dead.

The costs involved in volunteering for a political party can be staggering. After I resigned from the party I calculated that between the time spent delivering leaflets, attending council meetings or staying at party conferences and the lost earnings and career opportunities I had passed by, the personal cost to me was well in excess of £100,000 over 12 years! Who would want to be a vilified "militant party activist" when you take this into account? Have you ever wondered what would happen to democracy if no one joins our political parties? We are beginning to find out – rule by *The Prostitute State.*

Chapter 4

But party democracy does not suit the needs of the corporate state or the billionaire press. It threatens their capture of the party leaderships. If you only have to lobby one leader instead of thousands of party-members, you have a far higher chance of getting your way. Party volunteers used to be able to democratically influence party policy and so represented a direct threat to the corporate state. But such checks and balances have been destroyed by the party leaderships, at the urging of the right-wing media. In one of my more chilling moments in the Liberal Democrats, I heard Charles Kennedy tell conference in a fit of pique over the row about his appointment of non-elected nominees to the Lords, that no matter what it decided, he could do what he wanted.

Kennedy had appointed the owner of a political-lobbying firm (Dick Newby) to head his leader's office. But to be fair to Lord Newby, after the party voted to ban its peers from being professional lobbyists, unlike some others, he actually quit lobbying and worked for The Prince's Trust instead and he deserves respect for it. Other key members of Kennedy's inner circle were Lord Clement Jones, who worked for DLR Piper, the international lobbying firm and Lord Razzall, a director of a number of Channel Islands tax-haven based firms. They were normally referred to as "The Two Tims".

Whilst I knew and disapproved of Razzall's off-shore directorships, it was not until 2012 when The Observer did an exposé of the scandalous number of links between UK parliamentarians and offshore tax-havens that I finally learnt what Razzall's company did. He told The Observer that the company offered "tax mitigation" services to clients. He assured The Observer that they "had not indulged in aggressive avoidance". His Bachmann Group (Guernsey) also has branches in the tax-havens of Switzerland and New Zealand, as well as London. With no sense of irony, its website describes Guernsey as being "one of the most effectively regulated secure offshore jurisdictions". Revealingly, the company's website does not allow visitors to view its range of services. You have to be registered with them to see it. It states it "offers the full range of trust and company management services for both personal and corporate clients". But it does list the usual weird spider-web of subsidiaries that seems to plague all of these tax-haven entities.

Lord Razzall has been at the heart of the Lib Dem leadership for decades, having served as Party Treasurer for Paddy Ashdown from 1988 and is currently co-chair of the Liberal Democrat Parliamentary Committee on Business Innovation and Skills. He once sarcastically in an inebriated moment referred to my ear-ring as being a "halo". I assured him that at the other end of it there was a devil's tail!

The second of The Two Tims, Lord Clement Jones, has been a lobbyist for the nuclear, alcohol and arms industries and for the Cayman Islands tax-haven. He also seamlessly moved from Ashdown's to Kennedy's to Clegg's inner circle, serving as

Party Treasurer at the 2010 general election. Clegg's father, like David Cameron's, also had tax-haven connections. Sir Nicholas Clegg was a director of Hill Samuel, now a subsidiary of Lloyds TSB's Offshore Private Banking and is chair of the United Trust Bank.

Looking at the Labour Party, Blair's leadership election was largely funded by the billionaire David Sainsbury, as was his think-tank Progress, whose first director was the disgraced lobbyist Derek Draper. Having won the leadership, Blair got the supposedly working man's trade-union 'hero', John Prescott, to deliver the crucial symbolic Clause 4 deletion from the Labour Party's constitution. The Lord Sainsbury funded New Labour project then proceeded to gut the party's democratic policy-making processes, removing nearly all democratic decision-making powers from party members at conference and replacing them with the nebulous "consultative" process of the Policy Forum.

The demonization of volunteer party members by the billionaire press enabled this authoritarian coup within the Labour Party, easily crushing any resistance. This ensured that the leadership's lobbyist and media-baron inspired changes to party policy could not be democratically challenged. One consequence of this was that the UK equality gap rose by 50% during Labour's 12 years in power. Blair then proceeded to also destroy an enormous amount of the democratic power of the next tier up in the Labour party. Britain's 20,000 local councillors are a crucial voice for local people within Britain's democracy. Blair neutered that power by abolishing council committees which had majority and opposition councillors and replacing them with a one party mayoral or cabinet system.

At a stroke, this eliminated the power of the majority's backbench and all opposition councillors, reducing the number of councillors with any meaningful power to about 1,000 across the UK. This facilitated the concentration of even more power in the leader's office as it was far easier to neutralise this smaller number of potential opponents to HQ diktats. This seriously damaged the ability for local councillors to provide any checks and balances on the corporate control of centralised government. It also destroyed the public's power to influence council decisions, as votes are no longer taken at public committee meetings and the public cannot lobby opposition councillors to support them, as they no longer have any votes or speaking rights on most decisions. This has led to a large expansion of unaccountable corporate power even at local government level. Naturally, the billionaire media failed to inform the public about the amount of power being stripped from their elected councillors. It suits their needs to have all power concentrated nationally where they can more easily manipulate it.

Any party that now attempts open internal political debate not in line with the leadership's corporate agenda is instantly labelled as being "*divided and at war internally*". As a result, many members are now terrified of using any party democracy. This self-censorship has destroyed internal democratic discussions, as ordinary members turn on any member who disagrees with leadership diktats as *"being disloyal and damaging to the party"*. The Simon Hughes attempt to get me to keep quiet over RTZ at the party's conference was a classic example. Thus another layer of our democracy has been destroyed and the corporate power exerted through the party leaderships has become even more all-encompassing. The hollowed-out shells of our political parties are now almost entirely vehicles for the servants of the corporate state.

The master stroke in Blair's successful move to replace the Tories with a right-wing version of the Labour Party was the reported but denied deal he made with Rupert Murdoch, during his visit to News International's annual executive conference on Hayman Island in Australia in 1995. Very little media attention was given to the momentous revelation by Lance Price, who worked in Blair's Number 10 operation, in his book *"Where Power Lies"*, published in 2010, that there was a pact between News International and New Labour. *"A deal had been done although with nothing in writing"* wrote Price. Whilst Price did not provide the deal's details, two issues in particular would have been of crucial importance to Murdoch.

The first was the Conservative Party's pro-European Union position which he wanted reversed. Unlike the UK government, the EU is big enough to potentially regulate him, which is an anathema to this fundamentalist free-marketeer. In a unique glimpse of how the billionaire press bullies even Prime Ministers, John Major, the former Tory Prime Minister, revealed to the Leveson Inquiry in 2012 that Murdoch had in a private meeting in February 1997, warned him that *"If we could not change our European policies, his papers could not, would not support the Conservative government."* Later that year, the Tories lost to New Labour after 18 years in power. That defeat came after Murdoch's newspapers The Sun and the News of the World had switched their support to Labour, with even The Times remaining neutral.

To this day the Murdoch press continues its relentless xenophobic daily campaign of vilification of the EU's democratic institutions, abetted by the rest of the media billionaires. They have turned much of the naturally pro-European UK public into a snarling foreigner-hating British bulldog, creating a far-right nationalist UKIP party to represent their cause. After 30 years of their anti-European venomous propaganda, the poison finally resulted in large electoral swings to UKIP in the 2013 and 2014 English local and European elections. The miracle of three generations of a peaceful continent for the first time in European history is never celebrated. The EU has helped protect the lives of millions of young working-class men and women from the wars of their elites for the first time in history. These media billionaires have even got the working classes to hate the European Convention on Human Rights, which is often the only thing standing between ordinary workers and exploitative abuse by the ruling elite. The further irony is that the Convention has its roots in Churchill's vision for a post-war liberal democratic settlement for the continent, to protect it from ever again being ravaged by the evils of fascism.

The second issue crucial to Murdoch was the potential threat of legislation on cross-media ownership. Following the acquisition of the Times, Sun and News of the World (facilitated by Thatcher) and his Sky television network, Murdoch had come to dominate the UK media market by the 1997 general election. There was some discomfort about the unaccountable political power that this conferred on him, even within John Major's Tory government. Major favoured some limited controls on cross-media ownership.

The Leveson inquiry revealed that as early as 1994, in his wooing of News International, Blair had reassured Gus Fisher, a Murdoch lobbyist, that Labour was not a threat on cross-media ownership restrictions. Blair had sniffed the wind and understood how he could win the billionaire's backing by selling Labour's soul on cross-media ownership. By that general election, New Labour policy on cross-media ownership was more laissez-faire than the Tories. And Blair delivered for Murdoch in government. He not only refused to implement urgently needed restrictions on media ownership but actually relaxed some of those that had been in place under the Tories.

In his diaries, Blair's press spokesperson Alastair Campbell stated that during discussions at Number 10, Blair was in favour of total liberalisation of the UK media market! This would have removed all restrictions on Murdoch grabbing all of the remaining newspaper and TV markets. Campbell added that Blair in response to concerns about the further unchecked political power that this would give Murdoch, said *"we got nothing worse out of Murdoch than we did from anyone else"*. The fact that Blair was prepared to allow Murdoch to own all of the UK's media shows how far he had become a fully signed-up operative of *The Prostituted Media*

Following Blair's New Labour coup within the Labour Party, his fundraiser Lord Levy raised over £100 million from individual rich donors. This overwhelmed the party members' and trade unionists' individual membership fees, which reinforced corporate power at the heart of the hijacked political party. Many of these donors received seats for life in parliament, as Blair went on an unprecedented appointment spree to the Lords, exercising one of the most untrammelled powers of patronage available to any global democratic leader. No other democracy allows their Prime Minister to appoint unlimited numbers to life-seats in their legislature, with no elections whatsoever.

The usual mixture of lobbying, politics and tax havens were all present when another Blair donor scandal emerged in 2002. In July 2001, The Prime Minister wrote a letter to the Romanian Prime Minister in support of the billionaire Indian steel tycoon Lakshmi Mittal. It was just four weeks after a £125,000 donation had been given by Mittal to the Labour Party. Blair's press office said he would never hesitate to back a British company. But Mittal's LNM Holdings was based in the Dutch Antilles tax-haven and almost none of its 125,000 worldwide employees were located in the UK. It was, however a direct competitor with the steel manufacturer Corus, which did have thousands of employees in the UK.

But it was the Iraq War which demonstrated how far Blair had fallen into Murdoch's hands. Whilst millions marched opposing the war, Campbell's diaries revealed that Murdoch called Blair three times in March 2003, a week before the crucial vote in the House of Commons, urging him to invade. Murdoch assured Blair of the support of his British newspapers should he invade. The huge protests' failure to stop Blair declaring war was a body blow to the morale of British democracy and the point of peaceful protest. However, without those protests, it is unlikely that Parliament would have a decade later voted against another war, proposed in Syria by Iraq War supporter David Cameron in 2013.

The Iraq War chillingly demonstrated that even on war, it is usually not the democratic state which shapes such crucial decisions. Using non-existent weapons of mass destruction as a pretext, Bush and Blair ignored the UN Security Council and invaded Iraq. It led to the violent death of over 160,000 men, women and children, created over 1.2 million refugees and cost the US Treasury $800 billion and the UK Treasury £10 billion. It led to an ongoing brutal civil, the return of western oil companies to Iraq and eventually was directly responsible for the creation of the medieval horrors of ISIL. Corporate power has no qualms about the destruction of human lives when its financial interests require it and is very rarely held accountable for the devastation left in its trail.

The descent of Tony Blair from being the new bright young leader of a resurgent Labour Party after eighteen years of Thatcherism, to being a willing ally in a disastrous and bloody illegal invasion, demonstrates the moral hazard of sacrificing party principles to gain the support of the media billionaires. Inevitably, you will fail to rule with those principles, no matter how much you genuinely want to. Instead, whether you like it or not, you will govern in the interests of those with whom you did the deals. Eventually you will cease to have any links whatsoever with your original political purpose and supporters and you will morph into being a craven servant of those whom you set out to oppose.

After retiring from the premiership, Blair became one of the most highly-paid corporate political lobbyists in history. JP Morgan, the US investment bank, pays him £2million a year as a *"senior adviser"*. He also *"advises"* the international luxury goods corporation LVMH and Zurich Insurance. The JP Morgan connection reflects another recurring theme of **The Prostitute State** i.e. how lobbyists facilitate dictators' business dealings with the West. In 2011, The Telegraph revealed that Libyan officials had reported numerous visits by Tony Blair to Gadaffi's Libyan dictatorship, to promote deals for JP Morgan with the Libyan Investment Authority.

Blair also provided *"government consultancies"* to various Middle-Eastern Gulf dictatorships including Kuwait, Dubai and Abu Dhabi. The Telegraph estimated that his various commercial consulting and lobbying activities were then bringing in a cool £7 million a year. By 2012, The Daily Mail reported that his annual earnings had swelled to £20 million. It quoted sources stating that he had acquired an £8 million contract to clean up the Kazakhstan dictatorship's image. He now owns a £5.5 million stately home in Buckinghamshire and a £4.5 million home in Connaught Square in London. Ever since he appeared on the British political scene, he has reminded me of Oscar Wilde's The Picture of Dorian Gray with his altar-boy good-looks. But instead of the evil portrait of decay being hidden away in the attic, it was there for all to see on the ravaged faces of John Prescott and Gordon Brown.

Blair's successor, the Tory Prime Minister David Cameron, is **The Prostitute State** classically personified. In Cameron, we get on a grand scale the merger of lobbying, tax-haven wealth, billionaire-owned media and top-level British politics. He first worked as a researcher for his godfather, Tim Rathbone, the Tory MP for Lewes, and then for the Conservative Research Department. He later worked as a special adviser to Norman Lamont and then Michael Howard.

He used that job-experience to move into the political-lobbying sector, where in his only job outside politics, he became head-lobbyist for Carlton Television. He acquired the job after his mother-in-law-to-be (Lady Astor) asked her friend Michael Green, then head of Carlton TV, for a job for him. Green obliged by hiring Cameron directly as his Director of Public Affairs on a salary equivalent to £130, 000 in 2012 terms. A nice example of how rich elites can get astonishingly well-paid jobs for their children.

For the next seven years, Cameron used the resources this gave him, to pursue his political ambitions as a Tory candidate, like many parliamentary researchers who had switched to highly lucrative lobbying jobs before him. This combination of wealth, media access and parliamentary expertise is almost impossible to compete against for ordinary constituency party-members who want to represent their local community as a general-election candidate. Cameron thus duly became the Tory candidate for Witney and was elected in the 2001 general-election.

Cameron's connections with tax-havens are numerous. In April 2012, the Guardian reported that his father's wealth accrued from setting up tax-haven investment funds. Ian Cameron was chair of Close International Asset Management Jersey, a director of Blairmore Holdings Panama and a shareholder in Blairmore Asset Management Geneva. Blairmore Holdings was not named after the lucrative lobbying activities of Tony Blair but rather after the Cameron ancestral home in Scotland. In 2006, the hedge-fund's prospectus said it was basing itself in Panama, whose laws impose zero taxation on hedge-fund earnings made outside Panama. Investors had to invest a minimum of $100,000 in the fund, so it was explicitly aimed at the tax-avoiding super-rich. The Guardian said that the prospectus boasted that *"The Directors intend that the affairs of the Fund should be managed and conducted so that it does not become resident in the United Kingdom for UK taxation purposes. Accordingly the Fund will not be subject to United Kingdom corporation tax or income tax on its profits."*

In 2009, the Sunday Times Rich List estimated Ian Cameron's wealth at £10m. Yet when he died in late 2010, his will left only £2.7 million from which David Cameron received the sum of £300,000. A possible explanation lies in the fact that the family-will only details the estate's assets in England and Wales. The Guardian said his *"Offshore investments would only be listed in submissions to HMRC for inheritance tax purposes. It is unclear what those assets (if any) are worth and which family member owns them."* As with his father, so it was with his father-in-law Lord Astor. In June 2012, the Daily Record reported that Astor's Scottish estate was owned by a Bahamas tax-haven registered company.

Despite the government's rhetoric condemning tax avoidance, Cameron, like Blair before him, has rewarded his tax-avoiding funders with actual seats at the government table. Philip Green is one of Britain's ten richest billionaires, with a fortune estimated at £4.1 billion. He owns the Arcadia fashion empire which includes Topshop, Burtons, Miss Selfridge and British Home Stores. However on paper Philip Green does not actually own Arcadia. Instead, it is held in the name of his wife Tina Green. But she "officially" lives in Monaco, where she pays no income tax.

In 2005, Green awarded himself £1.2bn, the biggest pay-cheque in British corporate history. This dividend was paid through a network of offshore accounts, via tax havens in Jersey, to his wife's Monaco bank account. According to the BBC this saved Green £285 million in UK taxes. This single tax manoeuvre would pay the salaries of 20,000 nurses. Despite public outrage, this tax arrangement remains legal. The next time he fancies a billion pound dividend Green can do it again – no problem. Yet Cameron rewarded him by appointing him to oversee the government's cuts programmes. These are the same cuts to services for the poor, happening because billions in pounds of corporation tax are being legally avoided by people like Green. Meanwhile, The Sun, Express and Mail fan the flames of hatred against EU democracy or are totally up in arms over looters caught stealing some bottled water, rather than the real corporate thieves in our midst.

The head of the John Lewis Partnership, Andy Street, chillingly warned in November 2012 that the avoidance of corporation tax by multinational retailers meant companies like theirs could disappear within fifteen years. *"There is less money to invest if you are giving 27% of your profits to the Exchequer,"* Mr Street told Sky TV. *"Clearly, if you are domiciled in a tax haven you've got much more money. They will out invest and ultimately out trade us.* ***And that means there will not be a tax base in the UK."***

The Philip Greens of this world are leading us towards a zero corporate tax base where almost all taxes will be paid by the ordinary (non-billionaire) taxpayer. In 2011, UK Uncut claimed that much of Green's £4bn fortune was built on the back of sweatshop labour, using Mauritius sweatshops where Sri Lankans, Indians and Bangladeshis toiled 12 hours a day, six days a week, for minimal pay. At the heart of the corporate system is the ruthless transfer of wealth from the 99% to the 1%. Another infamous tax-avoider Lord Ashcroft (nominated to the Lords by William Hague) was appointed by Cameron to be government adviser on UK military installations on Cyprus. Ashcroft's status as a legal non-domiciled tax-avoider whilst serving in the House of Lords was exposed two months prior to the 2010 general election. The former Lib Dem MP Chris Huhne wrote in The Guardian that Ashcroft had avoided a staggering estimated £127 million in taxes whilst in the Lords.

Stephen Green is yet another Cameron tax-haven grandee. He is the Chair and former CEO of HSBC and was appointed a Tory life-peer by Cameron in 2010 and Minister of State for Industry and Trade in 2011. Green was also formerly director of HSBC Mexico and The Bank of Bermuda and a director of HSBC Private Banking Holdings (Suisse) for ten years from 2000. The Bank of Bermuda, which was bought by HSBC in 2004, operates in most of the world's major tax havens, including Bermuda, the Isle of Man and the Cayman Islands. Green refused to answer questions in Parliament about HSBC being found guilty of laundering billions of dollars from crime cartels in Mexico and Russia, during his time as its chief executive and Chair. His ministerial responsibilities are to supervise Britain's commercial economic diplomacy and business policy. Talk about putting the fox in charge of the hen-coop!

And the list of tax-haven habitués at the heart of the Cameron government goes on. In April 2012, the Daily Mail revealed that three members of the Cameron appointed Business Advisors Group ran businesses that had moved offshore to cut their taxes. The Mail reported that BT chairman Sir Michael Rake, one of Cameron's most senior advisers, chaired accountancy giant KPMG when it was fined $450million (£277million) for its promotion of illegal tax-shelters in America. Other Cameron advisers include James Dyson, who moved ownership of his vacuum-cleaner business to Malta in 2009, Eric Schmidt, chair of Google, which channels payments for its British advertising revenue through Ireland, avoiding an estimated £200 million in taxes in 2010 and Martin Sorrell, CEO of WPP which moved to Ireland in 2008 to escape paying taxes on foreign profits.

Not content with the billions of taxes avoided during the Blair and Brown years, the tax-haven elite has had plenty more rich cream poured down its throat since Cameron and Clegg came to power. Whilst Cameron issued the usual public condemnations of tax-avoidance, they passed budgets that gave major tax cuts on UK-based multinationals' overseas subsidiaries and huge cuts in domestic corporation tax. As a result, over the lifetime of the 2010 parliament, about £20 billion will be lost in tax receipts according to the Treasury's estimates. They are reducing corporation tax from 28% to 20% by 2015 which will result in further losses of more than £5 billion a year. This will be one of the lowest rates in the western world, shamelessly turning Britain itself into an on-shore tax-haven. These cuts directly transfer the tax burden from rich corporations to the ordinary taxpayers in the UK and lead to the further slashing of what was left of the Welfare State. For the investment of a few million in Tory party coffers and the advantage of having Cameron as Prime Minister, the returns in billions of pounds worth of cuts in corporation taxes and further legitimisation of international tax-avoidance were very profitable.

Another corrupt process by which the rich elite dominate our party leaderships is the notorious cash-for-access schemes that the various party leaderships employ. The blurb for Nick Clegg's fund-raising *"Leaders Forum"* exposes the level of prostitution to which our politics has sunk. Its launch in 2011 was sponsored by the previously mentioned notorious lobbyists Bell Pottinger, anxious for access to the Lib Dems now that they were part of the government.

PR Week reported that those at the launch included representatives of the Tobacco Manufacturers' Association, the Tobacco Retailers' Alliance, the global oil and gas firm BG Group, as well as a number of lobbying consultancy bosses.

Membership of Clegg's 'Leaders Forum' is restricted to fifty people paying £25,000 per year. Members are promised '*a regular programme of exclusive dinners and debates on issues such as the economy, the environment, international affairs and the media*'.

The launch blurb included this quote from Nick Clegg '*Dear Friend... We are in Government for the first time in almost 70 years. As we move forward, my colleagues and I want to listen to you and to continue this dialogue. This will be both with our own party supporters in the Liberty Forum and with leaders in business, entrepreneurs, cultural ambassadors and other like-minded individuals through both the Treasurer's and Leader's Forums.*

Pimps in Chief

'You don't have to be a Liberal Democrat to take part. In today's politics, all are welcome.' The last sentence is the most revealing – in other words if you want access to Nick Clegg MP, the UK's deputy Prime Minister, they do not care what your politics are, just pay your £25,000. Cameron operates a very similar cash-for-access group called *"The Leader's Group"*. But as he is the Prime Minister, the cash-for-access rate is doubled to £50,000.

However it is in his relationships with the billionaire press that Cameron's status as the key nexus through which the corporate state influences our government is quite breath-taking. Like New Labour before him, Cameron realised he had to get Murdoch and Rothermere back on board, if he was to become Prime Minister.

The depth of the links between the media-billionaires and Cameron were exposed by the phone-hacking scandal. It forced him to admit how often he had met media executives during the first 15 months of his premiership:

Newspaper Group	Number of Meetings
News International	26
Telegraph	7
The Mail	4
Evening Standard	3
Guardian	2

Totals:

Billionaire-owned media:	40
Non-billionaire owned media:	2

The meetings with Murdoch's executives included fifteen private meetings, five News International events and three parties. The list does not include telephone conversations, e-mail exchanges or even the numerous personal texts between the Prime Minister and Rebekah Brooks, then CEO of News International and former editor of The Sun. That the Prime Minister should dedicate such a staggering amount of time to meeting these billionaire media executives in the first days of his premiership instead of business leaders, university provosts, pensioner representatives, trade-union leaders, anti-poverty groups, environmental leaders or other civil society and democratic representatives, demonstrates the raw unaccountable power wielded by these billionaires.

The Murdoch empire had sunk its tentacles deep into Cameron's inner-circle. Cameron admitted to the Leveson Inquiry that in the lead-up to the 2010 general election, he had met Rebekah Brooks 19 times, James Murdoch 15 times and Rupert Murdoch 10 times. Forty-four meetings with just three representatives of

Chapter 4

one foreign-based media baron! One of the most infamous was Andy Coulson, former editor of Murdoch's News of The World, who was subsequently in 2014 found guilty of criminal activities in the phone-hacking scandal. Following his resignation in January 2007, as editor of News of the World, following the imprisonment of one of his reporters for hacking the royal family's phones, Coulson was rewarded by Cameron with the lucrative post of Tory Head of Communications at the urging of George Osborne.

The Daily Mail reported in July 2011 that Rebekah Brooks had also urged Cameron to hire him. The Mail reported that an individual involved in the recruitment said: *'Cameron was told it should be someone acceptable to News International. The company was also desperate to find something for Andy after he took the rap when phone hacking first became an issue. The approach was along the lines of, "If you find something for Andy we will return the favour".'* When Cameron became Prime Minister, despite numerous warnings about the dangers, he immediately appointed Coulson to be Head of Prime Ministerial Communications. Meanwhile Cameron and Rebekah Brooks were close neighbours in the market-town of Chipping Norton in Oxfordshire. Along with their spouses Samantha Cameron and Charlie Brooks, Rupert Murdoch's daughter Elizabeth and son-in-law Matthew Freud and the fossil-fuel junky Jeremy Clarkson, who writes lucrative columns for Murdoch's papers, they became known as the Chipping Norton Set. They met regularly for parties, dinners and horse-riding. As every single member other than the Prime Minister and his wife were connected to the Murdoch empire, they were *de facto* the Murdoch Chipping Norton Set.

The former Education Secretary Michael Gove worked for Murdoch as the leader-writer and Saturday Editor at The Times. The Guardian reported in February 2012 that upon his election, The Times almost matched his MP's salary by giving him £60,000 a year to write a column for them. Murdoch's Harper Collins also gave him an undisclosed advance to write a book, which nine years later had yet to be written.

The Leveson Inquiry revealed that Gove had met with James Murdoch a number of times to discuss "*education reform*" and the setting up of News International-run "free schools". Gove also indicated to the inquiry that he favoured the opening up of education to for-profit corporations following the 2015 election. Despite all the criminal practices exposed at News International, Gove described Murdoch as a "*force of nature, a phenomenon and a great man*".

Cameron appointed then Culture Secretary Jeremy Hunt to oversee the proposed £8 billion takeover of the remaining share ownership of BSkyB by Murdoch, knowing Hunt had privately lobbied him in favour of the deal just a month previously. Hunt's appointment followed a sting operation, by two Telegraph reporters posing as constituents, exposing Lib Dem Business Secretary

Vince Cable's opposition to the deal, which he had been in charge of. The Telegraph said the story was possibly leaked by two of their own reporters who were subsequently hired by Murdoch's News International. This deal was hugely important to Murdoch's entrenchment of the near-monopoly grip he already had on the UK media and would have been enormously lucrative. It would have doubled his UK media operations. Having accumulated over 70% of the Australian media market, Murdoch was on target to do the same in the UK. The deal would have given Murdoch combined UK revenues of £7.9 billion. He could have blown away all remaining rivals, with the BBC at £3.6 billion and ITV at £1.9 billion and the rest of the newspaper groups as minnows in the low tens of millions.

This was the biggest consolidation of media and political power ever proposed in UK history. The consequences for what little remained of democratic decision-making in the country were truly terrifying. Hunt was finally forced to resign after a deluge of information emerged about the flood of secret communications between Hunt's assistant Adam Smith and Murdoch's chief lobbyist Frederic Michel. Whilst in charge of a quasi-judicial process of deciding on government competition approval for the bid, Hunt's office's communications were almost exclusively with Murdoch's representatives.

A coalition consisting of the publishers of the Guardian, Telegraph, Mail and Mirror opposed the deal as they feared the massive TV advertising power of BSkyB could make bundled subscription offers with Murdoch's newspapers, which could eliminate them. UK democracy faced the potential horror of Sky News being turned into a UK version of the malignant Fox News in the US, which has taken US partisan politics into a frequently fact-free gutter.

The opposition media coalition were granted what they called a single "*sham*" meeting with the culture secretary, three weeks after he had already given his provisional blessing to the £8bn offer. Meanwhile thousands of emails, telephone conversations, dinners, parties and meetings had taken place between the Murdochs, their lobbyists and the Cameron government. The deal only collapsed following the News of the World hacking scandal. The Guardian's extraordinary phone-hacking revelations saved Britain from Murdoch gaining the potential to create an almost total UK media monopoly and a UK Fox News. Cameron could not brush aside the deluge of disgust sweeping the country about the allegation of the News of the World hacking the phones of a dead teenager, 7/7 victims, dead soldiers' families and relatives of murdered children. Almost for the first time ever, Murdoch did not get want he wanted from his pet UK politicians, but only thanks to one of the last newspapers not owned by *The Prostituted Press*. But he has not given up seeking to complete his monopolistic stranglehold on the UK media market. In April 2014 Murdoch sought to buy the TV station Channel 5. And there is no knowing when he might again seek to revive the Sky deal.

Chapter 4

So what was Hunt's reward for his disgraceful behaviour in this Murdoch scandal? Cameron promoted him from Secretary of State for Culture to Secretary of State for Health. The billionaire press raised no objections to this travesty and the public shrugged its shoulders in despair, as this tarnished Murdoch acolyte took responsibility for their treasured NHS. In April 2012, The Telegraph reported that Hunt had legally avoided over £100,000 tax on the profits from his education company by a dividend payment made to him in property that was then leased back to his own company.

Rebekah Brooks had texted Cameron after his 2011 conference speech saying she felt so emotional listening to his speech that she 'cried twice', adding: "Will love 'working together' ". This reference to loving "working together" is the core of *The Prostitute State.* The chief-executive of a billionaire-owned media corporation gets the reward of "working together" with the country's elected Prime Minister following their endorsement of him and his party. We may never know what political favours Brooks asked for in her dealings with Cameron, despite these potentially involving crucial matters of public policy, which are supposed to be decided via open democratic procedures.

Despite the outrage about phone-hacking, Murdoch quickly returned to the centre of power in the UK. The News of the World was simply replaced by a new Sunday version of The Sun, which is already selling over two million copies every Sunday and was cheaper to produce than the News of the World. In April 2012, Murdoch's News International made a move to demonstrate they had not lost their political power. The Sun picked up three minor issues and labelled them emotionally The Granny Tax, The Pasty Tax and The Caravan Tax and launched wildly populist campaigns against them. The Pasty Tax campaign was over a legal technicality on pasties that resulted in them becoming liable for VAT. The Granny Tax was a change in tax-allowances for a minority of middle-income pensioners which meant they would lose just over a pound per week and the caravan tax was an extension of VAT from mobile caravans to include fixed-caravans.

Despite the minute nature of these changes, The Sun went into full battle-mode, raising over half a million signatures demanding the removal of VAT from pasties. The combined force of these campaigns, which were replayed across the rest of the tabloid echo-chamber and spread into the broadsheets, had within a month rocked the Cameron Government to its core. Commentators were tearing shreds off the government for these three tiny technical changes.

But nobody commented on what was really happening. News International had demonstrated its ability to destroy Cameron, even if he led a right-wing government of which it generally approved. To Murdoch's fury, Cameron had established the Leveson Inquiry and its revelations had resulted not only in the humiliation of Murdoch and his son, the destruction of News International's reputation but also crucially the loss of the hugely lucrative BSkyB deal. Many people naively thought that the phone-hacking scandal was the end of Murdoch's stranglehold on UK politics. But just months later, The Sun had brutally shown Cameron who was still the boss.

This was demonstrated again shortly after, at the 2012 Olympic Games in London, where Murdoch turned up as the guest of the Tory leadership contender and London Mayor Boris Johnson. To go from universally reviled employer of dead-children's criminal telephone-hackers to VIP guest of London's Tory Mayor, was an impressive turnaround in just a few months. Before the Olympics, Murdoch issued a tweet praising Boris Johnson to the sky.

The combined messages could not be mistaken in Downing Street. The Sun had demonstrated its power to bring Cameron down and Murdoch had shown that he could easily back a replacement leader should he choose to do so. After only a slight hiccup, Murdoch was back with a vengeance. Indeed just days after the UKIP surge in the 2013 local elections, newspapers reported Murdoch in London successively dining privately with all the various potential Cameron replacements. The political significance of these oligarchic dinners was revealed when a major row broke out in the spring of 2014 between the Gove and Johnson camps over what was said about Johnson by Gove to Murdoch at one of these dinners. When a foreign media-billionaire carries out the job-interviews and almost *de facto* appoints our Prime Ministers, our democracy is very, very sick.

Cameron had prior to the 2010 general election, condemned the influence of the lobbying industry saying *"It has tainted our politics for too long, an issue that exposes the far-too-cosy relationship between politics, government, business and money."* He promised an end to ex-ministers lobbying the government on behalf of corporate paymasters. But once in power, in a deeply cynical betrayal, Cameron employed Lynton Crosby, co-founder of the international tobacco, alcohol, oil and fracking lobbying firm Crosby Textor, in a reported £500,000 deal to be his lead 2015 general-election strategist. After his appointment the government dropped its proposals on alcohol minimum-pricing and plain cigarette packaging. Cameron refused over twelve times to answer questions on any involvement by Crosby in these decisions. As Cameron said in his 2010 speech *"It's absurd that a tiny percentage of the population craft legislation that will apply to one hundred per cent of the population."* Quite so. The pity is that he did not mean it.

But it would be remiss to finish this tour of how *The Prostitute State* controls party leaderships, without referring to Margaret Thatcher. A few anecdotes on the usual party leadership links to tax-havens, lobbying and media links that emerged upon her death in April 2013 should suffice. Tax-havens and lobbying also run in the Thatcher family veins. The Mirror revealed that her home was held by a British Virgin Islands tax-haven company. The Belgravia property was worth over £6 million. This potentially saved £2.4 million in inheritance taxes, as they were not due if the property was owned by a company rather than an individual.

The Guardian reported that around the time of the multi-billion-pound al-Yamamah arms deal negotiated by Margaret Thatcher; Mark Thatcher's multi-million-pound home in Mayfair was purchased on his behalf by another offshore company linked to those close to the deal. Mark had to move abroad to Dallas, following yet another scandal, when the Observer reported that his mother had been lobbying Oman for a £300 million building contract for the company employing her son as a lobbyist. He had to leave Dallas for South Africa due to a dispute with the US tax-authorities and is now banned from entering the US where his divorced wife and children live. Then in South Africa, he was found guilty of conspiring to overthrow the Equatorial Guinea government and fined £266,000. The fine was paid by his mother. He now lives in the Gibraltar tax-haven.

Mrs. Thatcher having enabled Rupert Murdoch's domination of the UK media market was subsequently paid £3.5 million for her ghost-written autobiography by Murdoch's HarperCollins publishers. After resigning, she took up various corporate-lobbying posts including with the infamous US tobacco corporation R J Reynolds. For this she was paid $500,000 per annum. The Sunday Times in July 1992 reported *"her advice will be sought on controversial issues including the penetration of tobacco markets in Eastern Europe and the Third World. She will also be asked to help resist attempts to ban tobacco advertising in the European Community and to fight cigarette taxes and state-run tobacco monopolies."* Thatcher, despite having campaigned whilst in government against lung cancer, had no problem taking the tobacco corporate dollar in retirement. Murdoch coincidentally was also a director of Philip Morris at this time.

The final word in this chapter goes to former UK diplomat Craig Murray, who wrote this anecdote after her death and which shockingly encapsulates how our political leaders are in reality the servants of corporate power and who kindly allowed me to repeat it here in full:

"Let me give one anecdote to which I can personally attest. In leaving office she became a "consultant" to US tobacco giant Phillip Morris. She immediately used her influence on behalf of Phillip Morris to persuade the Foreign & Commonwealth Office to lobby the Polish government to reduce the size of health warnings on Polish cigarette packets. Poland was applying to join the EU and the Polish health warnings were larger than the EU stipulated size.

I was the official on whose desk the instruction landed to lobby for lower health warnings. I refused to do it. My then Ambassador, Michael Llewellyn Smith (for whom I had and have great respect) came up with the brilliant diplomatic solution of throwing the instruction in the bin, but telling London we had done it.

So, as you drown in a sea of praise for Thatcher, remember this. She was prepared to promote lung cancer, for cash."

Chapter 5

MPs for Hire

The Prostitute State has inserted its tentacles deep into the supposed temple of our democracy, the UK Parliament in Westminster. Whilst MPs are no longer allowed to work directly for professional lobbying organisations, there are many other routes by which corporations access the heart of the House of Commons. These include hiring MPs as directors of companies, parliamentary consultants or corporate advisers, sponsoring All Party Parliamentary Committees, all-expenses-paid trips to corporate headquarters, visits to dictatorships, generously paid speeches to lobbying companies and so on.

An increasingly common route used by corporate lobbyists is the capture of parliamentary seats. Like David Cameron, ambitious well-off university graduates can afford to take low-paid or voluntary internships with an MP or at a party headquarters. They can then use this experience gained within government and our political parties to acquire well-paid PR jobs with a lobbying corporation or with the public-affairs department of a large corporation. Our major political parties have literally become corporate lobbyist production units!

They can then devote the time and money it requires to nurture a potential constituency party which might be replacing a retiring MP in a safe seat. The media contacts and skills that they will have acquired as lobbyists will give them a significant advantage over local-party candidates. The Electoral Reform Society calculated that in the 2010 UK general election that no matter who won the general election 382 out of 650 seats were safe, i.e. those seats would still be held by the same political party after the election, due to the UK's first-past-the-post electoral system. In these constituencies, no matter how the average 68,000 constituents vote in the general election, it is the tiny couple of hundred members of the holding local-party who *de facto* elect the MP.

These corporate lobbyists appear at constituency meetings well-dressed and articulate. The local volunteers may know them from when they worked as a party or parliamentary intern or feel their experience working for an MP gives them an extra edge. They often downplay their work as corporate lobbyists in their CVs. Local members will usually have no understanding that these candidates will have a record of repeatedly hijacking parliament for their corporate paymasters. All

Chapter 5

these guys have to do is win a few local-party members' votes in a safe seat and they are into Parliament.

A disturbing number of our current MPs have now worked as lobbyists prior to their election. In 2010, 15% of new Tory MPs and 16% of new Labour MPs had done so. They bring the culture of corporate lobbying with them into Parliament. There is no way of measuring the impact of this on legislation. But it helps explain why the party leaderships can get away with serving the corporate state rather than the electorate, when so many MPs have previously been in its pay. After these former lobbyist MPs retire or lose their seats in an election, they frequently slip seamlessly back into corporate lobbying. The knowledge and contacts they garnered as MPs is now an even more valuable corporate commodity.

Jeremy Browne MP, the former Liberal Democrat Minister for the Home Office, is a classic example. The son of Sir Nicholas Browne, he was educated at Badeles School (£30,000 per annum fees) and Nottingham University. He worked initially as an intern for Alan Beith MP. He then acted as Head of Press for both Charles Kennedy and Paddy Ashdown, where I had the challenging experience of dealing with him, when I was working to stop Paddy betraying the party's opposition to the deal with Blair.

Browne used his experience to get employment at Edelman, the world's largest privately owned PR firm. Their clients included Royal Dutch Shell, Microsoft, Walmart and Starbucks. Edelman has been criticised in the US for its astroturf tactics. It is credited with inventing the Flog – a pseudo "independent" blog sympathetic to a corporation and secretly paid for by their PR company. Bloomberg revealed how a blog called "*Walmarting across the USA*", was paid for by "*Working Families for Walmart*". This had been set up by Edelman on behalf of Walmart, to counteract a public outcry in the US over Walmart's pay and conditions. Walmart also own the ASDA super-market chain in the UK.

Browne was then able to target and win selection for the marginal seat of Taunton in the 2005 election. In the Liberal Democrats, a marginal seat is as good as it gets, as the party has almost no safe seats. In the 2007 leadership election he was a member of Nick Clegg's campaign team. He was rewarded with being Clegg's Shadow Chief Secretary to the Treasury and then with being a Minister of State in the coalition government.

Browne, along with many other public-affairs professionals, was at the heart of the Orange Book coup which captured the Liberal Democrats for **The Prostitute State,** just as it was about to reach government. It was heart-breaking for all those liberal local hard-working volunteers who had spent decades building the party up, to see their hard work hijacked just as it was coming to fruition. This capture of so many parliamentary seats by lobbyists in all parties is a reason why many people now feel politicians are all the same. There is some truth in the premise that no matter who we vote for the corporate lobbying party wins.

Whilst MPs are barred from professional lobbying, bizarrely they can act as paid "advisers" to corporations or alternatively they are nominated to their boards with a generous salary or even lucrative share options. David Miliband MP, former Labour Foreign Secretary, provides an example of both. In 2012 whilst still serving as a Labour MP he earned the following:

£	32,000	Adviser Oxford Analytica (Up to £12,000 per day)
£	116,000	Adviser Vantage Venture Capital (£23,000 per day)
£	65,000	Adviser United Arab Emirates (UAE) Foreign Office (£22,000 per day; Flight and accommodation for 3 days £5,000!)
£	15,000	Adviser Indus Basin Holdings (£15,000 per day)
£	102,000	Speeches at corporate dinners (up to £19,000 per speech)
£	500	Article for Rupert Murdoch's The Times Newspaper.
£	25,000	Teaching at Stanford University (one week)
£	75,000	Director Sunderland Football Club (£8,000 per day)
£	**430,000**	**Total**

This naturally dwarfs his £65,000 MP's salary. The Lib Dem blogger Iain Donaldson looked up Vantage Venture Capital after he became suspicious about Miliband advocating the UK switching to gas-powered stations from coal, on the BBC's Question Time in December 2012. As a former UK Climate Change minister one would have expected him to be advocating renewable energy. Donaldson found out that Vantage Venture Capital was investing substantially in the hugely controversial shale-gas fracking technology.

Oxford Analytica's website states *"Our private sector clients include financial institutions and hedge funds, energy and mining companies, technology firms, diversified conglomerates and professional services firms."* These organisations are willing to pay top dollar for the advice of a former UK government environment minister and foreign secretary. The frequent connection between *The Prostitute State* and dictatorships appears again on Miliband's list. The United Arab Emirates, whose Foreign Office paid him £65,000 for his work with the Sir Bani Yas Forum, is governed by seven dictatorial hereditary sheikhs.

The *Thieving Tax Haven Pillar* also embraces a significant number of serving parliamentarians. A 2012 Guardian investigation found that sixty-eight parliamentarians were directors of or had a controlling interest in companies based in tax havens. Whilst the majority were members of the Lords, six were MPs, including Peter Lilley and Nicholas Soames.

Chapter 5

Lilley was a director of the Cayman Islands registered Tethys Petroleum Company, which paid him £47,000 for 30 days work. In 2012 Leo Hickman in the Guardian reported that Lilley had received share options worth nearly half a million dollars. Lilley unsurprisingly is a climate-crisis *"luke-warmist"*. He was appointed to the Parliamentary Committee on Climate Change in 2012 to the alarm of the environmental movement. He is one of only three MPs who voted against the cross-party Climate Care Act. Lilley's oil company specialises in fossil-fuel exploration in the dictatorships of Kazakhstan, Uzbekistan and Tajikistan.

Former Tory Defence Minister and serving MP Nicholas Soames brings together many strands of the corporate state – the purchase of serving MPs expertise, dictatorships and tax havens. His only declared trip abroad in 2011 was to visit the Syrian dictator President Assad's deputy Prime Minister. In addition to his £66,000 MPs salary, in 2011/12 Soames earned an additional £220,000 from his various external roles including:

£	77,000	Adviser MMC Financial Services
£	20,000	Adviser Intrepid Capital Partners
£	91,000	Director Aegis Defence Services
£	21,000	Director Aggregated Micro Power
£	5,500	Paid Trip to Dubai

The Guardian revealed that the British security corporation Aegis Defence Services Ltd, despite being British, has its HQ in the tax haven of Switzerland and a subsidiary in the British Virgin Islands. It provides corporate security and lobbying services to a range of global corporations including the oil, gas, mining and tobacco industries.

It is not just the sizeable cheques that Soames collects that are noteworthy but the hours devoted to them. Remember he is supposedly a full-time Member of Parliament, for which he is paid an annual salary of £66,000 plus office staff and expenses.

Hours	Non-Parliamentary Work
180	Adviser MMC Financial Services
30	Adviser Intrepid Capital Partners
180	Director Aegis Defence Services
30	Director Aggregated Micro Power
21	Paid Trip to Dubai*
451	**Total Hours**

*number of days not declared but estimated at three workdays @7 hours/day.

Thus Soames was working for his corporate paymasters for an extraordinary three working months of the year whilst a serving MP.

The MPs register of interests reveals a similar story for Peter Lilley MP:

Hours	Non-Parliamentary Work
120	Director IDOX
150	Director Tethys Petroleum Services
220	Adviser Ferro Alloys Corporation
490	**Total Hours**

Lilley therefore devoted about 3.5 months of his year to his corporate paymasters. Thus the corporate state even hijacks the time of some of those elected by us to regulate and tax it.

The Guardian's list of parliamentary tax-haven company directors named many former MPs now serving in the Lords, indicating yet another route for *The Tax-Haven Pillar* into the legislature. It included Virginia Bottomley, former Tory Health Minister, who is a director of the private health corporation BUPA, with subsidiaries in Bermuda, Cayman Islands and the British Virgin Islands. Ian Lang is a director of hedge-fund Charlemagne Capital, registered in the Cayman Islands. But in another outrageous example of the fox being put in charge of the hen-coop, Lang is simultaneously Chair of the government's Advisory Committee on Business Appointments.

The Committee's Website states: *"The Advisory Committee acts independently to advise the Prime Minister, Foreign Secretary and former Minsters on applications made to it under the Business Appointment Rules, about appointments former Ministers, senior civil servants and other Crown servants wish to take up on leaving government. It is long-standing government policy that it is in the public interest that those with experience in government should be able to move into business or other areas of public life and it is equally important that in the taking up of an appointment, there is no cause for suspicion of impropriety."* The website naturally does not make any reference to their Chair being a director of a tax-haven based hedge fund.

The former Labour MP George Moonie, now Lord Moonie, is a director of Bwin.party, one of the world's largest gambling corporations. Like many UK gambling corporations it is based in the Gibraltar tax-haven. Moonie was caught up in the Cash for Influence scandal in 2009, where the Sunday Times quoted him offering to identify people who could put down an amendment. The Times said he named an annual fee for his assistance of £30,000 and quoted him as saying *"I did*

Chapter 5

not agree to amend the legislation. I agreed to seek to help to find a way of trying to amend the legislation."

The House of Lords' Report on the scandal found that "*on the standard of proof that we have set, we do not find that Lord Moonie expressed a clear willingness to breach the Code by promoting amendments on behalf of lobbyists in return for payment.*" This means that peers were happy for their fellow legislators to be hired to help get legislation amended but not to submit amendments themselves. Anyone other than the peers themselves will find this distinction bemusing.

Another former Labour MP and peer George Robertson sold his experience as general secretary of NATO and Blair's Secretary of Defence to become a director of the multi-billion-pound oil, gas and nuclear engineering corporation The Weir Group which had subsidiaries in the Bahamas and British Virgin Islands. His is also Deputy Chair of the massive oil corporation TNK–BP which is registered in the British Virgin Islands. Unlike the House of Commons Register of Interests, the Lords Register inexplicably does not report how much they are paid. But it is worth noting that Lord Robertson's secretarial costs are partly sponsored by BP!

Robertson is also paid as:

Senior International Adviser:	Cable & Wireless Communications
Senior Counsellor:	Cohen Group (US consultancy)
Adviser:	BP
Advisory Board Member:	Engelfield Capital (private equity)
Director:	Western Ferries

The Cohen Group is an international lobbying corporation whose website boasts of helping a U.S. company obtain government approval to pursue contracts with Chinese nuclear power stations. It is chaired by the former US Secretary of Defence and Republican Senator William Cohen.

David Steel, former MP and Liberal leader, was also on the Guardian list. As Lord Steele of Aikwood, he is a director of Blue Planet Investment and the luxury hotel group GMH, based in the Luxembourg tax-haven. When asked about this by The Guardian, GMH said "*he is of course a very highly respected and experienced individual and it was felt he would make a valuable contribution to the board of GMH.*" Having spent his entire working life since 1965 as an MP or MSP, it is clear they were paying for his political experience.

The Guardian only detailed parliamentarians who were directors of companies based in tax havens. It did not detail those who were employed by, were advisers to or were shareholders in such companies, such as the Lib Dem Peer Lord Sandberg, former chair of HSBC, who in addition to being the director of five Hong

Kong based companies, is also a shareholder in Telemedic Developments based in the British Virgin Islands.

An interesting example of how our rich elite use the UK government to facilitate the transfer of wealth from the taxpayer to itself is the Common Agricultural Policy of the European Union. It was created to help small farmers deal with wildly varying food prices. But the payments were never capped to prevent ultra-rich landowners from creaming off huge amounts in subsidies. George Monbiot reported in 2012 that it cost each UK family up to £245 every year in taxes. UK aristocrats receiving these farming welfare benefits included Queen Elizabeth II who received £10 million for her Sandringham Estate and the richest man in England, The Duke of Westminster, who received £6 million over the last ten years. There were estimated to be over two hundred millionaires receiving over £500,000 each every year in such subsidies.

Tory Minister Richard Benyon MP, whose twenty thousand acre estate is worth £125 million, is estimated to have received over £2million in such subsidies. As the land must be kept clear, any wild plants have to be removed, thus drastically reducing their wildlife benefits. The EU has for years tried to limit these payments to smaller farmers only. In 2012, despite Cameron demanding that the EU cut its budget, he opposed capping payments at €300,000 as he did not want to discourage *"consolidation"* of farms. When you remember that just 0.36% of the UK population already owns over two thirds of all UK land, it is clear Cameron will not be happy until they own one hundred per cent of it!!

Until 2002, MPs were barred from discussing in Parliament, matters of direct interest to a person or group employing them. MPs are now only forbidden to raise issues that would *exclusively* benefit groups in which they have an interest. The BIJ reported that four MPs who benefited from CAP payments contributed to the production of Parliamentary Reports or asked Parliamentary questions urging the retention of the payments in 2011 alone. Other examples included Tory MP Stephen Hammond who was paid £15,000 as "parliamentary consultant" to the Professional Contractors Association and was reported as asking questions related to their operations in Parliament. The Labour MP Nick Raynsford was paid £50,000 in 2011 by organisations including the Construction Industry Council and Triathlon Homes. He asked numerous Parliamentary questions about housing, planning and construction in 2011. Despite all the uproar over Cash for Questions and Cash for Influence, the corporate lobbying industry continues to find numerous legal ways around the regulations vainly trying to protect parliament's integrity.

But it is how the corporate state used parliamentarians to privatise the NHS (Britain's free National Health Service), despite overwhelming public opposition, that really takes the breath away. The details on the financial involvement of so many parliamentarians in private health corporations, amassed by blogger Dr Eoin Clarke and the Social Investigations Team are truly shocking. They starkly demonstrate the enormous breadth of the forces brought to bear to carry out this smash and grab on our most valued essential public service.

With an annual NHS budget of £106 billion, global private health corporations have been licking their lips over potential rich pickings for years. Gradually, during the New Labour years, they secretly laid the groundwork, penetrating every nook and cranny of parliament and the civil service, ready to go full speed ahead once they were ready. This ranged from donations to all the major political parties, to hiring a plethora of ex-ministers as lobbyists.

Clarke detailed three hundred and thirty separate donations totalling £8 million from the private healthcare industry to Tory coffers during the decade prior to the new Healthcare Act. Over half the major donations to the Liberal Democrats leading up to the 2010 general election came from a private health insurance company, Alpha Healthcare. The Times reported that Alpha Healthcare was a client of lobbying company DLA Piper, who employed former Lib Dem Treasurer and Cayman Islands lobbyist Lord Clement Jones. It is another example of Lib Dem hypocrisy, as they condemned for years Tory Party funding by Lord Ashcroft. Hundreds of thousands of pounds from the private health care industry also poured into the right-wing Labour group Progress. According to research by Social Investigations, over TWO HUNDRED parliamentarians had direct financial links with the health care industry. These included directors, advisers, lobbyists, publicists or suppliers who were MPs (71) or Lords (142) and who outrageously actually voted for the Bill privatising the NHS.

As well as the considerable minority of MPs who are directly part of the corporate state, the impact of the billionaire press on the rest of MPs cannot be overstated. At the most basic level, one cannot stand for parliament or even local government, unless one is prepared to have just about any aspect of one's private life strewn across the billionaires' tabloids. I experienced this in a small way when standing for election as a local councillor. The local press rang me up saying that someone from the local Labour Party had contacted them to say I was gay. I was taken aback but luckily was able to say that many of my constituents already knew and that it was impossible to out someone who was already out.

I also had to deal with it when going through the approval process to be a parliamentary candidate. To be approved you not only have to pass tests on party policy, media skills, campaigning, public speaking, fundraising et cetera, but you also have to undergo a special interview by an inner-core committee on any potential skeletons in your closet. And I had one!

Whilst in my twenties I had decided to see what it was like to be with a sex worker. He was a nice guy but it was not an experience I wanted to repeat. So when they asked me about skeletons I felt I had to tell them. I was afraid this could be the end of my political career. But I was delighted when the panel, which included the Newbury MP David Rendel, said if I was willing to endure it being splashed across the Daily Mail, then the party would not bar me from standing as a candidate. This was an occasion where I was grateful for the party's liberalism. But how many far better qualified people are deterred from standing due to unwillingness to risk, for themselves or their families, such merciless exposure, and what damage have the tabloids thus inflicted on our democracy?

I also had direct experience of the impact of *The Prostituted Media* on our MPs when I served on the Federal Executive. We were given regular updates from the Campaigns Department on the party's polling and focus groups and how this drove the party's election messages. Chris Rennard, as then Head of Campaigns, in my opinion surrendered the party's political power to the media barons without even a fight. Instead of asking focus groups how we could express our party values and policies in a way voters could support, he simply asked what their top priorities were. This made no effort to find out how to persuade people about our liberal values or policies but instead conducted simplistic consumer retail-polling and then used that to guide our MPs' messaging.

Reducing democracy to pure political consumerism is the ultimate victory for Thatcherism. If you abandon conviction politics and simply adapt your message to fit prevailing consumer polling, then you surrender vast unaccountable power to the media barons, who largely shape those consumer views and you help destroy democracy. Whilst I was a member, two examples demonstrated how corrupting this approach was on the party. From its formation the Lib Dems were far ahead of the other major parties on ecological issues and even in the early 1990's had policies to tackle the climate crises, including a carbon tax on electricity production.

But even the Tories had begun to realise the importance of ecological issues and Thatcher's background as a chemist had led her to being one of the first international leaders to understand the seriousness of the climate crises. In a landmark speech to the UN in 1989 she said: *"Change in future is likely to be more fundamental and more widespread than anything we have known hitherto. Change to the sea around us, change to the atmosphere above, leading in turn to change in the world's climate, which could alter the way we live in the most fundamental way of all. That prospect is a new factor in human affairs. It is comparable in its implications to the discovery of how to split the atom. Indeed, its results could be even more far-reaching,"*

In 1994 the Tories under Major introduced VAT at 8% on domestic gas and electricity bills. It was an ecological tax on carbon consumption, as natural gas is a fossil fuel and over 80% of electricity was produced from burning fossil fuels. The media barons went mental – declaring it a tax on *"little old ladies"*. This could have easily been dealt with through targeted winter fuel or benefit payments. But the best solution would be to insulate all UK homes to passive-house standards, slashing bills and carbon consumption at the same time.

Chris Rennard, with the backing of Paddy Ashdown, picked up this tabloid attack and mercilessly hammered the Tories with it, in the extraordinary series of by-elections that arose during the 1992-97 Parliament in safe Tory seats. Rock-solid Tory seats like Newbury, Christchurch and Eastleigh fell to the Lib Dems, establishing them as a serious third force in British politics for the first time in a century. But it was sheer hypocrisy. Whilst the Lib Dem carbon tax would not appear on *"little old ladies"* energy bills as VAT, the fact that it was imposed on the energy companies as a carbon tax meant that bills would still go up. The Lib Dem approach however would have encouraged renewable energy as well as home energy-efficiency, whereas the Tory tax merely encouraged energy-efficiency.

At the time I was friendly with the Lib Dem Environment Spokesperson Simon Hughes MP. I was acutely aware of the gutter politics being used in the by-elections by the Lib Dems, but Hughes himself had not publicly condemned the Tory VAT rise. Huge pressure was being put on him by Ashdown to adopt the populist attack on the Tories.

I was in the audience at the 1994 Party Conference where Simon had to give the keynote Environment speech. The hall was packed. Simon was the darling of the radical wing of the party and hugely popular. He gave a barn-storming speech and included a full-throated attack on the Tory's VAT rise. Simon appeared beside me a few seconds after he finished and asked anxiously what I thought. As a naive new member who was flattered to even know an MP personally, I said it was an excellent speech. He asked again what I thought of it and again I blithely said it was fine. When he asked a third time what I really thought of it, the penny finally dropped. He had caved in....the media barons had won yet again.

Ashdown had succeeded in breaking him and Rennard continued with the hypocritical by-election attacks on the Tories. The irony was that the Tories were so unpopular that the by-elections could have been won anyway, but not with such huge margins. Hughes was then so passionate about halting nuclear power that he lay down on the road in direct actions to try and stop the building of the Sellafield Nuclear Reprocessing Plant. History proved him right. The reprocessing plant closed years later amid hundreds of millions of pounds of taxpayers' losses. Gut wrenchingly sad, twenty years on he is part of a government ramming a new generation of untested Franco-Chinese nuclear power stations down our throats. Such is the power of **The Prostitute State** to neuter MPs with integrity in our democracy. If someone as strong as Simon can be absorbed by it, what hope is there for the rest of us, unless we band together to take it on.

The other example that I saw first-hand of how the media barons control the parliamentary party's agenda was on Europe. The Lib Dems are instinctively opposed to sectarian nationalism and are natural supporters of the European Union. So when it came to the EU elections, you would expect vigorous pro-EU campaigning. Extraordinarily, whilst I was in the party, with a few local honourable exceptions, there was almost no mention of Europe in its Euro-elections literature. Rennard dishonestly concentrated instead on making the EU elections a national referendum on whatever government happened to be in power.

Rather than tackle in its election leaflets, the endless anti-EU xenophobia being poured out by the billionaire tabloids, the party was silent on its pro-EU stance. Indeed Ruth Bright, who was the Lib Dem Parliamentary candidate in East Hampshire, reports that they were expressly told by the Lib Dem Campaigns Team to NOT even mention Europe in their Euro Election campaign materials! The irony that such vitriolic xenophobia comes from five billionaires who either do not live in Britain or legally avoid UK taxes was never confronted. I repeatedly raised this issue on the FE, when Rennard was presenting the Campaigns Department's European election plans to us. I was convinced that if even the pro-EU Lib Dems were afraid to mention Europe during European election campaigns, then the media billionaires' propaganda would win and eventually the British public would turn against European cooperation. This cooperation has helped ensure an unprecedented almost continent-wide peace for three generations, a fact recognised by the EU being awarded the Nobel Peace Prize in 2012.

But I got nowhere with my colleagues or MPs on the FE. They refused to include almost any mention of our support for Europe in the campaign plans. Sadly time has proven me right with the media billionaires enabling UKIP to win the 2014 EU elections. Clegg's final desperate attempt to campaign on a pro-EU ticket was far too late and Clegg's own reputation is now irrevocably associated with bare-faced lying on tuition fees. The Lib Dems' decades-long cowardice in the face of the billionaire-media's hatred of Europe has contributed to this hijacking of Britain's political agenda. What *The Prostituted Media* desperately does not want voters to realise is that the combined power of the democracies of Europe could, if we demanded it, rein in the rich elites and multinational corporations.

It is crucial that we wake up to the destructive unaccountable power this handful of media barons exerts over our MPs. The News of the World's phone-hacking scandal shockingly exposed the depth of this treasonous blackmailing of our political system. An independent free press is one of *the* fundamental pillars of a free democracy. But what we have in the UK at present is its antithesis. The billionaire press manipulates a considerable proportion of the electorate to the media owners' agenda. They dictate policies to our MPs on taxation, health, international relations, Europe, war, pensions, transport, environment, welfare etc etc. They anoint their chosen political party leaders.

Only those ambitious MPs who meet with their approval gain the oxygen of positive publicity. They have destroyed the power of local councils and decimated party membership. They have successfully waged a destructive war on our state institutions for generations, ensuring that nearly all former state assets have been grabbed by their fellow billionaires and corporations. They are a malign incubus feeding on the decayed entrails of what was once our proud democracy.

Murdoch's News of the World scandal exposed what was long known within the political world. If any MP, minister or Prime Minister wanted to support a policy which they believed was right for the country but which was opposed by News International or the other media billionaires, they knew they would have to risk having every aspect of their private lives trashed in public for daring to do so. Their medical history, taxes, income, emails, bank-accounts, telephone conversations, police records, texts, benefits history, drug-taking and sex life would all be trawled through by those working for Murdoch, Rothermere, or Desmond. That information would then be used to destroy them politically and to demolish the policy disliked by the corporate media. As Leveson exposed, MPs would also be taking on this risk on behalf of their partners, family members, friends, employees and even neighbours!

Consider this breath-taking list of shocking abuses of power, straightforward bullying and actual criminality exercised by Murdoch's employees at News International, many of the details of which are in Tom Watson MP's book Dial M for Murdoch:

- It created "naming and shaming" lists of MPs who did not support their newspaper campaigns.
- It threatened an MP with the following: *"My editor will pursue you for the rest of your life"*, for daring to oppose Tony Blair who had the support of The Sun.
- Large numbers of serving MPs had their phones hacked.
- Some of the most senior ministers in the government had their phones hacked, including Deputy Prime Minister John Prescott, Culture Secretary Tessa Jowell (responsible for overseeing media regulation), Home Secretary David Blunkett, Defence Minister Peter Kilfoyle and Cabinet Member Peter Mandelson,
- It hired a private investigator who hacked computers and targeted the Commissioner of the Metropolitan police John Stevens.
- It hacked the phones of then Tory frontbencher Boris Johnson and Respect leader George Galloway.

- Murdoch broke an undertaking given to the Secretary of State not to interfere with the editorial policy of the Times Newspapers, saying the undertakings *"were not worth the paper they were written on."*
- It persuaded the Thatcher government to exempt Murdoch's Luxembourg-based Sky satellite business from foreign ownership regulations.
- It privately demanded that the Prime Minister fire ministers they did not like.
- It bribed staff on competing newspapers for their news-lists.
- It stole other newspapers' exclusives.
- It paid senior politicians over £200,000 per annum to write newspaper columns.
- A senior executive was quoted telling a reporter *"This is what we do – we go out and destroy other people's lives."*
- It illegally purchased people's private and ex-directory phone numbers and itemised phone bills from corrupt phone-company employees.
- It illegally bought or blagged individual's medical records from corrupt NHS officials.
- It illegally bought individual tax and pension records, bank-statements, criminal records, car number plates, home addresses and benefit records from corrupt officials.
- It blackmailed individuals by agreeing not to expose embarrassing details in return for providing them with stories or co-operating with them.
- It put celebrities under surveillance including spy vans parked outside their homes with no public interest justification.
- It paid corrupt police for information. When Hugh Grant called the police when he had a burglary or a car broken into, the first people around were nearly always paparazzi photographers.
- Their senior executives lunched with senior Metropolitan Police officers whilst it was supervising the criminal investigations into NI.
- It hacked the phones of the senior police officers investigating NI, Andy Hayman and John Yates (both of whom were having affairs and so subject to pressure if revealed).
- Following Andy Hayman's resignation during an investigation into his expense account, he was employed by NI even as the various criminal investigations were ongoing.
- Trade-union leaders had their phones hacked during strikes and personal information used to damage their reputations.
- It targeted the parents, families and friends of tragic child murders, including Milly Dowler and Sarah Payne.
- The families of victims of other atrocities such as those of the 7/7 bombings in London had their phones hacked.

Chapter 5

- The phones of families of soldiers killed in action in Iraq and Afghanistan were hacked.
- It allocated a pool of cash to its Royal editor for paying contacts for stories – it paid for illegal phone hacking of the royal family and their employees.
- It corruptly paid special-branch officers for the private phone numbers of the Queen.
- They paid over £100,000 in total in illegal bribes to members of the Metropolitan police and Royal protection officers.
- Boris Johnson's Deputy Mayor for London, Tory Kit Malthouse, pressed the Met three times to scale back NI investigation.
- Despite being jailed for illegal phone hacking of the royal family, Clive Goodman received a payoff of nearly £250,000 from NI.
- Information Commissioner Richard Thomas told the Leveson Inquiry that the press were able to assert very substantial influence on public policy and the political process.
- James Murdoch at the 2009 Edinburgh Television Festival demanded the pruning of BBC budgets, abolition of the BBC Trust and curtailing of the BBC website and the muzzling of Ofcom (the broadcasting regulator). Not long later David Cameron wrote an opinion piece for the Sun promising to prune the BBC and to remove ALL of Ofcom's policy making powers. Jeremy Hunt, Tory shadow Culture Secretary duly promised the abolition of the BBC Trust. Suddenly James Murdoch's wish list was miraculously the Tory wish list.
- As Secretary of State the pro-NI Jeremy Hunt removed Ofcom's policy-making powers on media ownership and transferred them to himself.
- George Osborne cut the BBC's six year budget by 16% in his first budget. BBC Online was cut by 25%. James Murdoch's agenda was being delivered almost to the letter despite the hacking scandal.
- Prior to the Milly Dowler phone hacking scandal, NI had paid out over a million pounds to keep quiet legal cases that threatened to reveal criminal activities by journalists at NI.
- The convicted phone-hacker Glenn Mulcaire had been paid over £100,000 per year by NI.
- NI outrageously even placed the lawyers representing the phone-hacking victims under surveillance.
- A strategy document was leaked which revealed that NI intended to use the personal information gleaned about the victim's *lawyers* as a means to *"force compromise and settlement"*.
- Shockingly even the families of the lawyers were also put under surveillance with an ex-wife and young daughter of one lawyer being filmed.

- They allocated six journalists to investigate the private lives of the Parliamentary Select Committee investigating the criminal activities taking place at NI. They were ordered by the editor to find out everything about them *"who was gay, who was having affairs, anything we can use to get them"*.
- Tom Watson MP was told that Rupert Murdoch had lobbied the then Prime Minister Tony Blair to get Watson to halt his investigation of NI.
- Rebekah Wade informed Tony Blair's Director of Communications that NI were making it personal and would not stop until they got Tom Watson.
- NI launched a policy in 2009 to *"eliminate emails that could be unhelpful in the context of future litigation in which an NI company is a defendant."*
- Adam Price MP member of the Culture Committee stated that they were warned if they summoned the Chief Executive of NI to give evidence their private lives would be raked over.
- Senior Metropolitan Police officers who had been repeatedly dined by NI tried to persuade the Guardian's editor to drop the investigation into NI.
- NI paid an ex-criminal £150,000 per year to carry out illegal information gathering on its behalf. This ex-con had twice been charged with murder and had been released from a 7 year jail term for subverting the course of justice, after planting drugs on a businessman's wife to enable him to gain custody of their kids.
- NI put two police officers who were carrying out a murder investigation under surveillance in 2002. One of the police officers said that they believed this was because one of the suspects (the ex-con mentioned in previous item) had strong links with a senior NI executive who was doing them a favour by intimidating the investigators.
- The senior NI-friendly Metropolitan Police officers in charge of the original failed phone-hacking inquiry refused to supply evidence in their possession to the victims of the phone hacking, as the victims' lawyers tried to pursue NI through the civil courts after the police had failed to act.
- These same senior police officers were then forced by court orders to hand over the evidence, which they had redacted in such a way as to protect the NI journalists named on the materials.
- The victims' lawyers then had to get yet another court order to get the redactions removed so the victims could finally get justice from NI through the civil courts.
- The Director of Public Prosecutions (DPP) had numerous dinners and social meetings with top executives of NI whilst they were under investigation for criminal phone hacking.
- Following his retirement that same DPP was employed as an adviser by NI.

Chapter 5

- The BBC reported that Andy Coulson was paid his salary by NI for two years after he resigned in disgrace from NoW and was working for David Cameron.
- NI paid the publicist Max Clifford nearly a million pounds including costs to keep silent about the hacking of his phone and to renew his supply of exclusives.
- The NI-friendly Met Police Officers told Parliament in 2006 that they had evidence of only a small number of phones being hacked. The Guardian later discovered they had evidence of literally thousands of phones being hacked.
- The NI-friendly Met Officers made an agreement with the Crown Prosecution Service in 2006 to deliberately limit their prosecutions to "less sensitive" victims. This potentially helped protect NI from the scandal exploding at that time and allowed it to continue with the criminal activities up to 2009.
- The NI-friendly Met told high-profile victims that they had no evidence of their phones being hacked when they actually had.
- Despite being under investigation for various criminal charges, NI smashed up its reporters computers in 2010 when moving to new premises.
- Norman Lamb MP reported that NI had told him that they would turn The Sun on the Lib Dems, if they did not support Murdoch's bid for BSkyB.
- The former Prime Minister Gordon Brown told Parliament the reason for NI turning on him was because he refused their request to cut the BBC budget and the government order for it to sell the 16% stake it bought in ITV to stop rival media baron Richard Branson buying it.
- The Met Police employed the former deputy editor of the NoW to advise its press office, whilst NoW was under investigation.
- The Met press office complained about the Guardian's phone hacking investigation.
- 10 members of the Met Press Office had previously worked for NI.
- NI rewarded their disgraced chief executive and Sun Editor Rebekah Brooks with a parting package of nearly £11 million.
- The NI criminal phone-hacking operation started at least in 2002 and police believe it continued right up to 2009, years after their reporter Clive Goodman had been arrested for it in 2006.
- They blackmailed J K Rowling by promising to return the stolen copy of her unpublished 5th Harry Potter book if she agreed to a photo session.
- Journalist Sean Hoare admitted that phone-hacking originated first at the Sun and then spread to the NoW.
- Illegal computer hacking was also admitted by Murdoch's The Times and Sky News.
- NI paid for the almost continuous surveillance of various celebrities such as Jude Law, Charlotte Church and JK Rowling, for no reason other than fishing

for potential stories. They were followed for days at a time at home and abroad, as were their children, family members, friends and employees.

- Justice Vos stated that NI should be regarded by the police as *"deliberate destroyers of evidence"*.
- Despite John Prescott and other VIPs being told repeatedly by the Metropolitan Police that they had not been targeted, they finally admitted that they had behaved unlawfully in not telling them that they had been, when forced to by a judicial review funded on behalf of the victims by Max Mosley.
- NI former editor Andy Coulson was charged with committing perjury during the Tommy Sheridan trial, whilst serving as Cameron's Head of Communications.

The phone-hacking of the victim family phones was an appalling intrusion on human grief. But the fact that it was this revelation and not the blackmailing of almost our entire political system that brought down The News of the World indicates how far the corporate media has neutered UK public opinion. Nowhere was there any serious explanation or discussion in the tabloids about the catastrophic constitutional and democratic implications of the revelations.

For twenty years an Australian media baron had basically usurped the various organs of the UK state for his own ends. In another era, that would have been called treason and he would have been hanged for it, not that I am in favour of the death penalty. But Murdoch merely got his knuckles rapped by a parliamentary committee and his malign treason continues unabated. This was demonstrated by the humiliating sight of all three major party leaders posing like three Murdoch rent-boys with the front page of The Sun in their hands at the beginning of the 2014 World Cup.

The above chilling list of the abuse of power was by just one of the four major UK media corporations. How many decent MPs wishing to take on the corporate state, pursue an investigation or propose a policy in our Parliament on behalf of their constituents would be willing to risk exposing themselves to this brute force if quadrupled? Those who do, like Labour's Tom Watson MP or the Green Party's Caroline Lucas MP and Baroness Jenny Jones, deserve our full respect.

Taken together, whether our MPs sit on corporate boards, are employed as corporate advisers or are merely honest MPs trying to serve their constituents, there is no getting away from the fact that what we have is a prostituted parliament where the majority of our MPs are either owned, bribed or terrified into subservience by the corporate lobbying and media machines.

Chapter 6

The House of Lordly Prostitutes

The House of Lords is the British parliament's upper chamber. Almost uniquely among the world's democracies, it is completely unelected and as of January 2013 is made up of ninety two hereditary aristocrats (two female), twenty six male Church of England bishops and 666 appointed life peers. Only twenty-five percent of new peerages created since 1997 were granted to women. The current total of 784 peers compares to 650 elected MPs and makes it the largest parliamentary chamber in the world, other than the Chinese Congress which represents 1.4 billion people and has 3,000 members. There is no limit on the number of appointed peers, who sit for life.

Many hereditary peers are from the landowning aristocracy and are natural supporters of the corporate state. They are the descendants of the historical equivalent of today's corporate billionaires. Until the twentieth century, most members of the Lords were hereditary peers, whose title granted them membership of the legislature. However, the 1999 House of Lords Act reduced the number of hereditary peers from 753 to 92. Of these, forty-nine are Conservatives, with only four Labour and four Liberal Democrats. The remainder sit as unaffiliated crossbenchers. The Daily Mail reported in 2010 that the hereditary aristocracy, to this day, controls nearly a third of all the UK's land, with just 1200 families controlling most of this. Unlike most European countries, Britain has never undergone any major land redistribution since feudal times. In 2011, The Guardian reported that two thirds of Britain's land, about 40 million acres, is owned by a tiny 0.36% of the population or about 158,000 families. Increasingly, the hereditary landowners are being joined by a new generation of oligarchs, with Roman Abramovich, Stefan Persson (H&M) and even Madonna buying huge swathes of UK land.

In feudal times, the majority of members of the House of Lords were "princes" of the church, including bishops, archbishops and abbots, who owned vast expanses of land. Following the dissolution of the monasteries under Henry VIII, the House of Lords was composed largely of hereditary peers, with no abbots and a reduced number of bishops, who were now Church of England rather than Catholic. These were appointed by the King and not the Pope as previously. In some ways the dissolution of the monasteries represented a land-grab of a previous religious incarnation of *The Prostitute State* by its successor the crown and aristocracy, to whom Henry granted many of the monasteries' lands and new peerages in the Lords as rewards for loyalty.

The practice of creating hereditary peerages faded out in the twentieth century, with Margaret Thatcher being the last Prime Minister to create any. Following the 1958 Life Peerages Act, the Lords moved from a majority of hereditary peers to a majority of life peers. Life peerages cannot be inherited. Prime ministers now use their unlimited power to appoint life peers to shift the political balance of the Lords towards their own political party. Until recently, Tory prime-ministers did not have to do this, as the hereditary peers had ensured an inbuilt Tory majority. Tony Blair however appointed an astonishing 357 life peers, which meant that by the end of his term, a majority of the Lords had been appointed just by him. His successor, David Cameron, by January 2013 had already appointed 155 new life peers, at a record breaking 60 per year.

Established practice has been for the prime-minister to allocate some appointments to the Leader of The Opposition and recently to the Liberal Democrats, though not proportionate to the votes cast in general elections. The Prime Minister allows the other party leaders to select their own appointees. This system of patronage, which is a hangover from feudalism, is an ideal route for the corporate state to insert its tentacles into the legislature itself. This is ironic, as it was designed to end the hegemony of Britain's feudal landowning classes, but has merely complemented it with the new corporate elites. The prime-minister and the leaders of the opposition, without the requirement to consider anyone's views or hold any vote, can appoint FOR LIFE members of the Lords, unlike almost every other democracy where the voters elect their legislators. This unaccountable patronage is a fundamental flaw in the UK's so-called "unwritten constitution".

Once someone has been appointed to the Lords, they can then be appointed to be Ministers of State. This is an important but little publicised UK route into actual government. Thus bankers, corporate directors or major donors can become Ministers of State without having to face any election whatsoever. They are the cuckoos in the democratic nest.

The corporate state also exerts its influence in the Lords in many other ways:

- Corporations regularly appoint peers to lucrative seats or chairs of their boards.
- Peers are hired as "consultants" by private corporations.
- Peers are employed full time as "public affairs directors".
- Corporations or political lobbying companies subsidise peers' office costs and in return get free parliamentary passes, giving them carte-blanche access to Parliament.

Chapter 6

- These corporate peers can speak and vote on legislation that impacts directly on their corporate financial interests.
- Corporate peers are frequently appointed to oversee their own corporate fields as Ministers of State.

These practices continue despite the supposed ban on peers working as professional political lobbyists in 2010, following the *"peers for sale"* scandal in 2009.

After my first couple of years on the Liberal Democrat Federal Executive, I saw how corrupting the leader's vast powers of patronage were. It undermines both the power of the electorate and of party members, in favour of the elites in the leaders' inner circle. Patronage gives the leaders almost untrammelled control over all three sections of their parties, the parliamentary party, their party in the House of Lords and their party membership.

In the House of Commons, the Prime Minister appoints all Secretaries of State, Junior Ministers and all the way down to parliamentary private secretaries (first rung of the promotion ladder) or their shadow equivalents if they are an opposition leader. MPs must display loyalty to the Prime Minister or party leader if they value their career in parliament.

As the leaders can also appoint retiring MPs to the Lords, it ensures that even MPs, who are nearing retirement, generally also do not start expressing independent views. This deprives Parliament of crucial independent, patronage-free experienced voices. Otherwise they will lose any hope of having a nice comfortable sinecure in the Lords. Nearly a third of appointees are former MPs or MEPs. With almost all MPs thus shackled by patronage and not fully free to speak out, the concept of parliamentary "debate" becomes almost worthless.

In addition, leaders also have the same power of patronage over their party's peers as they do over MPs, as they also appoint all spokespersons or Ministers in the House of Lords. The power of appointment to the House of Lords, gives the leader almost dictatorial power over the party's democratic membership. When I was a member of the Lib Dems, it was established practice that only those loyal to the leader would be considered for peerages from party committees. The Lib Dem Federal Executive had a standing agenda item for questions to the leader at its monthly meetings. Almost invariably, I was about the only member to actually ask the leader what their positions on the current major political issues were and to put opposing viewpoints if I disagreed with them.

Many members who had long served on federal committees or who held senior party posts naturally often harboured ambitions for seats in the Lords. The quickest way to lose that seat was to oppose the leader's wishes. In practice, this meant that many of the supposedly elected posts in the party's constitution were actually leadership appointees. Almost nobody would dare stand against the leader's nominees for such posts and even in the rare cases when they did, the leadership's patronage vote would help ensure that they were defeated. Patronage-induced loyalty is also useful in silencing even those who have the courage to express an alternative viewpoint to the leaderships. If anybody does, they usually get so deluged with a barrage of attacks by patronage-seeking loyalists that they will think twice about doing so again. All of this is extremely useful to the corporate state, for if it can control the leadership, then through patronage, it can effectively control the rest of the party.

Following our huge effort to scupper Paddy Ashdown's Project, as well as the party's corrupt lobbying culture, we realised that the corrupt Lords patronage system also needed tackling. I decided to try and democratise the process of Lib Dem appointments to the Lords. My purpose was threefold. Firstly, as we were in favour of elections to the Lords, we could demonstrate our good faith by introducing elections for our own nominees. Secondly, I wanted to put an end to donors buying Lib Dem peerages. David Steel, former leader of the party virtually admitted to the inherent corruption in the Lords appointment process, by saying in November 2013 that *"not surprisingly each party leader finds that those doing nothing for the party except writing large cheques somehow manage to catch their eye"*. And thirdly, I wanted an end to the corrosive suppressive effect Lords patronage was having on internal party democratic debates.

Naively, I thought as the party was committed to an elected Lords, that people would think the introduction of internal elections for Lib Dem peers would be an exciting way to demonstrate that the party practiced what it preached. How wrong I was! Via *new radicalism*, we drafted a motion calling for an elected panel of potential life-peers, from which the leader would have to appoint his nominees to the Lords. Sadly, with the usual hypocrisy, the leadership tried to block the motion being debated. On the seventh attempt, we overcame the leadership loyalists on the conference committee and the motion was accepted for debate.

The leadership lined up the entire parliamentary parties in the Lords and Commons to oppose the motion at conference, with the Chief Whip lecturing the conference that patronage was far more democratic than elections! Despite the party's supposed commitment to an elected Lords, the addiction to patronage was too strong for the leadership to let go without a massive fight.

The MPs and Peers naturally backed the leadership, but the larger and more challenging group opposing us were the long-serving committee loyalists hoping to be next in line for the Lords. They were appalled that after years of slavish loyalty, they might now have to stand for election. Despite this powerful coalition and after a nail-biting debate on the conference floor, we won by a very narrow majority. We were exuberant.

Chapter 6

An amusing episode occurred later at a black tie dinner held to honour Paddy Ashdown's retirement. I was sharing a table with Rupert Mitford (Lord Redesdale) a cousin of the Mitford sisters, who had inherited the enormous 17,000 acre Redesdale Estate in Northumbria. He expressed his displeasure about the new system of elections to the Lords. The reason was that Mitford as a Lib Dem hereditary peer was in the process of losing that permanent seat due to the 1999 House of Lords Act.

Redesdale was a hard working peer and expected a life-peerage from Ashdown to continue his life membership of the legislature uninterrupted, without an election. We had destroyed that plan and he was now going to have to stand for election to the new panel of potential Lib Dem peers. He was not happy about it. I confess as I cycled home that evening my bicycle, to having a giggle about having helped force one of England's largest aristocratic landowners into finally having to stand for election like the rest of us. However, Rupert had the last laugh, as he duly stood for election to the panel, nearly topped the poll and was subsequently appointed by Charles Kennedy back to the Lords for life. I did not mind; the principle I was seeking to establish was that people should be elected and not that aristocrats should be banned.

Our victory over elections to the Lords happened during the leadership transition from Paddy Ashdown to Charles Kennedy. Kennedy had written a letter to the party's newspaper, Liberal Democrat News, saying he would respect the conference decision mandating such elections. For the first time in UK constitutional history, an election was held for political appointments to the Lords.

Sixty people were elected to the panel by a proportional voting system. As I regularly came near the top of the elections for the FE, I stood a good chance of being elected to the panel, as it was the same electorate. But I knew the establishment would accuse me of fighting the campaign merely to get myself into the Lords. Indeed, Lord Maclennan made such an accusation to my face. That would have undermined the battle for democratic integrity which we had just won and so I did not stand.

Rumours then started swirling that Kennedy was going to renege on his promise to respect the elections. Blair had given eight new peerages to the party, a fraction of the number needed to provide proportional representation for the party in the Lords and a betrayal of his agreement with Ashdown. Having got rid of most of the hereditaries, Blair was now packing the Lords with his own ultra-rich donors and loyalists. This was something even the Crown had not been able to do since late medieval times.

Kennedy duly announced the party's eight nominees. In a blatant betrayal of his promise, only two were from the party's elected list and one of those was the partner of a donor to his leadership election. It is a criminal offence to steal even one vote in a local council election but it is perfectly legal for a party leader to steal life seats in the national legislature from those duly elected by their own party. Unsurprisingly, it was not reported in the billionaire-owned media.

Among those awarded peerages by Kennedy were rich millionaires such as Iain Vallance, Chair of BT, who subsequently became Lib Dem spokesperson for Trade and Industry in the coalition government. The radical wing of the party erupted in outrage but Kennedy shrugged it off and imperiously stated that he did not have to do anything conference mandated. This was an extraordinary thing for a liberal to say, especially when it came to elections. I formally complained to the party's Federal Appeals Panel. Kennedy's defence was that he appointed life-peers in his role as leader of the Parliamentary Party and not as party leader. He argued that therefore the committee had no jurisdiction over his decision to appoint those not elected by the party.

Having exhausted the party's internal complaints system, I then complained to the Commissioner on Parliamentary Standards, Sir Philip Mawer, stating that the leader had failed to uphold parliamentary standards by dishonestly stating that he would respect the elections and then betraying that promise by appointing un-elected peers instead. In a classic heads we win, tails we win, British establishment trick, Kennedy told Mawer that his appointment of Lib Dem life-peers was done in his capacity as party leader and not as an MP and therefore the Commissioner had no jurisdiction on this matter. Mawer found against my complaint and ruled he had no jurisdiction over Kennedy's appointments to the Lords.

Think about that for a second. The Commissioner for Parliamentary Standards claimed that the power of appointment for life of members of parliament by a single member of parliament, who happens to be a party leader, with all the wide range of corruption this can and has entailed, was not subject to the Code on Parliamentary Standards! No wonder Parliament's reputation is in tatters.

A couple of years later, not content with just ignoring the elected list, Kennedy proposed scrapping of the elections completely. The loyalist majority on the FE kowtowed to his demand but it had also to be passed by conference. The leadership's spokespeople had the ignominious task of lecturing a liberal conference on how Kennedy's power of patronage was more democratic than elections. They were jeered with laughter. Our defence of democracy was led by Lord Greaves (one of the very few peers to be nominated to the Lords from the elected list).

Unlike the first debate establishing the elections, when we won by the tiniest of margins, this time conference overwhelmingly re-endorsed democratic elections. Since then, the party has regularly held elections to refresh the panel of potential peers and the leaders including Nick Clegg, generally just keep ignoring them! In September 2013 Clegg appointed only one out of ten new Lib Dem peers from the elected potential peers list. Clegg gave the legally stolen peerages instead to the usual party donors, party treasurer, lobbyists and his own former aides.

Chapter 6

Gareth Epps, chair of the party's Social Liberal Forum, told The Huffington Post: *"There's a complete stench over the way patronage is used in these appointments."*

This abuse of patronage by party leaders is systemic and enormously destructive of democratic accountability in all our major political parties. It is another reason for the collapse in party memberships over the last half-century, as members realised that they were increasingly just leaflet deliverers and donation appeal targets rather than democratically empowered equals.

In the UK, the link between party donations and the infamous sale of peerages goes back to the early twentieth century, to David Lloyd George, then Liberal Prime Minister and the founder, with Herbert Asquith, of Britain's ground-breaking welfare system for the poor. Ironically, as the Chancellor who with The People's Budget of 1909, took on the Tory landed gentry then dominating the Lords, his sales of peerages established an unfortunate pattern, as subsequent party-leaders continued to grant life-peerages to ultra-rich donors, thus replacing one corrupt elite with another.

These bought seats means that these party donors can participate in parliamentary debates, serve on parliamentary committees on their areas of vested interests, submit amendments to legislation and most importantly vote! These are not minor powers. In 2007, for example, the Lords tabled 7,000 amendments to legislation of which 2,600 or 40% became law.

Labour Party donors who were granted peerages include Lord Hamlyn, who in the run up to the 1997 general election donated more than £500,000. In January 2001, Hamlyn donated a further £2 million, which paid for a full tenth of the election campaign. What hope have ordinary members of influencing the party leaderships in such circumstances?

The lobbying industry is as enmeshed in the House of Lords as it is in the Commons. Peers are hired as lobbyists in various ways. The most common route is for them to be appointed to the boards of large corporations where they can act as private political advisers. This is a lucrative source of income for many peers. Tory Peers have been especially adept at securing such directorships. A quick glance through the Register of Lords Interests online is quite an eye-opener, with some peers having long strings of corporate directorships. So, it is not surprising many hardly ever speak in the Lords, as they are so busy attending paid board meetings.

Some peers actually own lobbying companies, like the Tory Lord Bell, who chairs Chime Communications, which owns lobbying giant Bell Pottinger and Labour peer Lord Mandelson, who owns the lobbying firm Global Counsel. Others work directly for corporations, like the Lib Dem peer Lord Richard Allan who was hired as Facebook's director of public policy. The Tory Lord Blencathra worked directly as a lobbyist for the Cayman Islands. It is against the Voluntary Code of Practice for the lobbying industry to employ peers, as they rightly regard it as unethical practice to hire someone who votes on legislation to be paid to affect it.

Lord Blencathra proved what a sham the new rules are on peers lobbying parliament, adopted by the Lords in 2010, following numerous lobbying scandals. The BIJ reported that in 2012, David Maclean (Lord Blencathra) had:

- Lobbied the Chancellor George Osborne to reduce the burden of air passenger transport taxes on the Cayman Islands.
- Facilitated an all-expenses-paid trip to the Caymans for three senior MPs, including the chair of the Conservative backbench 1922 Committee.
- Followed an Early Day Motion in the Commons calling for the Caymans to be closed down as a tax-haven, by trying to introduce the MP responsible, John Cryer, to a Cayman Islands delegation.

Lord Blencathra's shameless defence was *"You have confused lobbying Parliament, which I do not do, with lobbying the Government which I do."* The subsequent inquiry by the Lords Parliamentary Standards Watchdog found that Blencathra had been lobbying in his paid role for the Cayman Islands, rather than in his role as a peer and so disgracefully cleared him of breaking the rules.

To add to the farce, the Lib Dem President Tim Farron piled in saying *"It is astonishing that a Tory peer is now the lead advocate in Britain for one of the world's biggest tax havens. If Lord Blencathra is using his very privileged position in the House of Lords to lobby for a government that wants to see money that should be for our schools, hospitals and our armed forces sailing off in luxury yachts to be stored on the Cayman Islands, it is yet another mockery of the Parliamentary system and reinforces a need for an elected upper chamber."* Farron's statement itself mocked the Parliamentary system, as the Lib Dem Treasurer for the 2010 general election, Lord Clement-Jones, had been a lobbyist for the same Cayman Islands for years.

Being a peer brings many practical benefits for corporate lobbying purposes. Peers have the right to hire parliament's facilities for receptions and meetings. The Palace of Westminster's bars and restaurants are useful places to entertain or lobby for their rich clients. A peer also has the right to allocate passes to the Houses of Parliament which provide the bearer with the security clearance to access Parliament and its facilities. Each peer is allowed to grant three such passes for their research and clerical assistants. In practice many passes are corruptly granted instead to corporate lobbyists. This gives them a privileged advantage over the ordinary citizen that lobbyists crave.

Chapter 6

The Guardian revealed in 2010 that more than one in four parliamentary passes granted by peers were given to lobbyists. Examples included passes for BP's head lobbyist Richard Ritchie granted by Tory Peer, Lord Howard, defence lobbyist Robin Ashby, granted by Lib Dem Peer Lady Harris and corporate lobbyist Dorothea Hedge, by Labour Peer Lady Amos. The Taxpayers Alliance (a right-wing secretively funded think-tank dedicated to lowering taxation and reducing government services for the poor) had a pass granted to its lobbyist Jonathan Isaby by Tory Peer, Lord Flight.

And it is not just the passes; a subsequent Guardian report in 2011 found that 20% of the people working for peers had connections with the lobbying industry! Whilst not relevant to the corporate state, it's interesting to note the right-wing religious groups that the 26 Church of England Bishops, with unelected ex-officio peerages grant parliamentary passes to include the Evangelical Alliance, SPUC (Society for the Protection of Unborn Children) and the Conservative Christian Alliance.

The 1997/98 Paddy Ashdown appointments to the Lords demonstrate how even the Lib Dems ennoble the corporate state. These were granted to the party by Blair after the 1997 general election. Among the list of 16 peers appointed were:

Anthony Jacobs: Lib Dem donor and former Party Treasurer. He is reported to be worth £128 million pounds. In 2012, he demanded greater tax cuts for the rich.

Michael Sandberg: A former chair of global banking corporation HSBC.

Tim Razzall: Another former Party Treasurer and tax-haven director in Guernsey. His 2012 list of interests in the House of Lords register included directorships of: Bridge Hall Holdings plc (stock-broking), Barton Brown Limited (financial services), LawAlert Ltd (litigation alert service), Edge IPK Ltd (computer services), World Wide Pay Ltd (debit card processor), Premjet plc (airline), Square Mile Capital Investments plc (investment company), London Mint Development Limited (property holding company), Finurba Corporate Finance Ltd, North Atlantic Mining Ltd, Ardel Holdings Ltd (Guernsey) (formerly Concordia Holdings Ltd (Guernsey)) Gameday Enterprises (Australia) Ltd (mining company), Arctic Water Resources Ltd (water company).

Emma Nicholson: Granddaughter of the Earl of Crawford and former deputy chair of the Tory Party. She is a trustee of Lord Lawson's notorious climate crisis-denying Global Warming Policy Foundation.

Dick Newby: Was a political lobbyist. He became chief whip in the coalition government in the Lords.

Veronica Linklater: Granddaughter of Viscount Thurso.

Timothy Clement Jones: Political lobbyist and director of Political Context Ltd. Up to 2012 he was a partner of the lobbying firm DLA Piper. The DLP Piper website boasted of his lobbying for the Cayman Islands tax haven and his extensive contacts with City institutions. His clients included the nuclear and US arms industries. He lobbied for the EU alcohol industry against health warnings on alcohol whilst Lib Dem Spokesperson on Health in the Lords. He was key to ending the ban on corporate supermarkets opening on Sundays through their Sunday Trading Campaign, a legislative victory that helped kill off of thousands of small corner shops.

Andrew Phillips: Was the founder of the commercial law firm Bates Wells & Braithwaite. He was Paddy Ashdown's personal solicitor and it was his safe that got bizarrely burgled and the notes about Paddy Ashdown's affair stolen.

Alan Watson: Watson was chair of Havas Media UK (the 6th largest global communications corporation) and the Coca-Cola European Advisory Board.

The rest of Ashdown's appointments reflected the usual practice of rewarding loyal party committee members and MPs. It is ironic that Ashdown, who remains a passionate supporter of an elected Lords with a stated abhorrence of the corrupting power of patronage, was himself a classic practitioner of it.

His successor Nick Clegg's attempts to introduce elections for the Lords as Deputy Prime Minister were destroyed by a combination of a Tory backbench rebellion betraying the coalition agreement to introduce an elected upper chamber and a Labour Party playing shameful party politics with a policy that has been core Labour policy for generations. Of course, it meant that Ed Miliband continued to benefit from his power of Lords patronage. It is valid to apply Gandhi's maxim of *"you must be the change you wish to see in the world"* to Clegg's failure. How could someone pilot elections for the House of Lords through Parliament, when he himself had done the exact opposite as party leader?

The same blatant link between party donations and peerages is present in all the major parties. The surest way of entering parliament without undergoing an election, is to be a party treasurer or a major donor. The premise that one's ability to raise or donate political donations is the best qualification for being a legislator is frankly morally corrupt.

Chapter 6

Although the Liberal Democrats' Treasurer is elected annually by the party's Federal Executive, due to patronage, almost any nominee of the leadership invariably gets elected. There was hardly a single election during the seven years that I served on the executive, as almost no one dared stand against the leader's nominee. The role is almost always granted to a rich member of the corporate elite, as their main job is to wine and dine other rich people to sweet-talk large donations out of them.

The Treasurer of the Conservative Party is appointed by the leader without any pretence at an election. Invariably he (they are invariably male) is a bona fide member of the rich elite. Tory Treasurers who have been made peers include Lord Fink in 2010 by David Cameron. He donated over £2.5 million to the Tory Party and was CEO of The Man Group, the world's largest listed hedge fund. He has been described as the "*godfather*" of the notorious hedge fund industry and his personal worth in 2008 was listed as £118 million. Andrew Feldman, made Deputy Treasurer in 2005, was ennobled by David Cameron in 2010. Feldman was also Treasurer for David Cameron's leadership-election bid. His family owns the Jayroma textile business.

One infamous Treasurer was Michael Ashcroft from 1998 to 2002, who was appointed a peer by William Hague in 2000. At the time of his appointment Ashcroft undertook to abandon his non-domiciled status, but 10 years later he had still failed to implement the undertaking. Ashcroft retained dual Belizean/UK citizenship and is also a "Belonger" of yet another notorious British Overseas Territorial tax haven, the Turks & Caicos Islands. A Turks & Caicos estate agency listed the following advantages for living on these islands on its website:

"No Income Tax, No Real Estate Tax, No Capital Gains Tax or Capital Transfer Tax, No Value Added Tax, No Estate Duty Tax or Inheritance Tax, No Land Tax, No Withholding Tax, No Tax Treaties and Therefore No Exchange of Information with Foreign Countries, No Exchange Controls, No Restriction on How Much Can Be Brought into or Out of the Country, Strict Secrecy Laws, British Dependant Territory, Laws Conducive to Conducting Business in a Tax Free Environment".

What an attractive location for the denizens of *The Prostitute State*! Ashcroft was listed as the 37th richest person in the UK in 2009, at a personal net worth of £1.1 billion. He also owns the influential Tory internet blog-sites, Conservative Home and Politics Home, harnessing the internet for his billionaire right-wing agenda. He funds significant amounts of polling on behalf of the Tories, knowing that those who control the questions that polling actually asks wield significant political power. Ashcroft also gave a $1,000,000 donation to the right-wing climate-sceptic Liberal Party in Australia prior to their general election in 2004, making him also one of Australia's largest political donors. Management Today reported in 2009 that Ashcroft had reportedly given the Belizean Opposition another $1,000,000 donation. They were subsequently accused of doing deals when in government that directly benefited Ashcroft. According to BBC Panorama he has donated a staggering £10 million to the UK Tories. Ashcroft epitomises how tax-haven money has hijacked our democracy.

George Magan, who was appointed Tory Treasurer by Iain Duncan Smith in 2003, was duly rewarded with his peerage by David Cameron in 2011. He is a director of a number of private-equity companies. His net worth was estimated to be £60 million. Jonathan Marland was appointed Tory Treasurer by Michael Howard in 2003 and got the usual peerage in 2006. He is the founder of the international insurance corporation Jardine Lloyd Thompson. William Hague granted a peerage to Graham Kirkham in 1999, following his appointment as chair of the Conservative Party Treasurers in 1997. Kirkham was the founder of DFS sofas and was reported to be worth over £1 billion.

The Labour Party actually has genuine elections for their Party Treasurer. John Prescott was defeated in 2010 by a trade-union candidate, Diana Holland. However, Tony Blair demonstrated that such party democratic procedures are easily circumvented. He simply announced Michael Levy to be his chief fundraiser and later made him Lord Levy. Without any election, Levy *de facto* carried out the Party Treasurer function of milking rich donors. When the Labour Cash for Honours scandal broke, Jack Dromey, the then Party Treasurer, astonishingly claimed that he had no idea that £14 million of the £18 million spent on Blair's last general election was funded by secret loans from multi-millionaires!

Michael Levy met Tony Blair in 1994 and was the party's chief fundraiser between 1994 and 2007, raising over £100 million. These donations from the ultra-rich enabled Blair to pursue a right-wing agenda, independent of Labour's traditional funders in the trade unions. Levy, along with Rupert Murdoch, was crucial to suborning the Labour Party to the needs of the corporate elites, whilst in power. Many of these rich donors were subsequently appointed life-peers by Blair, including Alex Bernstein and Robert Gavron. Suspicions about the links between the donations and loans raised by Lord Levy and subsequent appointments to the Lords became so great that they erupted into the Cash for Honours scandal that tarnished so much of Tony Blair's final years as prime-minister.

Labour had come up with the wheeze of getting large donors to make loans to the Labour Party's general election campaign. This was a clear attempt to get round the law requiring the declaration of all political donations above £1,000 that Tony Blair himself had brought in after the 1997 general election. This added a whopping invisible extra £14 million to Labour's general election war-chest. It was this revelation and that a number of those making the secret "loans" had been subsequently awarded   life-peerages that led to the outrage. Lord Levy was arrested by police in 2006 but later released. The Crown Prosecution Service never proceeded with any charges. Other than his maiden speech in 1997, Levy is reported to have spoken in hardly a single debate in the Lords since then.

Undeclared Labour Party Loans, Negotiated by Lord Levy:

Rod Aldridge	£1 million - former Executive Chair Capita
Richard Caring	£2 million - owner of The Ivy, London
Gordon Crawford	£500,000 - Chair of London Bridge Software
Sir Christopher Evans	£1 million - Founder of Merlin Biosciences
Sir David Garrard	£2.3 million - Property Developer
Nigel Morris	£1 million - Co-Founder of Capital One
Sir Gulam Noon	£250,000 - Chair of Noon Products Ltd
Dr Chai Patel	£1.5 million - Chair Elysian Capital Private Equity
Andrew Rosenfeld	£1 million - Chair of Minerva (Property) plc
Baron Sainsbury	£2 m – Former Chair Sainsbury's (also made a donation of another £2 million)
Barry Townsley	£1 million – Chair Insinger Townsley (Stockbrokers)
Derek Tullett	£400,000 - Chair London Hong-Kong Exchange

Total Undeclared Loans: £13,950,000

Thus, these secret loans by just twelve millionaires made up the vast bulk of Labour's total general election campaign expenditure of about £18 million. None of this was public-knowledge at the time of the general election. It only came to light when Blair tried to award four of them peerages, David Garrard, Gulam Noon, Chai Patel and Barry Townsley. Following the revelations, all four withdrew their nominations. In 2007, the Crown Prosecution Service announced that they would not bring any charges against those involved. Their decision stated that while peerages *may* have been given in exchange for loans, it could not find direct evidence that this had been agreed in advance, which would be required for a successful prosecution.

The Declaration of Members' Interests in the Lords is like looking at an exclusive membership list of the UK's corporate boards and their chairs. One particular subset of note is the number of Labour and Tory former Secretaries of State who take up lucrative corporate directorships directly related to the government department that they led. These include Lord Reid (Labour Home Secretary) director of security firm G4S Regional Management, Lady Bottomley (Tory Secretary of State for Health) director of private health giant BUPA and Lord

Hutton (Labour Energy Secretary) chair of The Nuclear Industry Association and a paid "special adviser" to PricewaterhouseCoopers. Kevin, Lord Reid's lobbyist son was at the centre of another *"Cash for Access"* scandal in the early days of the Scottish Parliament.

A useful case study of **The Prostitute State** operating in the Lords is the Labour Party member Peter Truscott. Truscott's journey began as a Labour councillor on Colchester Borough Council. He was subsequently elected to the European Parliament in 1994, where he became Labour's Foreign Affairs and Defence spokesperson. He was a member of the European Parliament's delegation for relations with Russia. He lost this seat in 1999 but like many other UK politicians rejected by the voters; he was rewarded with a seat in the House of Lords in 2004. Blair then appointed him to be Energy Minister and Government spokesman for the Department of Trade and Industry in the Lords, between 2006 and 2007 and made him his special envoy to the Russian Federation. So what did Lord Truscott do with all this knowledge and expertise garnered as a public servant?

Following his stint as Secretary of State for Energy, he went to work for the corporate state in earnest. Through his consultancy, Energy Enterprises Ltd, he sells his political knowledge to fossil-fuel and mining corporations in Europe, Russia and Africa. The knowledge gained as EU and UK representative to the Russian Federation has been put to good use, with Gazprom (the largest fossil-gas extractor in the world) becoming a lucrative client. He was also a director of Gulf Keystone Ltd and consultant to African Minerals.

In January 2009, Truscott along with three other Labour Peers was exposed in a sting by Sunday Times journalists in the *"Cash for Influence"* scandal. The Murdoch owned Sunday Times did not do a simultaneous exposé for Tory Peers. Exposing the occasional minor scandal, especially in the opposition parties, lulls readers into a false sense of complacency that the billionaire media is doing its duty, whilst the rot continues to eat away at our democracy.

Demonstrating how much can be made by politicians who sell themselves to the corporate state; Truscott was reported to have asked for £72,000 to help influence a single piece of legislation that the undercover journalists were pretending to seek to change. He said that he had done similar work for another client. A Lords investigation in May 2009 found him guilty of breaking rules on exercising parliamentary influence in return for money, by agreeing to make introductions to other peers and ministers and to lobby officials. For the first time since the seventeenth century, Truscott and one of the other accused peers Lord Taylor were suspended from the Lords for six months.

Think about that. For corruptly selling the ability to amend parliamentary legislation Truscott received no criminal record, no jail sentence, no financial penalty AND was allowed to retake his seat in the Lords just six months later. He sits there to this day. Throwing further salt in the wound, he was exposed in the expenses scandal for declaring a small flat in Bath to be his main residence, instead of his £700,000 London Mayfair residence. This enabled him to claim an extra £125,000 in living expenses at taxpayers' expense over four years. Unlock Democracy reported that in 2011, he voted nineteen times (out of one hundred and thirty one divisions), spoke in one debate, submitted no written questions and was not a member of any parliamentary select committees but still claimed £44,100 tax free in expenses. And in a sign that selling parliamentary influence is acceptable, the Lords' Register of Members Interests reported that he still remained the Parliamentary Ambassador to Russia.

Those who despair at the failure of parliament to tackle the planet's catastrophic climate crises need to know what people like Peter Truscott are doing in parliament. For example, in 2008, the accountability website Public Whip reported him to have voted "very strongly against" efforts to strengthen the Climate Change Act 2008, namely he opposed all of the following:

- The target of an 80% reduction in emissions by 2050
- The aim to prevent warming of more than 2°C
- Making the UK's annual statement on emissions the Prime Minister's responsibility
- Reporting on the international impact of the UK's emissions

What Truscott was exposed doing is just the tip of the iceberg of what is going on day after day in the Lords. In 2013, over seventy members of the Lords were directors or shareholders in fossil-fuel companies. Twenty three held shares or directorships in the dirtiest fossil-fuel industry of them all – the coal industry. Fifty were directors or shareholders in oil and gas corporations. As Truscott serves his fossil-fuel paymasters, so are others serving the banking, private equity, tax-haven, nuclear, genetic engineering and financial auditing industries. Murdoch's News International, EdF, SSE, HSBC, KPMG, Shell, BP, Rio Tinto Zinc, McKinsey's and so on, all have their directors, consultants or shareholders in the Lords. Whilst there are many decent honest peers in all parties, it is hard to avoid the conclusion that this truly is *The House of Aristocratic Prostitutes*.

Chapter 7

Tax Haven Pimps

Campaign groups like UK Uncut and campaigners like Richard Murphy and Nicholas Shaxson have done sterling work exposing how the corporate state and the rich elites are avoiding paying their fair share of taxes, through the use of tax-stealing havens. But there is also a little-known but crucial reason why so many scandals around the funding of Britain's major political parties have been linked with the international network of tax-havens. This is the fact that at the top of the fundraising efforts for all of the major parties have been many people with direct involvement with tax-havens. To protect the tax -avoidance system, the rich need to have access to the highest levels of the political structure. Donations are the key that allows them to avoid wasting their time with internal party democracy. *The Thieving Tax-Havens* are another crucial pillar of **The Prostitute State**.

Whilst our political leaderships repeatedly say in public that they are cracking down on tax-avoidance, it has continued almost unabated under all recent governments. Tax-haven lobbyists and beneficiaries have captured and corrupted our party political fundraising. It took me some time to realise that some of the key people involved in the Lib Dems' fundraising operations, who were opposing the reforms I was seeking, to make our fundraising more honest, were linked to tax-havens. I then realised that this was also the case in the other major parties. The former Tory Treasurer, Lord Ashcroft, who funded the Tories crucial target-seat strategy in the 2010 UK general election was, as mentioned, a non-domiciled tax-haven resident based in Belize, despite being a member of the Lords.

Bernie Ecclestone, one of New Labour's largest donors, was accused in a German court case of benefiting from £1.4 billion in offshore tax -avoidance. The Labour Peer Lord Myners, a donor to Gordon Brown's leadership campaign and his Minister for the Corporation of London, had been chair of two off-shore companies based in Bermuda and Jersey. In 2009, The Daily Mail reported that the Bermuda company Aspen Insurance, which Myners had set up, was avoiding over £100 million in taxes every year. Tory MP Zac Goldsmith, whose family has numerous offshore trust-funds, was able to use his wealth to unseat the Lib Dem MP Susan Kramer from her Richmond constituency in 2010.

This capture of our political parties by the tax-haven elite is crucial to how the ultra-rich are grabbing a greater proportion of our nations' wealth:

Chapter 7

- By using tax-havens, the rich pay a net tax rate that is zero or substantially lower than their own country's tax rate, which means they get significantly richer.
- Meanwhile ordinary working families whose taxes pay for crucial public services such as health, public transport and education become poorer, as they have to both pay more taxes and suffer from cut public services and welfare-benefits to make up for the missing corporate taxes.
- The money saved from avoided taxes allows the elite to buy an even greater proportion of our economies, particularly small and medium-sized companies who pay their legitimate taxes and so consolidate the elites' massive market-share.
- If a country's corporate tax rate is for example 24%, (UK 2012 rate), the tax-haven based corporations have that competitive advantage over ethical tax-paying companies, making it almost impossible for them to compete. Our remaining legitimate tax-paying companies are being quickly swallowed up by these tax avoiders. It is destroying the corporate tax base in nations across the world and leading to a vast concentration of wealth by the corporate elite.
- The theft of developing-world resources channelled through UK and international tax havens dwarfs global aid programmes to the world's poorest people and is a shameful stain on Britain's reputation.

According to a report by Car, Dev and Curcio, $7.2 trillion (i.e. $7,290,000,000,000) in illicit funds was spirited out of developing countries between 2000 and 2008. The wealth of the world's poorest people is being diverted into the tax-haven bank accounts of the super-rich.

The following list by the Tax Justice Network provides some idea of the amounts involved in the UK and internationally:

$6.2 Trillion: Amount of developing-country wealth that is held offshore by individuals.

$1-1.6 trillion: Annual cross-border flow of the global proceeds from tax evasion, corruption and criminal activities.

$160 billion: Taxes lost by developing countries through trade mispricing and false invoicing by multinationals in 2008. This was the equivalent of 1.5 times ALL aid to the developing world in 2007.

$124 billion: Lost each year by developing countries through the use of tax-havens by wealthy individuals (not including corporate tax evasion). Oxfam 2009

£75 billion: Lost in *illegal* tax evasion in the UK

£25 billion: Lost per year through *legal* tax avoidance by rich individuals and the 700 largest corporations in the UK.

18,857: Number of registered businesses at one address in the UK's Cayman Islands.

8,492: Number of the UK's FTSE 100 overseas subsidiary companies located in tax-havens.

1,649: Number of tax-haven subsidiary companies owned by the 'big four' UK banks.

611: Number of tax-haven companies operated by the UK based, but Jersey incorporated, international advertising corporation, WPP.

600: Number of companies in Jersey operated by FTSE 100 multinationals.

556: Number of tax-haven subsidiaries operated by UK bank HSBC

174 Number of companies operated by the UK Bank Barclays in the Cayman Islands.

98: Number of FTSE 100 companies with operations in tax-stealing havens.

0%: Effective corporate tax rate in UK Crown Dependency, Jersey.

0%: Effective corporate tax rate in the UK's Cayman Islands.

This list does not convey the horrific price being paid by the poor for the theft of their tax revenues. For that we would have to witness those dying of malaria in Sub-Saharan Africa or those poisoned by oil and gas pollution in the Niger Delta or those living on $2 dollars a day on the streets of Cairo. Because these stolen taxes should be paying for health, education, infrastructure, renewable energy and environmental protection for the world's poor. Millions of people are paying for this theft literally with their lives through malnutrition, poverty, pollution and disease, not only in the developing world but in the developed world also.

One of the most repellent aspects of **The Prostitute State** is its genocidal collaboration with this stratospheric theft from developing countries, by their dictators and colluding corporations. Riggs Bank regularly accepted deposits from members of the Equatorial Guinea government of between $400-$700 million dollars at time! Meanwhile, their population suffers from a life expectancy that is barely fifty years. President Mubarak of Egypt was reported to have up to $5 billion stashed in bank accounts in Switzerland and the UK. The deposed President of Yemen stole billions of dollars from the Yemeni people. President Abacha stole over $2 billion from the Nigerian state coffers, secreting it through banks in Britain, Jersey and Switzerland. The list is endless but the consequences are deadly for the poorest people on the planet.

Martin Sorrell is CEO of WPP, the global advertising and political lobbying conglomerate. It is a classic case study on the inter-relationship between political lobbying and tax-havens. Sorrel, whose estimated personal net worth was over

Chapter 7

£174 million, is a chilling example of the ultra-rich lobbying for lower taxes for themselves and slashed government programmes for the 99%.

Sorrell has ensured that WPP pays hardly any tax. In 2010, it paid just 1.6% of its £7.4 billion global turnover in corporate taxes, despite being the world's largest advertising-agency holding company, employing over 100,000 people. It also owns the global political lobbying giant, Burson-Marsteller. Sorrell moved WPP's headquarters to Ireland to avoid paying UK corporate taxes. He was described by the Financial Times as a long time Tory Party supporter. He lobbied the Tories prior to the 2010 general election for a reduction in UK corporation tax. George Osborne complied when he became UK Chancellor of the Exchequer. Action Aid reported that WPP had the highest number of tax-haven subsidiaries of any of the FTSE100 companies at a staggering six hundred and eleven!

Budget deficits and vicious welfare cuts are not just the result of government spending decisions. They also occur when governments are unable to collect taxes from their corporations and rich citizens. Over recent years Sorrell, who says he hates the phrase *"corporate social responsibility"*, has made sure that the U.K. government collected as little tax as legally possible from the supposedly British WPP. Sorrell then shamelessly lectures the US and other governments about the necessity to reduce government debt.

In another gift to the tax-haven elite, Osborne promised in the 2011 budget not to change taxation rates for non-doms for the rest of the parliament! These tax-haven elites do not agree with their free-market hero Adam Smith's belief that *"it is not very unreasonable that the rich should contribute to the public expense, not only in proportion to their revenue, but something more than in that proportion"*

As mentioned, the legal avoidance of corporation taxes also means that corporations like WPP can use the money that ethically should have been paid in taxes, to buy up the decent companies whose payment of national taxes puts them at a competitive disadvantage. Sorrell and WPP have led the "consolidation" of the global advertising industry over the last decade, snapping up national advertising agencies in markets all over the planet.

But it is not just corporation taxes that the tax-havens steal from us. Sainsbury's, by basing its online CD sales in the Channel Islands in 2010, avoided UK VAT, thus giving it a 20% price advantage over local high-street music shops and so helping to bankrupt yet more of these local tax-paying businesses. The UK online betting industry has decamped *en masse* to the grubby tax-haven of Gibraltar to take advantage of its non-existent betting taxes and low VAT rates.

Amazon is another example of these corporate-tax cowboys. It is the UK's largest internet retailer but paid ZERO tax on its three-year UK turnover (2010-12) of over £7.6 billion, by moving the ownership of Amazon UK to Luxembourg.

Whilst forcing the closure of a great swathe of our local bookshops which were paying their rent, rates and national taxes, Amazon luxuriates in the competitive advantage of paying almost no corporate taxes whatsoever. It additionally undercuts UK VAT rates of 20% on e-books by using Luxembourg's 3% VAT rate. When you buy from Amazon UK you are actually "buying" from Amazon Luxembourg. Amazon UK is referred to as the "*order fulfilment business*".

UK Uncut exposed that Starbucks UK paid just £8.6m in corporation tax on £3,100 million worth of sales over 14 years (0.28%). The company used a series of legal accounting loopholes to report supposed losses, despite telling investors the UK operation was profitable. The Telegraph reported in November 2012 that Amazon, Facebook and Google together paid less than £30m of UK corporation taxes, despite sales of £3,100 million over the previous four years. And it is not just the international tech companies who are tax-raiders. Great swathes of the UK's corporate world are up to their necks in the tax- avoidance industry. Basically almost any company with a recognisable logo is likely to be involved, including our leading supermarkets, oil corporations, water companies, electricity suppliers and service industries.

It is really important to realise that combined tax avoidance and illegal tax-evasion is costing the UK about £100 billion every year, whilst welfare fraud, which is almost permanently on the front pages of *The Prostituted Press,* is costing just about £1.2 billion. Due to this tabloid fixation with the latter, most people think the numbers are the other way round.

These annual UK tax losses are the equivalent of more than the entire 2010-15 coalition government austerity budget-cuts! On top of these debilitating tax losses, it is crucial to note that all these statistics by the Tax Justice Network, Oxfam, Christian Aid and others, exclude the enormous tax losses due to the fact that countries around the globe have been forced to reduce national corporation taxes in a vain attempt to stop the haemorrhaging of their national corporate tax base abroad. This figure is difficult to quantify but is again in the hundreds of billions if not trillions of dollars.

This haemorrhaging of taxation revenues has forced many countries to shift their tax base from corporations to employees and purchase taxes *and* to implement savage cuts in public services, all of which hit the poor hardest. *The Thieving Tax-Haven Pillar* is a key mechanism by which global wealth is being transferred from the poor and middle classes to the rich elites.

In addition to corporate tax avoidance, tax avoidance by rich individuals is also a major challenge to democracy. A report in the Evening Standard in 2013 revealed that only a fraction of Britain's super-rich are paying income tax. They estimated that the 400 richest people in the UK avoided paying about £2 billion in taxes. But they can relax, as the coalition government has slashed the HMRC workforce and sought to disrupt EU reforms to tackle tax-avoidance.

Early on in my innocent attempts to help the Liberal Democrats practice what they preached, I decided to tackle party funding. Party policy was that all political donations should be declared. But like everything else, they refused to declare their own donations unless the other parties did so also. We proposed that the party would in future declare all its political donations over £5,000. The establishment, led by lobbyist Lord Clement-Jones and tax-haven company director Lord Razzall, fought the proposal tooth and nail. On the fourth attempt, the conference committee overruled their objections and allowed the debate at conference, which we won.

Razzall and Clement-Jones then employed the establishment's usual method of scuppering democratic decisions that they were opposed to, by simply refusing to implement the conference requirement to reveal the party's donors. They only finally caved in, years later; when it was clear the government was going to legally require them to do so.

When I was elected to the party's Federal Finance and Administrative Committee, I was shocked to discover that it really only supervised the professional in-house fundraising operation. The Party Treasurer's role in obtaining donations from high-value donors was not thoroughly vetted and the committee spent most of its time deliberating organisational minutiae. Believing that the party's "high-value donor" operation compromised the party's integrity, as Deputy Chair, I proposed the setting up of a Federal Fundraising Committee, which would have 50% of its membership elected by conference. I also wanted our elected MEPs, MPs and councillors to donate 10% of their political salaries to the party, which would relieve the party of its dependency on high-value donors and their corrupt access to the leadership.

Predictably Kennedy's leadership team were absolutely opposed to such a fundraising committee being set up and squashed the proposal at birth. So you can imagine my astonishment when a year later, whilst chatting at a birthday party at the National Liberal Club for a leading party member, a woman there told me that she was a Deputy Treasurer of the party! Despite being Deputy Chair, I had no knowledge that such a role even existed, never mind there being any democratic process of appointment. It turned out that the Party Treasurer and leadership had decided, without telling the Federal Executive, to appoint eight Deputy Party Treasurers, who could assist the Treasurer in his wining and dining of rich potential donors.

In my anger at the secretive appointments, I asked on the party's internal email system (called cix), how would a successful black businessperson become Deputy Treasurer of the Liberal Democrats, if they did not personally know the

Party Treasurer Reg Clark? Surely such a secret appointment process was institutionally racist. Kennedy went ballistic and instead of putting open procedures in place, he threatened that my statement was legally actionable and I must withdraw it. Kennedy twisted my comments into a false accusation of personal racism against the Party Treasurer.

For a few days, I was in terror that Kennedy was going to take action against me, as I knew that even if I won the case, I would be destroyed by the legal costs. I wavered but decided that as I was speaking the truth, I refused to withdraw my remarks. To my relief Kennedy did not take legal action but instead created a huge row at the Federal Executive, again demanding their withdrawal. I calmly stated that the comments were valid, as they had appointed the Deputy Treasurers in a manner that broke all accepted equal opportunity procedures and again refused to withdraw them. The FE rejected Kennedy's demand that they censure me.

Around this time another row flared up when I discovered that Lord Clement-Jones was not only breaking the party rules adopted by party conference, barring Liberal Democrat peers from selling their services as political lobbyists, but that one of his numerous clients was the notorious Cayman Islands tax-haven. This also broke the professional lobbyists' code of conduct which bans the hiring of peers for political lobbying.

Angered at the party being dragged through this dirt by one of its most senior elected officers, I referred to Clement-Jones on cix as *"Lord Cayman Islands"*. But instead of taking disciplinary action against Clement-Jones, Kennedy again went ballistic against me, bizarrely stating that using such a sobriquet for Clement-Jones was legally actionable. Kennedy, in a tantrum, went so far as to threaten the closure of the party's entire electronic email network cix, due to these two messages!

The refusal to set up a properly constituted Fundraising Committee, helped lay the groundwork for the disaster that followed, when the party pursued the multi-million pound donation from international fraudster and tax-haven resident Michael Brown. Those involved in the key negotiations with Brown on the party's behalf included Reg Clark, Lord Clement-Jones and Lord Razzall. Brown wined and dined with Kennedy and Kennedy even flew in his private corporate jet.

Brown donated £2.4 million to the party through a company called 5th Avenue Partners. He turned out to be a bogus dealer in international-bonds and was jailed for stealing £36 million pounds from his clients, including £8 million from former Manchester United chairman Martin Edwards. Brown's stolen millions, which helped fund Charles Kennedy's general-election campaign, were funnelled from his offshore accounts into a front company in the UK and hence to the Lib Dem bank account. Lib Dem leader Nick Clegg said the party had done all the necessary checks and was *"totally unaware"* of the fraud. *"We took that money in good faith, everyone recognises that,"* he told the BBC.

In my early days on the Federal Finance Committee, I had another row with Clement-Jones, one of the key Brown negotiators, which had undermined my trust in his judgement. The party was adopting a system of elections for its candidates to the European Parliament, that some of us felt could fall foul of equality legislation. We requested officers to seek legal advice on the issue. The advice, obtained from Cherie Booth, was conveyed verbally to the FE stating that the system could be legally defended.

However, the party later received a legal challenge from a male candidate John Hemming, challenging the procedure under the equalities legislation. I then received an anonymous tip from a party employee, with the explosive information that the legal advice conveyed to the FE had not been in line with the written advice provided by Cherie Booth! The Finance Committee had to approve the expenditure to fight the legal challenge, which was estimated to initially cost £30,000. As I was a member of the Finance Committee, I requested that we be provided with the written legal advice prior to us voting to approve the expenditure. I had not believed the tip-off about the alleged deception but presumed that like so many legal opinions it could probably have been interpreted both ways. I was astounded when Clement-Jones refused to allow us view the legal advice that we were basing our financial authorisation upon. I asked that it be put to a vote but I lost.

Unhappy, I referred the issue from the Finance Committee to the FE, which overruled Clement-Jones and authorised myself and fellow FE member Lembit Opik to see the written advice. To my consternation, we found that the verbal interpretation of the legal advice which had been provided to the FE was completely at odds with that provided in writing. It clearly stated that the party stood a good chance of losing the legal challenge if we fought it. That experience destroyed my trust in Clement-Jones's judgement and I believe this episode should have barred him from holding any official post in the party.

My trust in the judgement of the second Brown negotiator, Lord Razzall, had likewise been destroyed, when he had helped block implementation of the party's rules on declaring political donations. As mentioned he was also a director of offshore companies based in tax-havens. Reg Clark was the Treasurer who had refused to set up a Fundraising Committee to supervise/help the Treasurer's work but had appointed without any notice the eight new Deputy Treasurers.

These were the main people negotiating with Brown. In addition, I received another personal tip-off from an employee of the fundraising department who personally had witnessed events around the Brown donation, who said that the judgements taken by various people involved needed thorough investigation. They said they were seriously concerned about what had happened. The disastrous misjudgement in relation to the Brown donation was exactly the type of disaster that I had tried so hard to help avoid. Unbelievably, even following the conviction of Michael Brown, the party has carried out no independent investigation into what went wrong. Nor has it taken any action against those who made the mistakes. Even more shamefully, Clegg refuses to return the stolen money to Brown's victims. In strictly legal terms, they are not required to, but morally it really is incumbent on them to do so.

The Electoral Commission considered whether there was a basis for concluding that either Michael Brown as an individual, or 5th Avenue Partners GmbH (the parent company of 5th Avenue Partners Ltd, incorporated in the tax-stealing haven of Switzerland) was in fact the true donor. Neither of them would have qualified as permissible donors under the Political Parties, Elections and Referendums Act (PPERA). The Electoral Commission had ruled in 2009, that it was *"reasonable"* for the party to regard his donation as *"permissible"*. This ruling was an extraordinary negation of the laws banning foreign donations to political parties and brings the Electoral Commission into disrepute. This is a key extract from their judgement exonerating the party:

"3.9 The source of funds for the donation of approximately £1.54 million can be traced as having originated with investments into the parent company. Funds were transferred from the parent company bank account to the UK bank account. E-mails prior to the transfer confirmed that the transfer was for the purpose of an onward transfer of those funds to the Liberal Democrat Party. The sum €2,250,000 was transferred to 5th Avenue Partners Ltd. Shortly after, €2,225,000 was transferred from 5th Avenue Partners to the Liberal Democrats."

The Commission bizarrely concluded that there was no reasonable basis to conclude that the true donor was someone other than 5th Avenue Partners Limited!! This, despite the fact that the above mentioned e-mail clearly stated the funds sent from the parent company in the Swiss tax-haven to 5th Avenue Partners Ltd, were to be transferred to the Liberal Democrats. It was also despite Detective Sergeant Nigel Howard of City of London Police's Economic Crime Department telling The Times *"It's just a company that didn't trade in anything. He just had it as an off-the-shelf company."* This raises the question, what in goodness' name what would comprise the Electoral Commission's view of *"reasonable evidence"*?! In the light of this, it is hard to see that the Electoral Commission itself is fit for purpose, as it was created by a political system infected by the corporate state.

Since I left the party, the Lib Dems fundraising links to tax -havens and ultra-rich hedge-fund millionaires have continued. Hedge-funds are notorious for their use of tax-havens, with over 70% of them estimated to be located in the Cayman Islands alone. Paul Marshall is described as one of the most powerful men in the City of London, with personal wealth over £200 million. He is a close adviser to Deputy Prime-Minister Nick Clegg and co-founder of the enormous $14 billion hedge-fund Marshall Wace, whose senior directors shared a bonus pool of £55 million in just 2009 alone. Marshall Wace was based in the Cayman Islands up to 2010. Marshall told a parliamentary inquiry into the 2008 financial crisis that hedge funds had nothing to do with the crisis!

Marshall was the editor of the infamous Orange Book, which was a catalyst for the successful right-wing neo-liberal free-market takeover of the Liberal Democrat leadership. With many disturbing echoes of Blair's New Labour hijacking of the Labour Party, it jettisoned the social-liberal tradition advocated by the party in previous general elections, just in time for the Liberal Democrats' entry into government. Marshall fulfils a similar role in the Lib Dems to that served by the billionaire David Sainsbury in the Labour Party. They both funded leadership election campaigns and think tanks from the right wings of their parties, which in effect hijacked the parties' policy agendas from the democratic control of their memberships.

Over half the major Lib Dem donations, in the lead-up to the 2010 election, came from Alpha Healthcare whose major shareholders, according to the Telegraph, were not domiciled in the UK for taxes. On a turnover of £57 million in 2009, it paid only £170,000 in UK taxes. It did pay, however, management bonuses of £2.7 million. The controlling company for Alpha Healthcare is Harberry Investments, based in the British Virgin Islands. Harberry's major shareholders were Bhanu Choudhrie and his brother Dhruv. Bhanu was arrested in February 2014 in connection with an alleged bribery case at Rolls Royce. The Times subsequently exposed former Lib Dem Treasurer Lord Clement-Jones as being the man who nominated Khalid Hameed for the Lords, after the peer had originally said he had 'no idea' who had nominated him. Lord Hameed is the Chair of Alpha Hospitals, part of the Alpha Healthcare group.

The tax-haven party-funding nexus is even greater in the other two major parties. The Tories tax-haven connected fundraising has been dominated by the previously mentioned Belize tycoon Lord Ashcroft whose multi-million-pound Tory target-seat programme prior to the 2010 general election, was crucial to unseating many Labour and Lib Dem MPs and bringing the Tories to power.

But Ashcroft is the just the tip of the Tory addiction to tax-haven funding. In 2012, yet another tax-haven scandal erupted when the Tory Party Treasurer Peter Cruddas was secretly filmed by the Sunday Times speaking to reporters posing as staff from a fake wealth-fund based in the tax-haven of Liechtenstein. The Times alleged that Cruddas told these potential donors that a donation of £200,000 or

£250,000 gave "*premier league*" access to party leaders, including private dinners with Cameron and Chancellor George Osborne. They also claimed that Cruddas indicated that such donors could have their views on political plans fed back to the party's policy committee. He went on to discuss what access different-size donations would get. He said: "*Two hundred grand to 250 is premier league... what you would get is, when we talk about your donations the first thing we want to do is get you at the Cameron/Osborne dinners.*" He said they would be able to ask Mr Cameron "*practically any question you want*" and they claimed he told them their views would be relayed to the No 10 policy committee. Cruddas successfully sued The Times for libel, but in April 2014, The Times was successful in getting the Court of Appeals to grant it the right to appeal and was standing by the story.

Cruddas is yet another Party Treasurer with a former non-dom status. He is the founder of the financial spread-betting and foreign-exchange trading company CMC Markets. It is now worth £1.25bn. He owns a £10m apartment in the Monaco tax-haven and his estimated personal wealth is around £850m. Monaco is also home to other major Tory donors including Lord Laidlaw who donated £5 million over the years to the party. HMRC estimated in 2012 that the UK loses about £1 billion in avoided taxes to this one tiny enclave every year!

The 2010 Electoral Commission list of the largest individual donors to the Tory Party demonstrates the political strength of the tax-haven and hedge-fund pillars of *The Prostitute State*:

- **£1,999,967 - David Rowland:** Appointed Treasurer by Cameron in 2010. Tax exile based in Guernsey tax-haven for 40 years. Personal worth £730 million.
- **£553,000 - Michael Farmer:** Hedge fund manager – Founder of Red Kite, one of the world's largest industrial metal hedge-funds. Appointed Treasurer by Cameron in 2012. Personal worth £120 million.
- **£500,000 - Jonathan Wood:** Manager SRM Global Hedge-fund Monaco. A former non-dom in the tax-haven of Switzerland.
- **£335,000 - Michael Bishop:** Given a peerage by David Cameron in 2011. Personal worth estimated at £440 million.
- **£300,000 - May Makhzoumi:** Wife of Lebanese-based former arms dealer and billionaire Fouad Makhzoumi. Most of the family fortune is based offshore.
- **£250,000 - Paul Beecroft:** Venture Capitalist, Chair of Wonga.com Estimated worth £100 million.
- **£250,000 - Mark Bamford:** Joint owner of the JCB empire, most of which is owned by a series of offshore tax-haven based trusts.
- **£250,000 - Chris Rokos:** Hedge Fund Manager. Personal worth £230 million.
- **£250,000 – Lord Sainsbury:** Sainsbury's, despite only selling to the UK market, has 14 offshore tax-haven subsidiaries.

Donors are invited to meet Cameron and other senior party figures at dinners, post-Prime-Minister's Questions' lunches, drink-receptions, election-result events and important campaign launches. Cameron has even handed the writing of various government reports to top party donors. Adrian Beecroft was asked to report on employment law, which shockingly recommended the abolition of almost all workers' employment rights and Anthony Bamford on UK manufacturing, which unsurprisingly recommended even further reductions in corporation tax and taxes on rich individuals. Other than the very high-donor informal route reported by The Times, the Conservatives have several official levels of donor schemes, with the top being the Leader's Group.

Stanley Fink is a former CEO of the Man Group hedge-fund. In January 2009 Fink paid £1m to the Conservatives and two days later he was Party Co-Treasurer. His personal worth is £118 million. In 2013, The Guardian reported that Fink was a director of three firms with subsidiaries or a parent company in the Cayman Islands, Luxembourg or Guernsey. He was made a life-peer by David Cameron in 2011. The tax-haven cabal have now become so emboldened that some are making their demands in public. Fink was reported in 2012 in the Guardian, as saying that he had lobbied the chancellor George Osborne for a cut in taxes on invisible earnings so that he and other hedge-funders no longer feel *"obliged"* to set up companies in places such as the Cayman Islands. In other words, he wanted Britain itself to become a tax-stealing haven. His farcical excuse was the supposed loss of UK jobs to the Cayman Islands. The Cayman Islands has a total population of 56,000 people. Fink naturally did not refer to the millions of public-sector jobs in health, education and infrastructure being lost across the UK and other countries due to the hedge-fund industry's use of such tax-havens. He thinks society is stupid enough to think that grabbing a few tax-haven banking jobs would justify the further decimation of the UK's financial tax base. Fink found political support when Francis Maude, Minister for the Cabinet Office, shockingly told the Tory Party Conference that it would be a compliment if Britain were known as a tax-haven!

As mentioned, the UK's Cayman Island tax-haven is home to 70% of all the world's hedge-funds. Channel 4 estimated that a mind-boggling £1.5 trillion pounds passes through this tiny enclave every year. Its zero corporation tax rate enables the hedge-funds to pick off national-based tax-paying companies, and hence their need to influence British politics to protect that advantage. As the Cayman Islands lobbyist and Tory peer Lord Blencathra put it when he told the islands' media: "*I've been appointed as I have 27 years' experience as an MP, 10 to 12 years' experience in a British government **and I'm still a parliamentarian in Westminster.**" He added: "*My role is to make sure I can feed that advice in to government ministers, to the Civil Service ... on behalf of the Cayman Islands government."

The importance of the tax-haven links to British politics can be judged from the fact that over HALF of the Tory Party donations between 2010 and 2012 came from hedge funds, private-equity companies and individuals working for finance businesses, which entitle them to face to face meetings with the Prime Minister and chancellor. So successful have these lobbyists been that they persuaded the Tory Chancellor, in 2012, to announce an exemption on profits of offshore finance-company subsidiaries, as well as on those offshore subsidiaries whose major activities are not in relation to the UK. As former tax inspector Richard Brooks said in the Guardian, this will make the UK's arrangements more lenient than almost **ALL** other jurisdictions. So whilst Osborne and Cameron are pledging a crackdown on tax-havens at G7 and EU summits, they are making the UK itself into a tax-stealing haven. If you abolish the corporate taxes due from tax-havens, whilst forcing them to be transparent, it becomes nothing more than a posturing PR farce that maintains the tax-stealing status quo.

Labour likewise has been up to its neck in tax-haven associated donors. Despite receiving significant funding from the trade unions, they have also raised large amounts of money from rich tax-avoiding donors. Ed Miliband has appointed the millionaire property tycoon Andrew Rosenfeld as his fundraising adviser for the 2015 general election. Rosenfeld avoided paying UK taxes by taking up Swiss residency for a number of years. Lewis Hamilton is another infamous UK tax avoider domiciled in Switzerland, refusing to pay UK residency taxes to support UK education, social services and the NHS, now that he has made it rich.

The Times reported that the multi-millionaire Patrick McKenna with Tim Levy, is believed by HM Revenue and Customs to be responsible for most UK film schemes that have enabled investors to avoid £5 billion in tax. Ed Miliband's Labour Shadow Culture Secretary appointed McKenna to advise on how to expand the film tax scheme to *other* areas such as music, computer games and advertising, as if the advertising moguls Martin Sorell and his ilk have not got enough legal tax-avoidance schemes available to them already. McKenna is a former partner with Deloitte and Touche and is worth over £520 million. Deloitte & Touche is infamous for having sold tax-avoidance advice to international corporations along with the other Big Four accountancy firms. Labour like the Tories think the reward for avoiding the payment of tax, should qualify you as being clever enough to advise on what government policy should be! It is the equivalent of asking drug dealers what the laws on drug-dealing should consist of.

Tony Blair's first major scandal involved Formula 1 billionaire and New Labour donor Bernie Ecclestone. He was the focus of a comprehensive article by the Tax Justice Network in 2011. Even though a Labour donor, Ecclestone exhibited some of the extreme right-wing views held by many of the ultra-rich when he was quoted saying "*(Hitler) brought a country that was bankrupt into a country that was very strong and that was really demonstrating what someone could do if they had the power and didn't have to keep back and referring every five minutes*"

The profits raised by Formula 1's worldwide monopoly are often funnelled through companies headquartered on the Channel Islands. According to the study by David Cay Johnson, a number of the English based companies in the Formula One empire took out large loans at 15% interest from subsidiaries in Jersey. As a result, the companies in Jersey post high earnings, which are only subject to the Channel Island's low tax rates. In return, profits are reduced for the companies registered in Great Britain, which pay higher taxes. This is the classic legal transfer-pricing tactic. You post your profits in the tax-havens and your subsidiaries make loans to your company located where the business is actually taking place at exorbitant interest rates. It thus makes an apparent loss and removes liability for taxes on the UK profits or wherever they are actually making their earnings.

Ecclestone was worth $4.2 billion in 2011, which makes him the fourth richest person in the UK. His twenty-two year-old daughter Petra bought a third home in the US for $85 million in 2011 and then had five hundred workers refurbish it in nine weeks flat. She also owns a $91 million London residence. Ecclestone transferred his Formula One assets to his wife Slavica in the 1990s and then to a family trust in Liechtenstein. Ecclestone said his tax bill would be about £1.2bn if he was shown to be involved in the trust.

The tobacco advertising ban scandal provides a classic example of the advantages in access to politicians that party donations can potentially facilitate. Unhappy that a proposed EU directive would ban tobacco companies from advertising in Formula 1, Bernie Ecclestone appealed over the head of the pro-ban Labour Minister for Public Health Tessa Jowell to Jonathan Powell, Tony Blair's chief of staff, who arranged a meeting with Blair. Ecclestone and Max Mosley, then President of FIA (Fédération Internationale de l'Automobile), Formula One's governing body and also a Labour donor, met Blair on 16 October 1997.

On November 4th, the "*fiercely anti-tobacco*" Minister for Public Health Tessa Jowell, then had to humiliatingly argue in Brussels for an exemption for Formula One. Then on November 6th, three newspapers asked whether Labour had received donations from Ecclestone; he had donated £1 million in January 1997. This led to a public outrage. On the 17th November, Blair apologised for his government's "*mis-handling*" of the affair and stated "*the decision to exempt Formula One from tobacco sponsorship was taken two weeks later*". In 2008, internal Downing Street memos revealed that, in fact, the decision had been made at the time of the meeting and not two weeks later as Blair had told Parliament. In addition to Ecclestone, Stephen Glover in the Daily Mail reported that between 2001 and 2008, Labour accepted donations worth £8.9million from eight non-domiciled donors.

Labour donor Sir Gulam Noon (estimated worth £65 million in 2006), gave up his lucrative non-dom tax status to become Assistant Treasurer to the Labour Party in 2010. His fellow Assistant Treasurer, the late Nigel Doughty (estimated worth £130 million in 2011), was again from the private-equity industry, being the founder of Doughty Hanson & Co which manages over £8 billion in assets. Labour's largest donor was Lord David Sainsbury, who had given a staggering £18 million pounds by 2012. He received his peerage from the party leadership that he had donated to and became a government minister for eight years, without having to stand for election. Who needs to lobby when you can get your own permanent seat in the legislature and actually run a ministry?!

Sainsbury is a large investor and enthusiast for genetically modified organisms. Throughout his time as Science Minister, unsurprisingly he supported genetically modified foods. Jack Cunningham (later Lord Cunningham) was appointed to lead the government's propaganda campaign on behalf of the GM food corporations to an energetically-opposed electorate. Cunningham was in 2013, exposed in yet another lobbying scandal, when the Sunday Times reported him seeking £124,000 a year to lobby the government on behalf of a South Korean firm. *"Knocking on doors, introductions and getting to see the people, including if necessary the Ministers – this is part of the package,"* he allegedly said. He was suspended from the Labour whip but not the party.

The extraordinary web of links between David Sainsbury, the genetic engineering lobby and government quangos were the subject of the following exposé by Spinwatch:

"He owns 2 genetics companies, Diatech and Innotech Investments (his shares in these were put into a 'blind trust' when he became a minister). He put millions of pounds into the study of Genetically Modified Organisms through his Gatsby Charitable Foundation, set up in 1987 and which gives £2 million a year to the Sainsbury Laboratory/John Innes Institute in Norwich.

Since 1998, the Sainsbury Laboratory has also received 6 Government grants, worth £1.1 million, from the Biotechnology and Biological Sciences Research Council (BBSRC). The BBSRC is part of the Government Office of Science and Technology, which answers to Sainsbury as Science Minister and has won an extra £50 million in funding since he became Minister. Officially, he is supposed to leave the room when GMOs are discussed at meetings. The Chairman of the BBSRC is another of Tony Blair's friends, Peter Doyle, former Executive Director of biotech company Zeneca (which also gives money to the John Innes Institute).

When Lord Sainsbury travelled to America in 1999, to research a report into Biotechnology, he was accompanied by members of the Bio Industry Association, a lobbying group for companies involved in GM foods (the DTI helped pay their costs). Diatech is a member of the Bio Industry Association. Eight days before he became Science Minister he loaned Diatech money to buy a £2 million office in Westminster. The Chief Executive of Diatech, Christopher Stone, owns 5% of Sainsbury's shares. "

This exposé provides a revealing example of how the corporate state manipulates the government. Throughout all this time, the British public was adamantly against the pollution of our crops and wildlife with GMOs. They understood that once the genie is out of the GM bottle for a particular crop, it eventually irreversibly contaminates all the non-GM plantings of that crop. It thus destroys the human rights of people to choose to eat organic and GM-free crops. Yet at the heart of government there was a fabulously rich pro-GM billionaire and so the Blair government, despite massive public opposition, were major cheerleaders for GM food contamination, as is the Cameron government.

The Sainsbury family are reported to have made extensive use of trusts in the British Virgin Islands tax-haven, which were exempt from corporation tax. The Independent newspaper reported that whilst science minister in the Labour government David Sainsbury benefited from such a trust. His personal worth in 2012, according to the Forbes World Rich list, is $1.3 billion. Another minister in the Labour government, Geoffrey Robinson, also had a £12 million offshore trust based in Guernsey. The Independent reported that this Orion Trust was *"just the sort of secretive avoidance device the Government wants to outlaw".* Following another scandal Robinson had to resign but remained a close adviser to Tony Blair for years after.

The Labour Party tax-haven links continued under Gordon Brown, who was Tony Blair's successor as Labour Prime Minister. Brown was bankrolled by another rich private equity fund owner, Ronald Cohen. Cohen donated over £2 million to New Labour and helped fund Gordon Brown's leadership campaign. He refused to answer repeated press questions asking if he was non-domiciled at the time. Cohen admitted to the Evening Standard that tax breaks mean he pays a lower tax-rate than his cleaner. Other hugely rich non-dom Labour Party donors included Lakshmi Mittal who donated nearly £5 million and Lord Paul who donated £0.5 million, as well as £45,000 to Brown's leadership campaign.

So it is clear the tax-haven cabal not only frequently become Party Treasurers but they also bankroll all three major parties and buy parliamentarians to lobby on their behalf. In the light of this political tri-partite lock by **The Prostitute State**, is it any wonder we get government after government saying in public that they will crack down on tax-haven based tax-avoidance, but nothing serious is ever done to close them down. After all, unless forced to by public pressure, why would they ever bite the tax-haven hands that feed them? *The Thieving Tax-Haven Pillar* remains rock solid, with disastrous consequences for UK companies, the middle classes and the poor, not only in the UK but across the globe.

Chapter 8

The Prostituted Media

Tom Watson MP, Hansard, UK House of Commons, September 9, 2010:
"The truth is that, in this house we are all in our own way scared of the Rebekah Brooks's of this world. It is almost laughable that we sit here in Parliament, the central institution of our sacred democracy – among us are some of the most powerful people in the land – yet we are scared of the power that Rebekah Brooks wields without a jot of responsibility or accountability. The barons of the media, with their red-topped assassins, are the biggest beasts in the modern jungle. They have no predators. They are untouchable. They laugh at the law: they sneer at Parliament. They have the power to hurt us and they do with gusto and precision, with joy and criminality. Prime Ministers quail before them, and that is how they like it."

A fair, free and diverse press is an essential pillar for a liberal democracy. But in the United Kingdom, just five largely non-domiciled, tax-haven linked billionaires own the vast majority of newspapers sold in the UK along with substantial chunks of our television, internet, film production, cinemas and book markets. Other than The Guardian, nearly all the rest, are in the hands of financial institutions or other billionaires. This gives the ultra-rich an almost complete monopoly on shaping our thinking, national culture and political agenda, diverting it from the concerns and needs of the majority. They control almost everything that we read, see or hear.

As this tiny band of elite owners have the crucial power to appoint the key newspaper editors and through them their journalists, our media has become *de facto* a manipulative propaganda system. This power ensures the press reflects the values and vested interests of the rich corporate elites and seeks the elimination of any democratic processes that could threaten it. *The Prostituted Media* is a core pillar of **The Prostitute State**.

One challenging concept to get across about the corporate state is that the thoughts, conversations and political dialogue that we as individuals and as a society are having, are not necessarily the thoughts that we would be having in a genuinely free liberal democracy. They are profoundly shaped by these billionaires. It is almost impossible to imagine what conversations we would be having, what political systems we would be discussing or what positive shape our society could be in by now, if they were not dictating our political debate. We naturally are frequently unaware that we are being manipulated. We have endless trivial political debates, whilst having no idea we are frequently simply discussing the issues that this tiny group of media barons have distracted us into debating.

The corporate press perverts the campaigning and policy-making agendas within all our political parties. This was dramatically exemplified by New Labour's determination in 1997 and the Cameron's Tories in 2010 to tailor their policies to get Murdoch to back them for the general elections.

The Electoral Reform Society estimated that if an election had been held in 2007, the difference between a Labour and a Conservative victory could have depended on how as few as 8,000 voters, across 30 to 35 key marginal seats, cast their votes. This means that the impact of the right-wing tabloids on a tiny number of swing voters in these constituencies can literally determine general-election outcomes.

Below is the full UK national press circulation breakdown for August 2011 (source ABC):

Daily Newspapers	Owner	Circulation
• The Sun :	Murdoch	2,795,601
• The Times:	Murdoch	449,938
• Daily Mirror :	Trinity Mirror	1,174,924
• Daily Record :	Trinity Mirror	307,794
• Daily Star :	Desmond	703,218
• Daily Express :	Desmond	629,764
• Daily Mail :	Rothermere	2,063,738
• The Daily Telegraph :	Barclay Brothers	632,070
• Financial Times :	Pearson Group	331,883
• The Herald :	Gannett Corporation	48,629
• The Guardian :	Scott Charitable Trust	241,287
• i :	Lebedev	191,077
• The Independent :	Lebedev	180,470
• The Scotsman :	Johnston Press	42,581

The total daily circulation therefore was about 9,388,000. Of these 7,451,600 were sold by four companies owned by five oligarchs – Murdoch, Desmond, Jonathan Harmsworth and the Barclay Twins. They thus control about 80% of all UK national newspapers sold. Just two of them own 57% of the market with Murdoch owning 35% and David Cameron's supporter, Jonathan Harmsworth, (Lord Rothermere) owning 22%. Most of the remainder were owned by a mixture of international corporations, financial institutions or other billionaires. This leaves only The Guardian not owned by the 1% but by the not-for-profit Scott Trust Ltd. Its percentage share of the daily market was a minnow's 2.6%.

The Sunday newspaper market is similar. Below are the Sunday newspaper sales in May 2012, following Murdoch's replacement of the News of the World with a "Sunday Sun". Despite the Milly Dowler phone-hacking scandal, Murdoch retained his grip on the Sunday newspaper market:

Daily Newspapers	Owner	Circulation
• Sunday Telegraph:	Barclay Brothers	447,428
• The Sunday Times:	Murdoch	924,312
• The Sun (Sunday):	Murdoch	2,242,132
• Sunday Express:	Desmond	512,596
• Daily Star Sunday:	Desmond	480,247
• The Mail on Sunday :	Rothermere	1,802,491
• Sunday Mail (Scotland):	Trinity Mirror	318,567
• Sunday Mirror:	Trinity Mirror	1,094,265
• The People:	Trinity Mirror	462,329
• Sunday Post:	Thomson Family	265,481
• Independent on Sunday:	Lebedev	125,373
• The Observer:	Scott Trust	252,780
• Scotland on Sunday:	Johnston Press	48,225
• Sunday Herald:	Gannett Corporation	27,897

Of the 9,000,000 Sunday sales, 71% were sold by corporations owned by the same five media oligarchs. The Murdoch/Rothermere duopoly had a right-wing stranglehold of 55%. It is again left to the Guardian Media Group owned Observer to fly the flag for the 99%, with a tiny 2.8% share of the Sunday market. Trinity Mirror owns The Daily Record, Daily Mirror, Sunday Mirror and the People. Their papers are supposed to be on the side of the working classes and it is only the major newspaper group not owned by the five oligarchs. However, among its top ten shareholders in July 2011 were many of the usual ultra-rich corporate elites:

* Schroder Investment Management Ltd. (SIM)
* Aviva Investors Global Services Limited
* Standard Life Investments Ltd.
* Royal London Asset Management Ltd.
* Legal & General Investment Management Ltd. (UK)

- BlackRock Investment Management (UK) Ltd.
- JPMorgan Asset Management (UK) Limited
- Old Mutual Asset Managers (UK) Ltd.
- Dimensional Fund Advisors, LP
- Barclays Wealth

The Financial Times is owned by Pearson plc which has only a small share of the newspaper market in the UK but is a global media corporation, with annual sales of £6 billion in 2012. It is also the largest private-education corporation and the largest book publisher in the world, owning Penguin, Dorling Kindersley and Ladybird. It had 12% of the UK book market. It has no large dominant shareholders but is owned by banks, investment funds and rich individuals.

The Guardian Media Group also owns The Observer and GMG radio stations. It also owned, up to June 2014, 50% of Auto Trader magazine, with the other half owned by Apax Partners, a private equity firm. The Guardian Media Group in turn is owned by The Scott Trust Ltd. It sold its regional newspapers to Trinity Mirror in 2010, which meant it lost its link to the Manchester Evening News, now also sadly in corporate hands. Only the presence of the Guardian gives the 99% a voice in a world where otherwise, almost 100% of our national newspapers would be owned by the billionaires. To lose it would be a calamity indeed for what remains of our prostituted democracy.

The Scott Trust was founded in 1936 by the then owners, the Scott family, to protect it from being closed due to death duties, after a number of family members died in quick succession. The purpose of the new non-charitable trust, according to CP Scott, was to protect the liberal editorial line of the *Guardian* from interference by future proprietors. The Trust is responsible for appointing the editors of *The Guardian* and *Observer* but apart from enjoining them to continue the papers' editorial policy along "*the same lines and in the same spirit as heretofore*", has a policy of not interfering in their decisions. In 1992, the Trust identified its central objective as being the following:

"To secure the financial and editorial independence of The Guardian *in perpetuity: as a quality national newspaper without party affiliation; remaining faithful to liberal tradition; as a profit-seeking enterprise managed in an efficient and cost-effective manner."*

The trust was wound up in 2008 and all its assets handed over to the Scott Trust Ltd, in which all the then trustees held shares in a process that received very little coverage or discussion in the wider media. However, even the Guardian is not immune from the tax-haven cabal. Lord Myners was chair of the Guardian Media

Group for 8 years from 2000 to 2008. As mentioned in the previous chapter, in March 2009, the Sunday Times reported that Myners had, for five years, also been chair of Aspen Insurance Holdings Bermuda. It reported that Aspen had avoided more than £100 million a year in tax. Myners was also chair of Liberty Ermitage, based in Jersey and of Gartmore, a fund management company which ran a Jersey-based offshore business. Outrageously, Lord Myners was appointed Financial Services Secretary by Gordon Brown when Prime-Minister and put in charge of overseeing a review of tax-havens. It was another clear case of putting the fox in charge of fox regulation!

Also on the Guardian board in 2011, was entrepreneur Brent Hoberman, who was appointed by George Osborne to be a member of the Conservative Party's Enterprise Council to advise the Tories on business policy. He was a venture capitalist and internet multi-millionaire from his sale of lastminute.com. The 2012 board included John Scott, who is chair of Ambac Assurance UK. He was previously a director of KPMG Corporate Finance and SBC Warburg. Another board member was Anthony Salz who was an investment banker and vice-chair of Rothschild. Formerly a corporate lawyer, he was employed to facilitate the legal aspects of the merger of Murdoch's Sky with BSB.

In 2008, the Guardian set up a new company in the Cayman Islands to facilitate the co-purchase of Emap that it carried out with the private equity company Apax Partners, which has a complete network of Cayman Island entities, like most of the rest of the hedge fund industry. So even in The Guardian *The Prostitute State* seeps in. This is a possible explanation as to why the business and advertising pages of The Guardian bear almost no relationship to the editorial policy of the paper and reinforce the mainstream corporate state.

Let's take a closer look at the media moguls who dominate our democracy. With 37% of the newspaper market, Rupert Murdoch is the leading force. But it is not just the newspaper industry that Murdoch dominates. He is the largest shareholder in BSkyB, which controls not only Sky News but also Five News and the news bulletins to over three hundred UK commercial radio stations. BSkyB had over ten million subscribers by 2012, giving him direct access into 40% of UK households. It has almost as much revenues as ALL the terrestrial TV channels put together. BSkyB revenues in 2010 were £5.6 billion, dwarfing its nearest rival the BBC's £3.6 billion and ITV's £1.9 billion. These revenues give it an enormous market clout, with £1 billion to spend on sports programming alone. It floods the market with advertising and is the fourth largest advertiser in the UK at £127 million annually.

He is a joint owner of the Press Association which supplies nearly all news outlets in the UK. The PA put very little attention into the News of the World phone hacking scandal. When Tom Watson MP mentioned this to one of their journalists, their reply was ."*You know we are partly owned by News International, don't you?*" Reuters, the other major international news agency, which had been independent, was gobbled up by the global Thomson Corporation which was worth $17 billion in 2012. It is largely owned by the Thomson family and so the ultra-rich control another of the major news sources for newspapers across the globe. They also own a 20% stake in the UK's ITN.

Murdoch also has a powerful influence on the rest of our cultural media including through his ownership of the publisher Harper Collins, which sells one in every ten books sold in the UK. Even the movies that we watch, not just through Sky Films, but the actual movies produced by Twentieth Century Fox are Murdoch owned. In one way or another, whether it is via his books, films, television, newspapers or sports, he controls much of what the collective UK psyche thinks. And through this he has an overwhelming impact on our democracy.

After Murdoch, the most powerful of the media billionaires is Jonathan Harmsworth, the successor to one of Britain's first media moguls Harold Harmsworth. Harold served in the UK government under Lloyd George from whom he received his peerage. The Daily Mail supported Nazi Germany in the 1930s and championed Mosley's British Union of Fascists in 1934. Harmsworth wrote to Hitler congratulating him on the invasion of the Sudetenland and the annexation of Czechoslovakia and urged him to invade Romania!

Jonathan Harmsworth is now the chair and controlling shareholder of The Daily Mail and General Trust (DMGT) which owns the Daily Mail, The Mail on Sunday and the free Metro newspapers handed out at metropolitan railway stations across the UK. The Metros are estimated to have a readership of 3.5 million people. DMGT is now one of Europe's largest media conglomerates. In the UK, it also owns 120 regional newspapers and has shareholdings in television and radio, including a 20% share of ITN. It has extensive activities outside the UK including DMG Radio Australia, DMG World Media and DMG Information. Its biggest markets are in the UK, US, Eastern Europe and Australia.

And for those who claim that the web will defeat the media barons, unfortunately they need to know that The Daily Mail Online is already the world's busiest news and newspaper website. The Audit Bureau of Circulation reported that it had 105 million unique visitors in August 2012. That is double BBC News online worldwide and beats the New York Times into second place for newspaper websites.

Rothermere became the 4th Viscount at the age of 31 following the death of his father. His net worth in 2011 was $1 billion. His sister-in-law married Margaret Thatcher's son, Mark, in March 2008. Rothermere is reported as being a supporter of the Conservative Party leader David Cameron. Despite being almost totally unknown to the wider public, he wields immense power via the Daily Mail on UK politics. With daily sales of over 2 million it is by far the most politically influential newspaper for middle England.

Its current editor, Paul Dacre, was appointed in 1992 by Jonathan's father. The academic, John Lloyd, labeled his editorial style as being a unique form of libertarian authoritarian Conservatism. He complains about the Tories not being conservative enough. He earned £1.6 million in 2008 as editor-in-chief. Whilst he avoids giving interviews, he nevertheless is one of the most powerful men in UK politics. When the Daily Mail thunders, government ministers truly tremble. Though Murdoch acts as a powerful Prime-Ministerial kingmaker, Dacre is more the policy dictator-in-chief, constantly forcing government policy further and further to the corporate free-market right.

A classic mini-example of the power of *The Daily Mail* was when, by simply labelling government efforts to improve home-energy efficiency as a 'conservatory tax' in a screaming headline, they were within days able to force a statement from the Prime-Minister ruling out the measure, despite the Department of Energy being in the middle of a public consultation exercise on the proposal.

A useful example of how the think-tank/lobbying/billionaire media nexus operates is the reported lunch between the infamous climate-sceptic "think tank" founder and fossil-fuel lobbyist Lord Lawson and Paul Dacre, which reportedly led to the major campaign by the paper against government support for renewable energy technologies and home insulation schemes, giving momentum to the UK Chancellor George Osborne's campaign against the green economy. This was immensely helpful to the gas industry's campaign to persuade the UK government to use more fossil gas rather than renewable energy to generate electricity over the coming half-century.

The Mail's campaign led to government cuts to onshore wind and solar electricity subsidies, £500 million granted to UK offshore gas development, a commitment to using fossil gas for electricity production post 2030 and greater powers for communities to block wind-turbines but not nuclear power-stations or gas-fracking drills. In 2014, the government introduced a Bill to abolish the requirement for planning permission for fracking companies to drill under people's own homes and promised the best taxation environment for gas-fracking in the world. Ed Miliband and Labour endorsed fracking even before the coalition did. Game and set to the lobbying Lord Lawson. The Mail achieved all this despite the government being supposedly committed to cutting UK emissions by 80% by 2050. This would be impossible if new gas power stations were built. Paul Dacre's single vote on behalf of the ultra-rich fossil-fuel criminals is millions of times more powerful than yours or mine.

Next on our list of media moguls is Richard Desmond who owns 100% of Northern & Shell, whose subsidiary Express Newspapers owns The Daily Express, Sunday

Express and The Daily Star. He is the third most powerful newspaper billionaire in the UK, owning 14% of the newspaper market. He also owns an international magazine-publishing business, including the world's largest selling magazine OK!, with 31 million readers. He owned Channel 5 up to 2014, one of the five main terrestrial TV channels in the UK and he owns a number of adult television channels including Television X and Red Hot TV. He was worth $1.53 billion dollars in 2011.

Along with Murdoch's Sun and Rothermere's Mail, his right-wing Daily Express feeds its readers an almost uninterrupted diet of anti-immigrant, anti-European, xenophobic stories that have profoundly damaged the UK's culture of tolerance. At the Leveson Inquiry into Media Ethics, Desmond, when asked about what actions he took to ensure the ethical running of his newspapers, said *"Well ethical, I don't quite know what the word means."* This would be amusing if his papers did not have a deadly serious influence over the public's views and on government policy.

The Barclay twins, David and Frederick, are the final two in our quintet of media billionaires. They own The Daily Telegraph, The Sunday Telegraph and the right-wing magazine The Spectator, many of whose editors have gone on to be Tory government ministers or high-profile politicians like London Mayor Boris Johnson. Their worth was listed as £2.2 billion pounds in 2011. Their purchase of Littlewoods and its destruction by breaking it up, to profit from the sale of its property portfolio, is classic ruthless cut-throat capitalism. They cannibalised long established companies and jobs in the pursuit of maximum personal gain.

It is noteworthy from a Scottish perspective that neither of its leading upmarket daily papers are Scottish owned but are firmly in the hands of the ultra-rich. The Herald is owned by the Gannett Corporation, America's largest newspaper corporation, founded by Republican Presidential candidate Frank Gannett. Its largest shareholder in 2012 was JP Morgan. The Scotsman and the Scotsman on Sunday are owned by the Johnston Press whose largest shareholder in 2012 was the Malaysian billionaire Ananda Krishnan. The Scottish Sunday Post is owned by the Thomson family through their holding company DC Thomson. The family's net worth was estimated at £540 million in 2009. They are a well-known bastion of Scottish conservatism, refusing to allow trade unions in their companies and even banning Catholics for decades.

Almost every single one of these media billionaires are up to their eyeballs in tax-havens or legal tax-avoidance of one form or another. Having the billionaire media within the tax-haven cabal, makes it easier for the tax-havens' client politicians and lobbyists to protect the UK's infamous network of tax-stealing havens, from what would otherwise be a far more outraged public.

Let us go through their tax-haven links one by one. According to a US Government Accountability Office study in 2009, News Corp has the third largest number of tax-haven subsidiaries, among the one hundred largest companies in the US. The Huffington Post reported, in 2011, that News Corp's total of tax-haven subsidiaries came to 136, including 16 in the Cayman Islands, 26 in the British Virgin Islands and one in Panama which has a zero corporation tax rate. This is where Murdoch had located his Twentieth Century Fox Films. The Huffington Post reported that between 2003 and 2006, according to the data available in News Corp's SEC filings (Murdoch moved his company from Australia to the US at this time); it paid US federal tax rates below 5%.

In another example of three pillars of *The Prostitute State* operating in tandem, the Huffington Post reported how Murdoch's News International lobbied the US government in favour of a free-trade agreement with the Panamanian tax-haven where its subsidiary is based. Thus you have a media corporation lobbying the government for the tax-haven where its subsidiary is based! But the low tax rates legally paid by Murdoch since he moved his corporation to the States are not new for him.

Paul Vallely reported in The Independent in 2011, that News Corp paid ZERO net UK corporation tax between 1988 and 1999, despite being the country's largest newspaper corporation. The BBC reported that this was despite pre-tax profits of nearly £1.4bn. So whilst his newspapers thunder about slashing help for refugees and the unemployed or the cost of the EU's modest bureaucracy, his companies are legally avoiding taxes. In one year alone, the BBC estimated that legal tax avoidance by Murdoch's companies cost the British taxpayer £92 million. Again the key reason why global media giants can pounce like vultures on individual national newspaper and media companies, paying their fair share of national corporation taxes, is their use of tax-haven subsidiaries.

Jonathan Harmsworth, despite being one of the most powerful British newspaper moguls, was registered in 2011 as "non-domiciled" in Britain, like his father, who spent most of his life "officially" as a resident of France. This status allows him not to pay income tax in England, despite having a £40 million palatial home at Ferne Park, Wiltshire. The Guardian reported that in 2004, through two Bermuda-based companies, Rothermere Continuation and the Coman Trust, his family owned 88.5% of DMGT's voting shares. Meanwhile, his papers demand that the government slash the welfare state to tackle the deficit largely caused by tax avoidance.

In 2012, BBC Panorama reported that Richard Desmond's Northern and Shell had subsidiaries in the UK, which up to 2009 had been lending each other £804m. Northern & Shell then set up a company in Luxembourg and transferred the loans there, which meant the interest payments were paid from the UK to it, leaving lower profits for UK taxes. In Luxembourg, that money was effectively taxed at less than one per cent. This scheme avoided £6 million in UK corporation taxes. Richard Brooks from Tax Research UK neatly summed up the practice saying: "*The company puts its money into Luxembourg and borrows it back. It just sends money round in a circle and picks up a tax break on the way*."

The Guardian reported in 2003, how Desmond had cut his corporate tax bill by another £2.7m in 2002 by basing his broadcasting businesses, including his profitable porn channels, in Jersey. His holding company, RCD1, even qualified for a UK £1.58m tax *rebate!* This was because despite showing pre-tax profits of £8.98m, its most profitable businesses were "based" in the tax-haven. According to an investigation by the Financial Times, four staff worked in two small rooms in a shabby office behind an Indian restaurant in St Helier. This profited from a Channel Islands 2% tax rate, compared with the 30% payable in the UK at the time. The FT naturally questioned whether Mr Desmond was genuinely running his businesses out of Jersey.

RCD1's accounts shamelessly suggested the company intended to continue exploiting offshore locations declaring: "*The group expects certain profits to be subject to lower levels of taxation in future years*". The TV businesses transferred to Jersey in 2000, after being set up in Britain in 1995. Content for the porn channels is filmed at a studio in London's Docklands.

The Telegraph's Barclay Twins' wealth was estimated in 2011 to be £2.3 billion. They have taken legal tax-haven exploitation to a new depth by buying an entire island (Brecqhou) belonging to the medieval fiefdom of the Channel Islands tax-haven of Sark. They also have a registered home in the Monaco tax-haven.

The Russian billionaire oligarchs, the Lebedevs (Alexander and his son Evgeny), whilst small players in the UK compared to Murdoch and Rothermere, own three national newspapers, The Independent, the "i" and The Independent on Sunday and London's only evening newspaper The Evening Standard. Alexander Lebedev is a former KGB officer, who after his KGB career, in 1992, bought a bank just three years later and heads a massive Russian conglomerate. His net worth in 2012 was estimated at $3.1 billion. He owns huge chunks of the Russian airline, gas, aircraft manufacturing, banking and construction industries. He is one of many former communist-era officials who grabbed chunks of Russia's nationalised industries after the fall of communism.

Like other Russian oligarchs, Lebedev quickly learnt the rules of the corporate state and used his enormous wealth to buy media power and the political influence that goes with it. He owns one of Russia's leading newspapers Novaya Gazeta. He was elected to the State Duma and is a leader of the Fair Russia Party. Owning UK broadsheets and the UK capital's only evening newspaper buys the Lebedevs prestige and political influence in one of the world's leading financial centres.

They appointed former Daily Telegraph Editor Sarah Sands to edit The Evening Standard in March 2012, just months prior to the London Mayoral Election. The Guardian reported that it was understood that the Tory Mayor of London Boris Johnson lobbied for her appointment. Sands and Johnson had been friends for years, since Sands had managed Boris's weekly column for the Daily Telegraph. Despite being paid £140,000 per year as London Mayor, Johnson also gets paid £250,000 per year for his weekly Telegraph column. Johnson dismissed this amount in an interview as "chicken-feed".

The Evening Standard played a crucial role in getting Johnson re-elected in the May 2012 London Mayoral election, by launching a blistering attack on Johnson's rival, the Labour candidate Ken Livingstone's tax-arrangements. The Standard tried to make out that Livingstone's perfectly legitimate practice of setting up a company to run his private office was the equivalent of tax avoidance.

Due to its ownership, the capital's only evening newspaper is dominated by the interests of the ultra-rich rather than the needs of Londoners. Sands wasted no time in launching a campaign to double the capacity of Heathrow Airport with an extra 260,000 flights per annum. The horrendous noise and pollution as planes land and take off almost every two minutes makes life hell for millions of Londoners. That London's only evening newspaper should support the doubling of this horror is an example of how the corporate state does not care about the negative environmental consequences, as it seeks ever greater wealth. It is a classic example of how the billionaire media manipulates its readers against their own interests.

Johnson then took insouciance into the stratosphere, when almost to the day that Murdoch's former News of The World editor was being charged in court with conspiracy to hack the phones of hundreds of victims, ranging from the families of killed soldiers to senior government ministers, he invited Rupert Murdoch to "*schmooze*" with him at the Olympics, as Murdoch was continuing his search for potential alternative Tories to replace Cameron, if necessary.

Whilst the media barons have not yet succeeded in eliminating the UK's public broadcaster The BBC, their guns are permanently aimed at it. Front-page headline after front-page headline screams about some scandal or another at the BBC or about some BBC presenter. It is hard to see how, in the medium term, it can survive in public ownership with the full weight of The Prostituted Media being thrown at it. It has already had significant cuts and privatisations forced on it by the Murdoch-captured Tory government. Its historic role of providing unbiased reporting naturally led to it giving more coverage to progressive issues than the captured press.

However, the tabloids are pressing hard to ensure increased coverage of their right-wing issues. Of course, this radically swings the BBC's coverage onto the media barons' agenda rather than one genuinely in the public interest. This swing to the right in the BBC's coverage has been exacerbated since under the Tory appointed BBC Chair Chris Patten, the two top managerial slots in BBC News were given to two former Murdoch executives. Many BBC editors start the day going through the papers to see what stories they should be covering. Likewise, BBC Online has a prominent section about what the front pages of the newspapers are saying and some programmes also directly report on stories being covered by the press. Therefore, as the vast majority of papers are owned by this tiny band of media barons, they get to set the agenda not only in their own newspapers but disastrously now, to a significant extent, on the BBC also.

To understand how this capture of our media manipulates our views article by article and through our views our democracy, it is worth looking in detail at a single example, such as this article published in Lebedev's London Evening Standard, in July 2012. Whilst the article is about American politics, it is typical of the genre. It was written by Roger Kimball and was headlined *"The Reason Why the President Just Turned Nasty"* with a strap-line underneath of *"Economies with the truth: the Obama campaign has spent millions placing aggressive attack ads"*. It appeared a couple of weeks before the US Republican presidential candidate Mitt Romney was to host a fundraising dinner in London with single seats costing $50,000. It was a typical right-wing media hatchet-job on the Democratic President Obama. The article trashed Obama's job-creating record. The reality of course was that jobs had been haemorrhaging under Republican President Bush and the entire global economy was in the middle of a disastrous meltdown greater than the Great Depression. Almost miraculously, through the stimulus package and other measures, Obama managed to stabilise the markets and the US economy started gaining millions of jobs.

The article then implied Obama had promised *"a raft of tax-increases"*. The author could not refer to actual Obama tax increases, because he had actually introduced a raft of tax cuts for middle-class Americans. The promised tax increases were actually Obama's attempts to cut the $133 billion of government oil-industry subsidies and to end the Bush era tax cuts on earnings over $1 million which had helped explode the US's federal deficit. Obama had cut public-sector jobs by over 600,000 to deal with the huge Bush deficits resulting from the trillion dollar Iraqi and Afghanistan wars.

The article then denigrated Obama's health care reforms as a *"legislative behemoth"* whilst making no mention of the millions of poorer Americans who would get health coverage for the first time as a result of it. Countries such as the UK with a free national health-care system spend far less on healthcare than the US and with better results. In 2011, the US spent over 17% of its total GDP on its private for-profit corporate-run healthcare systems whilst the UK spent 9.6%. If you lose your US job, you generally lose your health-coverage. Obamacare bans health corporations from refusing cover to people who are ill and it is now also illegal to remove coverage from people who become ill. Healthcare costs were the single greatest cause of personal bankruptcies in the US.

This is just one example of thousands of such biased articles churned out every year by the billionaire-owned media seeking to manipulate their readerships to oppose what is in their own best interests and to support instead the interests of the billionaires. I was only able to understand what this writer was actually doing, as unlike some Evening Standard readers, I was quite familiar with US politics. Otherwise, I could have taken the article at face value. It would be impossible for all of us readers to have enough information, so that the flood of manipulative articles like this, on the wide range of issues that directly affect our lives, from healthcare to British politics, could not fool us at least some of the time. It is likewise impossible to overestimate the extent to which the captured media using such biased articles is perverting our own UK democracy.

As millions of UK voters get their information from reading the tabloids, it explains why so many of us often vote against our own interests, as millions of Americans also do. Instead of headlining on the corrupt sell-off of the NHS, the tabloids focus for weeks on a problem public hospital, whilst failing to subject private hospitals to the same scrutiny. Instead of exposing media-baron corruption, they constantly attack the publicly-owned BBC. Instead of focusing on the billions stolen by corporations in tax evasion they go on and on about the small amount stolen in welfare fraud. Instead of reporting on the fundamental protections that millions of workers and people across Europe now enjoy, due to the Churchill-inspired European Convention on Human Rights, they focus endlessly on a few small deeply unpopular groups such as prisoners whose human rights the Convention also rightly protects. And so people end up voting again and again for politicians who want to privatise our free health care, who protect tax-havens for the rich, who collaborate with the fossil fuel corporations waging war on our planet and who want to trash our collective human rights for their financial gain.

As mentioned previously, the tabloids have largely forced the switch from conviction politics to consumer politics. Party leaders now depend on polling and focus groups. They ask the focus groups what voters want rather promoting the policies that they believe in. Since a large amount of UK public-opinion is now shaped by the billionaire-owned press, this entrenches the elites' hold over the country's politics, as politicians abandon conviction politics for fear of losing their seats. Labour did little to tackle the increasing wealth gap whilst in power, for fear of being on the receiving end of a tabloid savaging.

As people are gradually waking up to the fact that in many cases, they are becoming poorer, as the rich grab an increasing share of the wealth, the corporate media in a clever but frighteningly pernicious manner are manipulating readers to

Chapter 8

take out their anger, not against the corporate takeover of our government, but rather at democracy itself. This is reflected in the anti-politics swell of support for UKIP, despite it being even more in the pockets of the corporate state. This is like successfully persuading an ill patient to hate their body rather than the disease which has infected it.

After a slow start the media billionaires are now building an internet monopoly also. Whilst they are competing with the TV stations' online presence, you have to remember that most of them own shares in these as well. In 2011, about 41% of the UK population accessed news via the internet. Research commissioned by Ofcom shows that of the 45.4 million unique readers of the top 12 internet news sites in March 2012, the ubiquitous 5 billionaires already had 39% of the market.

The top ten UK internet news sites visited in March 2012 were:

Websites	Millions of unique visitors
BBC	10.1
Mail (Rothermere)	6.5
Guardian	5.1
Telegraph (Barclay Brothers)	4.8
Yahoo News	4.2
The Sun (Murdoch)	2.7
Newsquest	2.6
Huffington Post	2.5
Independent (Lebedevs)	2.1
MSN	1.9
Sky News (Murdoch)	1.5
Google News	1.4

In addition to the 39% market share owned by the 5 media billionaires, Yahoo is an American global internet giant worth $17 billion dollars in 2013. Newsquest is owned by the US media giant Gannett, which was worth $9 billion in 2013. AOL owns The Huffington Post, which now has a UK edition. This American internet giant was worth nearly $3 billion in 2012. MSN News is part of NBC Universal Corporation, which is jointly owned by Comcast (worth $158 billion in 2013) and General Electric (worth $656 billion in 2013). Google News is owned by Google Inc (worth $111 billion dollars in 2013). Added together these billionaire corporations own another 28% of the UK internet news market. Thus the corporate media already owns 67% of the UK internet news market. So much for the internet heralding a new dawn of press freedom!

The publicly owned BBC, which is not a participant in the newspaper market, has the largest market share at 22%. Hence the attack by Rupert Murdoch's son, James Murdoch on the BBC's website in his infamous McTaggart Lecture entitled, in a bout of self-delusional un-awareness "*The Absence of Trust*", at the annual Edinburgh International Television Festival in 2008, in which he claimed: "*The only reliable, durable and perpetual guarantor of independence is profit.*" These words came back to haunt Murdoch after the Milly Dowler scandal but scandalously the Tories largely gave him what he requested anyway. He demanded that the government force the BBC to slash its website investments and this is what the new Tory Culture Secretary Jeremy Hunt duly delivered, following the 2010 general election. In an extract from the speech, that the Leveson inquiry showed was more applicable to his own family's News International rather than the BBC, Murdoch bizarrely attacked the BBC saying "*The Corporation is incapable of distinguishing between what is good for it and what is good for the country,*" he claimed.

On a positive note, The Guardian has 5.1 million readers, giving it an 11.2% market share. Thus the BBC and Guardian together give the non-billionaire section of the population a current 33% share of the internet news market. However, unless concerted action is taken to rein in the media billionaires, it may be only a matter of time before the billionaires squeeze the BBC and Guardian into a tiny internet ghetto, as in the newspaper industry.

In the light of the extensive media blackmailing of our government that was exposed at the Leveson Inquiry, it is clear that tackling the billionaire media is *the* most crucial political task facing the country. But the bitter reality is that the party leaderships are either already in hock to *The Prostituted Media* or are unwilling or too frightened to tackle it. David Cameron clearly is its servant. Nick Clegg made clear to Hugh Grant during the Leveson furore that he had no intention of tackling media ownership, despite the once-in-a-lifetime golden opportunity to legislate for a genuinely free press that the scandal provided. It was a deeply profound failure from a liberal party leader.

But to be fair to the Labour leader, Ed Miliband, after the News of the World scandal, he did attack the current system of media ownership. But his proposed alternative was truly derisory. He proposes to replace the current system, where five billionaires control most of the media, with one where the same five billionaires control most of the media but none could own more than 20% of the total market.

However, despite the huge outcry over the phone-hacking scandal, none of the major Leveson Inquiry recommendations for reform of the failed press self-regulatory system have been implemented. I had a personal experience of how bad the "self-regulatory" Press Complaints Commission actually was in 2013. I had formally submitted a complaint about a report in the Telegraph, which described the anti-fracking protests in the Sussex village of Balcombe as violent. I had seen first-hand the major commitment by the protesters to peaceful direct action despite provocation by some police. The Telegraph's defence was that as the policing of the protests had been violent, it was therefore legitimate to describe the protest as being violent! I replied that this meant no matter how peaceful protesters were, all the police had to do was to initiate violence themselves and then the press could malign the protest itself as being violent. Unsurprisingly, as The Press Complaints Commission was largely made up of representatives of the billionaire press, it agreed with the Telegraph and rejected my complaint.

If you still doubt the power of the media billionaires, then maybe the Lib Dem MP David Ward might convince you. When I made the case, at a fringe meeting at the 2014 Lib Dem Spring Conference, that these media billionaires exert huge unaccountable power over Parliament, in reply David unexpectedly said it was far worse than I had made it out to be. As an example, he related how the Parliamentary Party meets every morning during the party conference. The first item on the agenda is always the report from the press office. He said he had given up counting, that morning, at the tenth mention of what line the Daily Mail was taking about the current political issues!

The Prostituted Media is completely incompatible with a properly functioning democracy. Malcolm X put it succinctly when he said:

"The media's the most powerful entity on earth. They have the power to make the innocent guilty and to make the guilty innocent, and that's power. Because they control the minds of the masses."

Of all the pillars of *The Prostitute State,* the billionaire-owned media is the one that we need to tackle most urgently, so that democracy can recapture the levers of power from the hands of the Corporate State and put the Fourth Estate back into service for the good of all the people and not just the enrichment of a small elite.

Chapter 9

Our Perverted Academia

Over recent decades *The Prostitute State* has increasingly wrested control over our education and academic systems from the democratic state. If you control the production of thought, research and information, then allied with the control of the media which spreads those thoughts, the control of government which implements legislation arising from those thoughts and the tax-haven system which helps the capture of the resulting wealth, you have seized control on just about every aspect of a country's functions. Democracy then ceases to have any meaningful role other than to act as a camouflage for the corporate state or as a process to decide which particular elite vested interests are pursued.

There are three main routes by which the corporate state is capturing the creation of our intellectual thoughts:

- The establishment and funding of think-tanks
- The direct purchase of academics and academic studies
- The actual takeover of formerly public and not-for-profit schools and universities.

Think tanks are usually non-profit organizations that research various aspects of public policy and advocate solutions through various means such as publishing policy papers, hosting conferences and carrying out media work. They are frequently consulted by politicians for advice on proposed legislation and have a powerful role in a democracy.

Some are aligned to particular political parties and others are independent, but usually have an underlying agenda or political philosophy. For example, the Adam Smith Institute produces policy on free-market capitalism, whereas the Labour Party associated Fabian Society addresses social justice. They can be phenomenally influential when their associated politicians are elected to government, as their policy papers can then often be adopted wholesale into legislation. In addition, as they are not "officially" party political institutions, they are not required to reveal their donors. Corporations can thus fund "independent" reports on their industries' legislative agendas, without any corporate fingerprints being left behind. These think-tank "reports" are usually widely reported in the media, without the sponsors being mentioned. Thus, the public are tricked into thinking that corporate advertising is actually independent research.

Unlike the other major parties, the Lib Dems had no associated think- tanks prior to 1997. Then suddenly, The Centre for Reform arrived on the scene. Until then it was the party's democratic policy-making structures which developed its philosophy and policies. I was concerned about who was funding this new think-tank. Such a professional institution, with paid researchers and funds for press operations and conference events, would gain a powerful unaccountable policy-making role within the party. Rich anonymous donors could use it to hijack the party's policy agenda as they had already hijacked its leadership-election processes.

As a member of the FE, I demanded that it should reveal its donors. The leadership refused. They assured me that the think-tank's funder was "*a good liberal*". They offered to confidentially tell me who the donor was. I refused the offer, saying it was the principle of party transparency which was at stake. I did not want to know who the funder was if I was unable to let the membership know and let them decide who was an appropriate donor.

Whilst researching this book I finally discovered that it was the former Liberal MP and merchant banker Richard Wainwright who funded its establishment. When Wainright died in 2003, its funding was taken over by the hedge-fund manager and millionaire Paul Marshall, co-editor of The Orange Book. He appointed the former Goldman Sachs banker Jennifer Moses as chief executive. Marshall was described in a Times report in 2009, as being one of the most powerful men in the City of London and worth over £200 million.

The Centre for Reform then morphed into the policy-development vehicle for the right-wing Orange Book grouping which disastrously moved the party to the neo-liberal right. This was exactly what I feared when it was launched with anonymous funding. Even more than Thatcher, the Orange Bookers want to drastically reduce and privatise the role of the state. It even changed its name to the meaningless CentreForum, with no reference to the radical liberalism of the party. With its millionaire backing, CentreForum spends hundreds of thousands of pounds flooding the Lib Dem party conferences with fringe meetings dedicated to their agenda, drowning out the memberships' role in policy making. This process followed the classic pattern in the other two parties, where party leaders or small groups of senior figures with the backing of rich donors, hijacked policy-making from their party memberships using anonymously funded think-tanks.

It was reported on Lib Dem Voice in 2009 that CentreForum was the source of opposition in the party to the Tobin Tax, which would have put a tax on global financial transactions including those by the banking and hedge-fund industries, from which CentreForum gets funding. The Tobin Tax would raise billions of pounds for tackling the climate crisis, alleviating global poverty and funding other UN goals. It is referred to as the Robin Hood Tax. It would also help prevent dangerously large share movements during financial crises, as traders would have to factor in the costs of making trades. CentreForum has also urged building on green-belt land, a policy that a majority of party members would oppose. It would make the elite landowning classes billions of pounds in profits of course.

The CentreForum website in 2012 did not list its donors and scored only a C for transparency from whofundsyou.org. However, they did list their *"partners"* at the bottom of a website page. The list was revealing about their links with the corporate state. It included a plethora of oil, banking and lobbying corporations including BP, Citibank, General Electric, Diageo, KPMG, BAE Systems, Aviva, Serco, Bloomberg, Brunswick and Babcock.

The Tory-allied Centre for Policy Studies, who also refuse to reveal their donors, produced a report, *"Time to Bin the Tobin Tax"* and hosted a web-seminar with various speakers from the banking industry including Citibank and Barclays. Thus the banks were able to pose behind "independent research". Unsurprisingly, the UK government regularly vetoes the tax at EU and G20 summits.

One of the crushing realities of modern British politics is that as grassroots democratic, liberal or social justice movements build political momentum, they are subject to hijacking by the corporate state. Corporate lobbyists start joining opposition parties in droves, as soon as they start gaining or are likely to gain power. We used to call them *"the suits"* and their numbers at Lib Dem conferences were directly proportional to the party's proximity to power. The fact that this entryism goes unreported in the billionaire press ensures that it proceeds without objection. One of the key tools these lobbying entryists use to over-rule existing party memberships are think-tanks.

The Labour Party has a long tradition of respected membership-based think-tanks like The Fabian Society. However, New Labour under Tony Blair introduced the Tory practice of billionaire-sponsored leadership think-tanks. In 1996, Peter Mandelson, the co-architect of the New Labour coup, established the think-tank Progress. It was primarily funded by David Sainsbury. In 2012, the BBC reported that he had contributed over £2 million since its formation. Progress uses this money to promote its right-wing "modernisation" agenda throughout the Labour Party. Modernisation is a euphemism for handing over the state-sector to corporations, with reduced pay and conditions for workers, other than the senior managements whose wages skyrocket.

Progress exerts a huge influence on Labour Party policy. It sends a monthly magazine out to 4,500 party members, organises fringe meetings at party Conferences and hosts its own annual conference and weekends for party

Chapter 9

activists. Bizarrely, it states that one of its purposes is to promote "religion". This fits in with Blair's catastrophic promotion of religious schools, mimicking the worst of the sectarian education divide that had led to so much strife in Northern Ireland!

In 2011, the trade-union Unite produced a document stating *"Labour Party policies are often determined by a small group of advisers – far too often dominated by old thinking, neo-liberalism and the organisation Progress"*. Labour leader Ed Miliband dismissed the attack as a distraction but he did not address the excessive influence wielded by Progress's billionaire funder.

Peter Mandelson also established a second right-wing think-tank called The Policy Network. Whilst Progress has a UK focus, the Policy Network is international, seeking to force a right-wing agenda onto progressive parties across the world. Its 2012 board included the usual corporate lobbyists such as Matt Browne, head of public affairs for the lobbying giant APCO Worldwide, Vicky Pryce, managing director of global lobbyists FTI Consulting, and Susan Hitch, the manager of Sainsbury's pro-bono operations.

A Policy Network pamphlet released in December 2011, made the front page of The Guardian. It was urging Labour to avoid *"the temptation to appeal to its core supporters in the public services"*. No information was provided as to who funded the pamphlet. The Policy Network's own website does not reveal who funds it but it admitted to the WhoFundsYou.org website that it also is largely funded by David Sainsbury and has an annual turnover of about a million pounds. Most of the genuinely progressive think-tanks score highly on whofundsyou.org's financial transparency table.

The number of UK right-wing think-tanks has exploded since the beginning of the millennium, with more than twenty now in existence. Many were set up in association with one of the many leaders the Tory Party has had in that time. These include the Cameron-associated Policy Exchange, which was the source of the destructive "free schools" policy, the hard-right small government campaigning think-tank ResPublica and the anti-tax think-tank The Taxpayers Alliance. Most of these are bottom of the WhofundsYou.org transparency scale. We have no idea who is funding these hugely influential institutions, which often have more direct influence over legislation than MPs. It is crucial that we know who is buying the political and media agendas being set by these corporate lobbying front-groups.

For environmentalists, one particular "think-tank", the Global Warming Policy Foundation (GWPF), founded by former Tory Chancellor Nigel Lawson, has been especially destructive of UK efforts to tackle the climate crises. As Chancellor, he used the North Sea oil-fields bonanza to slash taxes for the rich by cutting the top rate from 60 to 40%. It was a key plank of the trickle-down economics that instead saw wealth flood upwards to the top 10% in the following decades. He squandered a unique opportunity to fund a renewable-energy economy that would have ensured British energy independence when the oil and gas started running out. He also refused to set up a UK sovereign investment fund to invest the surplus proceeds for the benefit of future generations, unlike almost every other oil-producing nation like Norway, Kuwait and Qatar. His disastrous Big Bang banking deregulations in 1986 laid the groundwork for the subsequent wild-west criminality that led to the 2008 financial meltdown.

Lawson re-emerged in the 2000's to play an equally destructive role on environmental issues, as an arch opponent of UK action on climate change. In 2009, he launched GWPF. The name is a classic black-art lobbying tactic imported from the US. Choosing a name that sounds like a pro-environment campaign group, confuses the public and media into thinking you are a charity, when you are a lobbying front for the fossil-fuel agenda. Lawson refuses to reveal who is funding the Foundation. But it is known that billionaire Tory donor Michael Hintze is one of the backers. His Cayman Island based hedge fund manages over £5.5 billion in assets and the Daily Mirror reported in 2012, that despite earning £125 million in just the UK, it paid only £77,000 in UK corporation taxes. Rubbing salt in the wound, David Cameron awarded him a knighthood on the day he was meeting the heads of the UK's offshore tax havens to supposedly to crack down on tax avoidance.

Being a think-tank, GWPF can provide paid interviewees and place articles in the media attacking action on the climate crises, without anybody questioning whether they are paid mouthpieces for the oil industry. When I was debating fossil-gas fracking on BBC2's Jeremy Vine Show with GWPF's director Benny Peiser, I challenged him to reveal who was funding them but he refused. The BBC really should ban think-tank spokespersons unless they declare who their funders are.

A plethora of such deceitful front-organisations were set up by the US oil industry in the 1990's to block US government action on the climate crises. Lee Raymond, chief executive of Exxon Mobil until 2006, poured money via the American Petroleum Institute (API) into think-tanks that attacked the Kyoto Protocol and discredited climate scientists, such as the deceitfully named Global Climate Coalition, to appear to be speaking "independently" without Exxon's branding. The API mimicked the PR campaigns of the tobacco industry, which sowed public doubt about the cancer risks of smoking, by funding pro-smoking scientists and think-tanks.

The New York Times in 1998, published the leaked *"Global Climate Science Communications Action Plan"* from the API. It is a spine-chilling document, laying out how they planned to destroy action on climate change. In their own words this is what "Victory" meant for them:

Chapter 9

"Victory Will Be Achieved When:

- *Average citizens "understand" (recognize) uncertainties in climate science; recognition of uncertainties becomes part of the "conventional wisdom"*
- *Media coverage reflects balance on climate science and recognition of the validity of viewpoints that challenge the current "conventional wisdom"*
- *Industry senior leadership understands uncertainties in climate science, making them stronger ambassadors to those who shape climate policy*
- *Those promoting the Kyoto treaty on the basis of extant science appear to be out of touch with reality.*

Unless "climate change" becomes a non-issue, meaning that the Kyoto proposal is defeated and there are no further initiatives to thwart the threat of climate change, there may be no moment when we can declare victory for our efforts."

It then lists the dark lobbying arts they proposed to use to achieve this victory:

- hiring of sympathetic academics
- funding of think tanks
- lobbying of politicians
- sending educational materials directly into schools
- paying for scientists to submit regular letters to the press
- the creation of pseudo-grassroots organisations
- Paid-for op-ed pieces by sympathetic scientists for local, regional and national newspapers.
- Funding of lawsuits against those trying to save humanity from the climate disaster was later included.

As you can see, many of these involve corruptly perverting academia and the press. If western civilisation survives the climate crises, when they look back on the history of the World War on the Climate, this will rank as one of its most evil documents! It is really worthwhile reading the full document on the web at: http://www.euronet.nl/users/e_wesker/ew@shell/API-prop.html (shortened URL http://goo.gl/0O2zjn).

Exxon Mobil held weekly meetings with two ex-US Senators in their pay, to monitor and act on any potential climate legislation by the US Congress. Their action plan can be boiled down to three main strategies:

- Manipulate scientific discourse
- Manipulate public opinion
- Manipulate government policy

It is only by knowing their methods can society develop mechanisms to protect itself from their destructive activities. Disastrously, the API battle plan was successfully implemented and has genocidally put the entire planet's ecosystems and humanity, in mortal danger. They blocked the Kyoto Treaty by a 95 to 0 vote in the US Senate and vetoed any meaningful legislative action by President Obama. This led to the catastrophic failure of the crucial 2009 Copenhagen climate summit, which was humanity's almost last gasp opportunity to avoid a climate apocalypse.

Nigel Lawson is now applying these tactics in the UK and has already successfully undermined billions of pounds worth of renewable energy investments, one of the few successful sectors of the economy following the financial crisis. The Guardian revealed Lawson's oil-industry background in January 2012. It reported that he had been President of the Shell and BP sponsored think-tank the British Institute of Energy Economics and had also been Chair of lobbying firm CET, whose clients included BP, Texaco and Shell.

Prior to the 2010 general election David Cameron sought to stop the Tories being branded *"the nasty party"*, by proclaiming its conversion to tackling the climate crisis. This was accompanied by photographs of Cameron visiting the melting Arctic ice cap and the slogan *"Vote Blue to Go Green"*. This green Toryism was brought to a shuddering halt by George Osborne's attack on the environment at the Tory Party Conference in 2011. This led to a disastrous decline in the growth of UK renewable energy investment. By 2012, Oystein Loseth, CEO of the Swedish wind-turbine manufacturer Vattenfall was saying *"if you look at the UK, not one supplier has established itself yet because of uncertainty in the future"*. The Tories by 2014 had moved towards ruling out all subsidies for land-based wind turbines.

This conversion of Osborne to the anti-environmental cause was again attributed to Lord Lawson. As Jonathan Porritt said in December 2011, *"George Osborne's recent conversion to the bizarre climate illiteracy of Nigel Lawson and Lord Young ("this is no time to be wasting our money on windmills") constitutes a far greater threat to economic growth in this country than whole battalions of bureaucratically-inclined planners"*. The BBC's Nick Robinson in September 2012 attributed the firing of a whole slew of pro-environment Tory ministers, to the influence of Osborne's Lawson-inspired anti climate-action zeal. The appointment of the climate-sceptic Environment Secretary Owen Patterson was described by Lord Lawson as *"brilliant"*.

In January 2012, in an unprecedented joint statement, the editors of The Lancet and the British Medical Journal stated that Lawson's GWPF was:

Chapter 9

"Perverting the course of evidence-based policy on climate-change adaptation and mitigation, damages our health resilience, our economic prosperity and our environmental stability". Yet it continues to be widely quoted in the media and even the BBC. It is hard to think of many other UK individuals who have created as much environmental, economic and social destruction in their lifetime as Nigel Lawson, a true enemy of our planet and social justice.

The financial-services industry also uses think-tanks to invisibly advance their vested financial interests with government and the media. In 2012, the BIJ contacted the eighteen top think-tanks that focused on the financial sector. Five refused to say who funded them. Seven refused to indicate what that money actually funded in terms of official reports or events. Of the remainder, the share of think-tank funding from the financial sector, varied from six-per-cent (Adam Smith Institute) to nearly a third (the Social Market Foundation).

Think-tanks were crucial to the banks successfully lobbying for deregulation in the years leading up to the financial crisis. CentreForum says its corporate sponsors *'don't have a massive influence but they do offer suggestions on areas of focus.'* Exactly! Who is going to pay think-tanks to focus on the need to regulate or tax their own industry?

As previously mentioned, when the BIJ filmed Bell Pottinger lobbyists meeting with undercover reporters posing as representatives of the Uzbekistan dictatorship, they told them that joint events could be held with influential think-tanks close to the Tory government, such as the Policy Exchange. The think-tank system as currently constituted is institutionally corrupt, as it ensures UK policy making is invisibly dominated by their rich donors and lobbyists. It is crucial that think-tanks are properly regulated. A minimum first step would be for all funding to be declared. Media coverage of think-tank reports should state who funded them. This would enable the public to judge the independence of their reports and the perspective from which it was commissioned.

An additional tool used by the corporate state to capture society's intellectual agenda is the use of massive corporate advertising budgets. One pernicious method is the swamping of mainstream liberal or progressive publications with feel-good Corporate Social Responsibility messages. The oil corporations flood UK papers like the Guardian and Independent or liberal US cable-news networks like MSNBC with advertising campaigns extolling gas-fracking or what they are supposedly doing to create new "cleaner" energy. Exxon Mobil, BP, Chevron and Shell do it *ad nauseum*. They seek to delude the public into believing the oil companies are pouring investment into renewable energy.

In April 2009, I reported in The Guardian on a Total advertising campaign. Total is the world's fifth largest oil company, with operations in over one hundred and thirty countries. It was running a series of adverts boasting about its solar-energy investments. They were festooned with cuddly pictures of giraffes and solar panels and said *"To meet growing energy demands and to prepare for the future, Total is contributing to the boom in new energies, which complement fossil fuels."* The adverts said Total was investing €100 million in solar energy that year.

Their 2008 annual report, said that one of their top four ambitions was *"Preparing for future energies i.e. innovating and pursuing our research efforts to support the development of new energies."* Whilst €100 million sounds impressive, the reality in the accounts, however, was that their solar investments were less than 0.18% of the total €13,500,000,000 investment they had planned for fossil fuels.

Annoyed at this manipulative advertising, I filed a complaint to the UK's Advertising Standards Authority. I was not successful. Their judgment stated: *"We don't consider that the ad implies that this is the main area or focus of their business."* They failed to address the consequences of companies constantly telling the public about the tiny proportion of their investments which are positive, whilst ignoring the massive investments they are making in yet more destructive fossil fuels. The urgency of the climate crises requires that all new fossil-fuel investments need to be immediately banned. These advertising campaigns make it almost impossible for the environmental NGOs to make this case as the advertising budgets of the oil corporations swamp their tiny budgets.

Their ads use sophisticated psychology to appeal to the liberal conscience. One Exxon advert slyly interchanged the phrase *"North American"* for *"American"* in the context of extolling the virtues of the Canadian tar sands for *"US"* energy independence. It then intersperses cuddly small-town American family-life images rather than pictures of the horrifying strip-mining rape of the indigenous people's forests and lands in Alberta.

Corporate oil also deploys large advertising budgets to manipulate public opinion on the web. In the US, their think-tanks teach supporters how to trash liberal and environmental authors on the Amazon book site. Shell sponsors advertorial on green websites such as businessgreen.org. It ran a front-page feature in August 2012 entitled *"Inside Shell Let's Go"*. It was presented in the usual editorial style of Business Green and was attributed to Business Green writer, Thomas Lake.

The introduction said *"A look at Shell's "Let's Go" campaign, working to make their own operations more energy efficient and helping customers to lower their emissions. Global energy demand is rising and so are consumer expectations - more people want energy from cleaner sources. At Shell we are unlocking new energy sources and squeezing more from what we have. With others we are finding ways to lower our emissions and helping customers to do the same. In building a better energy future we all have a part to play - let's go."* Only at the bottom of the article, in small print, was the statement *"This content is sponsored by Shell"*. The story-link remained on Business Green's front page for months under *"Resources"* rather than *"Advertising"*.

Business Green did allow the posting of my comment, stating *"This advertorial green-wash is for a company that is one of the world's largest sources of fossil-fuel carbon dioxide and one of the world's leading carbon-criminals. It is a leading extractor of Canadian Tar Sands - one of the dirtiest fuels on the planet which is destroying vast areas of the indigenous Indians' ancient forests."* If even environmental news websites are flooded with corporate oil propaganda, how can environmental groups hope to protect our planet?

The corporate state has also moved to capture the very font of our intellectual thought, training and education that is academia. Just as our media has been absorbed, so gradually academia is also being captured. University research is increasingly sponsored by the corporate sector. Take for example Dr Steven Blair, a widely published US expert on physical exercise. He receives millions in research funding from Coca-Cola. Aseem Mahotra reported in The Observer that Coca-Cola and Nestlé also pay to sit on the food policy board of the World Health Organisation. In the UK, the British Nutrition Foundation includes Coca-Cola, Kellogg's, McDonald's, Nestlé and Pepsi as members. Privately owned universities are now being established in the UK and even our state schools are increasingly being run by the corporate state. This is leading to a poisonous erosion of essential academic independence and impartiality.

The following extract from a letter to The Guardian, published in September 2012, lays out some of the serious concerns now held by many academics and the wide range of signatories shows the breadth of concern. The letter was entitled *"Market Driven Education is Destroying University Values"*:

"This process is eradicating the egalitarian and educational ethos of higher education and replacing it with the imperatives of individual and corporate calculation. Staff, students and applicants are to be driven by narrow, personal and pecuniary calculations in judging what to research and what to study.
In an increasingly market-driven sector, institutions are being forced to "rebrand" to compete for market share, rather than co-operate as collegial, scholarly adventures.
Society as a whole is being damaged. Research output is being skewed, while independent learning and critical thought are being erased by a creeping culture of "service provision", turning students into customers. Some institutions risk bankruptcy and being sold in their entirety. Widespread hostility to these policies exists in universities, but since the student protests against fees in autumn 2010, no comparable opposition has arisen."

Our Perverted Academia

It was signed by: Professor Terry Eagleton *Lancaster University,* Professor John Holmwood *University of Nottingham,* Professor Colin Green *UCL,* Michael Rosen *(author),* Dr Jim Wolfreys *King's College London,* Professor Jacqueline Rose *QMUL,* Professor Tom Hickey *University of Brighton,* Dr Kate Tunstall *University of Oxford,*Dr Nina Power *University of Roehampton,* Professor Jonathan Woodham *University of Brighton,* Priyamvada Gopal *University of Cambridge,* Professor Bill Schwartz *QMUL,* Professor Luke Martell *University of Sussex,* Professor Julian Stallabrass *The Courtauld Institute of Art,* Professor Raf Salkie *University of Brighton,* Dr Stathis Kouvelakis *King's College London*

Another exchange of letters in The Guardian demonstrated how deeply corrupting the privatisation of academia has become. Two American Professors, Earle and Gehlbach, wrote to the Guardian in December 2011 criticising a scientific paper in The Lancet demonstrating a link between the depth and speed of health privatisation in the former Soviet Union and mortality. A reply was published the following day from the authors of The Lancet study stating that they had comprehensively responded in the Lancet. They noted that Earle and Gehlbach had approached the evidence selectively and failed to offer any plausible alternative explanation for the enormous death-toll in the 1990s. However, what was most pertinent was the final sentence of the letter, which said *"They also fail to mention their extensive involvement in the privatisation process."*

The routes by which the corporate state is absorbing academia are myriad. They vary from the privatisation of our universities and schools to the corporate sponsorship of university professorships, research departments, conferences and academic reports. Direct provision of educational materials to schools by corporations is another route by which they seek to manipulate the next generation of voters. As well as their salaried work for their universities, many academics are now available for hire as corporate freelance researchers, report-writers or even op-ed authors, as seen in the American Petroleum Institute's war-plan on the Kyoto Treaty. The attraction of such unbranded academic endorsements for the corporate world's efforts to manipulate public opinion and legislation is obvious. Some academics, knowing that their research can be useful for major corporate interests, are thus tempted to bias their research in such directions, in the hope that they or their department may attract valuable sponsorship.

This has been especially destructive in the science versus propaganda battles over the climate crises, as fossil-fuel sponsored think-tanks paid sympathetic academics to write media articles undermining the science underpinning the urgency of the crises. Articles that the oil companies can get into the press or academic journals under the name of a professor engender greater public trust. Readers will have no idea that they are essentially reading corporate propaganda.

Steve Coll, in his book *"Private Empire: Exxon Mobil and American Power"*, outlined a case where an academic wrote about how Exxon approached him to write a paid-for article to be placed in an obscure academic journal. Exxon explained to him that this could be used later in evidence at the US Supreme Court when they needed to defend their interests! The previously mentioned BIJ sting at Bell Pottinger recorded lobbyists telling journalists that they could pass information to key academics, *"so that they are then blogging the right messages out there – so it's coming from an independent."* The corporate state is nothing if not all-encompassing!

Professor Derek Bok, a former President of Harvard University, wrote in his book *"Universities in the Marketplace – The Commercialisation of Higher Education"*, that universities, in their eagerness for money, were compromising basic academic values to the extent that some professorships were being awarded, not on the applicant's academic performance but on their ability to attract corporate sponsorship. In a 2014 cull of fifty seven Kings College London health researchers, the university admitted that the selection of those to be fired was made on their ability to raise research funds, rather than the quality or importance of their health research! Bok also reported concerns about the conflicts of interest and dangers for human health due to pharmaceutical firms sponsoring both the education of doctors and clinical research on patients.

Pharmaceutical sponsored education programmes for doctors have no incentive to teach about preventative care or non-drug based treatments. A paper in the Journal of the American Medical Association reported that 38% of clinical studies of new cancer drugs financed independently, reported unfavourable results, whereas only 5% funded by pharmaceutical corporations did. Another notorious example was the tobacco industry where over 90% of academics in the hire of the tobacco industry found that passive tobacco-smoking was not dangerous for human health, whereas only 13% of independent academics found it not to be dangerous.

Some academics in the pay of vested lobbying interests, just like their think-tank colleagues, give expert advice to governments. Stephen Glaister is an interesting example of a cross-breed of think-tank employee and academic. In 2012, he served simultaneously as Emeritus Professor of Transport and Infrastructure at Imperial College London and as the paid Director for The RAC Foundation, a pro-car think-tank. Glaister in a 2012 Guardian article expressed disappointment at a government announcement that public-transport fares would only rise by 1% above inflation rather than by 3%. Glaister did not mention that over the last two decades public transport had suffered rises well above inflation, whereas motoring costs in real terms had fallen. What chance has the poor cyclist or bus user of getting fair treatment from our government when lucratively paid motoring lobbyists can have senior professors in their pay, making high powered presentations on their behalf even in the non-billionaire press?

Also of concern is the corporate blocking of the publication of research papers damaging to their commercial interests. Bok gives two alarming examples. Researcher Betty Dong revealed that the expensive drug she was paid to research was no more effective than a cheaper generic drug. However her results were barred from publication for seven years by the commissioning company. And Professor Olivieri from the University of Toronto was threatened with legal action and had her research contract cancelled, when she discovered the drug she was researching was not only less effective than presumed but was potentially damaging to patients. This exposes how corporate sponsorship pressurises researchers to come up with results favourable for their sponsors, otherwise their funding could be threatened.

Exxon Mobil again demonstrates the dangers to the common good inherent in such corporate academic sponsorship. After the catastrophic Exxon Valdez oil spill, government scientists from the US National Oceanographic & Atmospheric Administration (NOAA) found elevated deaths among fish at low levels of oil pollution. Exxon then funded competing studies, ALL of which found the NOAA studies to be wrong. All subsequent independent scientific studies proved the NOAA study right. The American Association of University Professors unsurprisingly stated in 2014 that industry-funded research is far more likely to reach pro-industry conclusions than research that is peer reviewed and independently funded. In other words, corporate-funded research is often simply corporate propaganda.

Increasingly, rich donors such as the US oil billionaire, Koch brothers, are seeking to capture academia by even insisting on a role in the appointment of academics at some universities where they fund research. Cary Nelson, president of the American Association of University Professors, wrote in 2011 that donors were violating academic freedoms: "*Although the Koch Foundation's objectives are written so as to sound upbeat and cheerful, they amount to code words calling for the dismantling of the welfare state. 'Economic freedom' sounds like mom and apple pie until you realize it means the government shouldn't collect taxes, and 'free voluntary processes' means buy health care on your own if you can afford it. It is wholly inappropriate for an outside foundation to use a university to promote its ideological biases in this way.*"

One global negative consequence of the enormous research investments made by international pharmaceutical corporations in addressing rich societies' illnesses is that it means academic research is diverted from the horrific diseases affecting the developing world, despite the latter affecting vastly greater numbers of people. Worryingly, the Chief Medical Officer in England, also warned in 2013 that we faced a major health crisis, which was as serious a threat to humanity as global warming. She warned that many current antibiotics may be obsolete within ten years, with the world returning to the 19th century horrors of simple operations and childbirth again becoming potentially lethal, due to antibiotic resistance. This was due to the lack of investment by pharmaceutical firms in new antibiotics, due to the low profit margins for such products and the wholesale use of antibiotics in factory farming of animals, giving rise to antibiotic resistance. This latter insane practice is protected by extensive lobbying by the powerful industrial farming corporations and rich farming lobbies.

Corporate-funded research is often subject to severe secrecy conditions, as they naturally wish to capitalise on their investments. Researchers are sometimes banned from speaking at conferences or even communicating with colleagues about the corporate-funded research that they are carrying out. What should be academic research in the public interest is now increasingly simply research in the financial interests of the corporate state.

In another ingenious method to dictate government policy, some corporations can even penetrate civil-service training programmes. Leo Hickman reported in the Guardian, in 2012, that Shell Oil provides an annual two-day training programme for senior civil servants from nearly all government departments including the Department for Business, Innovations and Skills, which had Vince Cable, a former Shell chief economist, as Lib Dem Secretary of State. This is something no renewable-energy or environmental group has access to. Naturally the training sessions do not focus on how to end society's lethal fossil fuel addiction, but rather on how Shell can work "in partnership" with government. I knew Vince Cable when I was a member of the Liberal Democrats Federal Executive. However, despite my personal liking for him, I was opposed from the very beginning to his having a role anywhere near party policy on energy, due to his background as Shell's chief economist. But I never dreamt he would be a member of a government allowing companies like Shell and EdF the extraordinary access that they have to his and other departments.

Equally pernicious are advertising campaigns aimed at mothers by Nestlé. The use of formula milk-powder for babies, other than for the rare instances where it is medically necessary, can lead to increased infant mortality. The destructive environmental impacts of the associated carbon footprint of powdered formula milks are significant and the negative unnecessary financial impacts on poorer families can be debilitating.

The entire education system in the UK is now in the process of being privatised. There will soon be no limits on who can provide education or measures to prevent it being completely grabbed by the usual corporations and rich elites.

Primary schools, secondary schools and universities are all being handed over to the corporate state. In a breath-taking confluence of different strands of *The Prostitute State* (politics/tax-havens/academia) Tory donor Lord Fink, in 2009, became chair of the hedge-fund-backed Academy sponsor Absolute Return for Kids. And the Lib Dem hedge-fund millionaire donor, Paul Marshall, is also up to his neck in the government's handing over of state schools to academies. Whilst there is still a bar on running schools for profit, Michael Gove, the then Tory Education Secretary, made clear that he wants this abolished. In 2011, he had already legalised the running of Further Education Colleges by corporate for-profit providers and private equity corporations are lining up to buy them.

My local secondary school, The Peckham Academy, has been taken over from local council control by an academy network run by Tory donor, Lord Harris (whom the Guardian revealed in 2014 to have trusts with offshore deposits in tax-havens). A teacher, who taught at the school when it was taken over, told me that overnight, the teaching staff were excluded from developing the teaching strategies for the children. It was imposed from the top according to the ethos of Lord Harris. She retired soon after as she could not stomach the changes brought in by him.

There is also a corporate revolving door between government and private education corporations. Chris Woodhead was a controversial UK Chief Inspector of Schools. He now runs a chain of fifty private fee-paying schools called Cognita. Zenna Atkins, a former chair of Ofsted, now runs Wey Education, a private company with international and local government education contracts. Its aim is to *"take control of all aspects of the day to day running of such schools"*. This education privatisation process was begun under the Blair government which launched the Academy Schools programme, which handed public schools over to corporate sponsors and removed them from local government control.

This process speeded up under the coalition government, with over 66% of state secondary schools being removed from democratic local government control by the end of 2013. Ownership of billions of pounds' worth of public land and school buildings is being handed over to these business-controlled entities, representing another land-grab on our few remaining community-owned assets. The number of Academies rocketed from 200 in 2010 to over 3,300 in 2013, as Gove forced conversions against the wishes of many schools and parents.

An indication of the importance that the corporate state places on the capture of state education, can be deduced from the Guardian reporting that in April 2012, Gove, had dined with Rupert Murdoch, seven times in the year after being appointed Education Secretary in 2010! News International offered £2 million in sponsorship to create an academy school. It also reported that Gove's civil servant in charge of the "Free School" project went to News International's offices for a meeting with senior executives. The substance of these discussions between

Murdoch and Gove naturally remains unknown. The media billionaire Lord Rothermere also owns shares in the academic standards organisation NARIC!

One in ten of our state primary schools had been handed over by August 2013. Even the chair of the private-school heads association, Dr Timothy Hands, said in 2013 that state schools were *"increasingly at the mercy of much-favoured commercial providers who would like to expand their operations"*. Mr Gove dismissed the parents and teachers at Downhills Primary School in inner London, who were seeking to remain a local-authority school despite Gove's department seeking to force them to be an Academy against their will, as *"Trotskyists"*. This trickle will soon be forced into a flood of primary schools being also captured by the corporate state.

It is thus clear that the sources of our society's information and education are increasingly being captured by *Our Perverted Academia*. As Sir Keith Thomas, former president of the Royal Society put it, *"the very purpose of the university is being grossly distorted to create a market in higher education"*. He added, *"Academics are now viewed as producers whose research is expected to focus on topics of commercial value and whose output is measured against a single scale and graded like bags of wheat."* The remaining non-corporate spaces in education and academia are being destroyed, just like our wider natural ecosystems. The dangers inherent in this takeover of our education and intellectual creative systems should not be underestimated. It means that our entire system of thought, from academia to the media and think tanks, from childhood to adulthood, is being sold or handed over by our own government to a tiny band of the ultra-rich. It is a significant step to the creation of a version of society that George Orwell warned about in his book "1984".

This increasing loss of an objective independent academia is a disaster for the legitimate functioning of our democracy. It is to professors, academic researchers and scientists that society turns, when it needs independent expertise when making crucial decisions. Academics, should as a minimum, be required by law to report on their financial conflicts of interest. In a genuine liberal democracy, academia should be free of commercial bias.

If we do not act quickly, our precious tree of knowledge will be buried under a mountain of Coke cans, McDonald's wrappers and Sainsbury's coupons and our kids will end up having an enslaving McEducation instead of a personally liberating and empowering liberal education. And, if that tree dies, what remains of our liberal democracy will be buried soon after. Society cannot afford this *Perverted Academia*. Like the money changers in the temple, ***The Prostitute State*** needs to be urgently kicked out of what should be our hallowed halls of learning

Chapter 10

The Brothel's Revolving Door

Another key element of **The Prostitute State** is The Revolving Door. A democracy requires an independent civil service to deliver the laws and public-services laid down by parliament and a respected regulatory system to oversee their implementation. It is essential that the civil service be permanent, politically neutral and free from corruption. Up to the middle of the 19th Century, this was not the case in the United Kingdom, as positions in the civil service were often acquired through patronage or were simply bought.

Reforms were finally introduced by Lord Northcote in the 1850s. They were based on the professional civil service of the Chinese Imperial Court, which had an academic entry examination system. This led to an effective civil service for the elected government largely free of corruption. However its independence has not only been significantly reduced since Thatcher's premiership but in many ways, it has been captured by the corporate state to serve its wishes rather than the electorates.

The Lib Dem lobbyist Lord Newby, in a moment of prescience in the mid-nineties, referred to the untapped source that lay in the Civil Service for future valuable lobbyists for the industry. Senior civil servants are now frequently recruited into the private-sector fields related to their public duties, whether directly by corporations or indirectly as lobbyists, with many cashing in on their state-funded knowledge and top-level government contacts.

As civil servants can be recruited by the corporations they are negotiating with on behalf of the general public; it can be in their personal financial interest to err towards the corporation's advantage, as such corporations can provide them with a far more generous salary than the government. In addition, the high private-sector executive wages available to senior civil servants who facilitate the privatisation of the public services that they run, provide a massive financial incentive for them to privatise those services, rather than protecting the public good.

The Guardian reported in 2012, that Mark Britnell, as the Department of Health's Director General for Commissioning, was responsible for a new policy encouraging private-sector provision in the NHS. He drew up a shortlist of companies that would have preferential access to NHS contracts. KPMG was one of these. He was subsequently hired by KPMG as their "Head of Health". When corporations can buy our top civil servants lock, stock and barrel, how can the public interest be protected? Gladstone would be turning in his grave if he could see the raw greed of so many of today's senior civil servants who have betrayed the public service values of their colleagues. The rot started by Thatcher and fuelled by Blair, is reaching its apotheosis under Cameron and Clegg, as almost every last vestige of our public sector is sold from under our noses. They have destroyed the civil service's precious independence and its immunity from corruption.

A similar corrupt revolving door also exists between the army, secret services and police, and the corporations seeking to take over these core state functions for profit. Take for example these former police chiefs:

Original Police Role	New Private Sector Role
Ian Blair Commissioner, Metropolitan Police	Chair, Bluelight Global Solutions
Tim Godwin Commissioner, Metropolitan Police	Consultant, Accenture (Bidder for policing contracts)
Ian McPherson Assistant Commissioner, Metropolitan Police	Partner KPMG
Bob Quick Assistant Commissioner, Metropolitan Police	CEO, Bluelight Global Solutions
Paul Hancock Chief Constable, Bedfordshire Constabulary	Business Development Manager, Bluelight Global Solutions
Bill Hughes Director, Serious Organised Crime Agency	International Director, Bluelight Global Solutions
Sir John Stevens Commissioner, Metropolitan Police	Chair, Quest (Global Corporate Intelligence) Chair, Axiom International (Private forensic corporation)

The Brothel's Revolving Door

Original Police Role	New Private Sector Role
Sir John Stevens (cont'd)	Chair, Protector Group (Private security-firm) Columnist, News of the World
Andy Hayman Assistant Commissioner, Metropolitan Police	Columnist, News International
John Yates Assistant Commissioner, Metropolitan Police	Adviser to Bahrain dictatorship (Advising Bahrain Police during suppression of protests)

All of these are now free to lobby their colleagues still in the Association of Chief Police Officers, to privatise all of their remaining police services. Lucrative rewards await them in the private sector if they do so. This aids the usual cacophony organised by think-tanks, such as the Policy Exchange and lobbyists advocating privatisation, despite there being no public demand for the privatisation of policing.

Former Metropolitan Police Commissioner, Sir John Stevens, is a particularly good example of this revolving door. Despite his many lucrative private-sector roles, Stephens was not only promoted to the Lords by Gordon Brown, giving his corporate employers direct access to Parliament, but he also appointed him as his Senior Advisor on International Security Issues. David Cameron had previously appointed him Chair of the UK Borders Policing Committee in 2007. After his retirement, he was employed by Murdoch to write columns for the News of the World at £7,000 a column, at the same time as his former police force were investigating the News of the World for criminal involvement in phone-hacking and bribing of public officials!

In 2011, he was appointed by Yvette Cooper MP, Ed Miliband's Shadow Secretary of State for Home Affairs, to chair Labour's Independent Commission into the Future of Policing. What hope has the public of saving our public police force from wholesale privatisation, when both the Tories and Labour hand responsibility for new policing policy to the director of a private security corporation? New Labour, the Orange Book Lib Dems and the Conservatives are all part of the same incestuous political lobbying class, hijacking our public services for their corporate backers, with the connivance of their former civil-service senior managers.

Have you ever wondered why we keep having massive cost overruns at the Ministry of Defence (MoD)? The Express reported in 2009, that arms-procurement

Chapter 10

costs were typically 40% higher than the Ministry's forecasts. The coalition announced in January 2013, that the UK was, despite the recession, going to spend an eye-watering £159 billion (£159,000,000,000) on arms purchases from defence corporations over the next decade. In 2012, the UK was the world's fourth-highest spender on arms procurement and defence.

The revolving door between the armed forces/MoD and the arms corporations spins really fast. In October 2012, the Guardian reported that in the last sixteen years, over 3,500 senior military and MoD officials have left public service to work directly for the arms manufacturers and security corporations. In one year alone, three hundred and sixty senior defence public officials changed sides.

There actually is a regulatory body called the Advisory Committee on Business Appointments (ACOBA) that is supposed to oversee all senior corporate public-sector recruitment. However, it is as usual dominated by the corporate state. In 2013, its all-male membership included former Chair of Mercury Asset Management, director of Standard Life and Shell Oil shareholder, Sir Hugh Stevenson, as well as Director of Scottish Power and a paid adviser to Macquarie Infrastructure Assets, Lord Macdonald. Its Chair was Lord Lang, Chair of MacLennan Group and SI Associates, Director of Charlemagne Capital and SoyuzNefteGaz and a Shell Oil shareholder.

Whilst all private-sector hiring of senior army officers and MoD officials are referred to this committee, the process is a typical British establishment deception. Its rulings can be totally ignored by the Army top brass, as they leave for lucrative directorships and lobbying consultancies. This is because the committee has only an advisory role with no powers whatsoever to enforce its rulings on officers who ignore the committee's decisions.

The Sunday Times in October 2012 exposed a brace of former army top brass willing to sell lobbying services to reporters posing as South Korean arms salespersons. Those incriminated included Lord Dannatt, former head of the army, Lieutenant General Richard Applegate, former head of procurement at the MoD, Lord Stirrup, former chief of the defence staff and most dramatically Lieutenant General Sir John Kiszely, who was President of the Royal British Legion. Kiszely was filmed by the Times boasting that the Remembrance Day ceremonies were a "*tremendous networking opportunity*".

The Cenotaph ceremony is one of the most solemn of UK state occasions, marking the dead from two awful World Wars. Turning this into a tawdry sales promotion opportunity was something which even the corporate state could not avoid some accountability over and Kiszely duly resigned his Presidency of the British Legion. Kiszely's comment reveals the brazenness of our army top brass as they literally convert that brass to gold! These were the very officers who had been entrusted with protecting the nation and yet were happy to promote Asian arms corporations in return for the corporate shilling.

The Brothel's Revolving Door

In a glimpse of the nepotistic details that oil the defence lobbying wheels, Kiszely told the sting that he was spending Christmas with the armed forces minister Andrew Robothan. No wonder arms manufacturers can run billion-pound rings around the MoD when they can hire the top brass negotiating with them. It is the poor and the general taxpayer who pick up the bills, whilst former top brass and MoD officials enjoy the corporate high life.

The Revolving Door even operates at local council level. I live in the London Borough of Southwark. For a generation, the council has almost completely abandoned the building of new social housing, despite having one of the largest housing waiting lists in the country. The council's Regeneration Department ("The Bulldozing Department") has embarked on the demolition of vast swathes of council housing built in the 1970's.

Some of the initial projects resulted in some good quality new replacement social housing. But the net result has been a loss of over 7,000 social housing units, increasingly replaced with expensive apartments aimed at the international elite who want a pad in London with its favourable non-dom tax regime. The recent enormous demolition project of the Heygate Estate at the Elephant & Castle is a prime exemplar of the local council Revolving Doors.

I attended the project's planning application hearing in January 2013. The chair banned all filming, recording and photography by the press. The developers, an international corporation called Lend Lease, who had been convicted of local-authority fraud in New York in 2012, wanted to build 2,500 luxury flats to replace the existing 1,200 social housing units, even though they were structurally sound.

I was horrified at what else was being proposed:

- Despite the council having a policy of 20% renewable energy, the developer included none.
- Out of the 2,500 new homes proposed only a token seventy-nine were to be social housing units, even though the existing 1,200 council tenants had been promised a right of return.
- Despite the council having a policy of zero parking at major transport hubs, the developers were given 600 parking spaces.
- Despite the council having a policy of protecting trees, over 300 mature trees were to be bulldozed.
- Despite the council having a policy requiring space for cycling, not a single meter of cycle lane was included.
- Even the streets and the reduced public open space were to be privatised.

Chapter 10

I was shocked that a supposedly Labour council proposed to kick out 1,200 local families in return for just 74 social housing units. The developers were able to tear up the council's planning regulations with complete impunity. I had not reckoned on the corporate state's tentacles reaching down so deep into my own community. I discovered that Lend Lease had legally hired many of those overseeing the project on the council's behalf over the previous decade. They included:

- Lend Lease hired the lobbying firm founded by the former leader of the council who had initiated the Heygate demolition proposal.
- Lend Lease's lobbying firm employed the councillor who was Chair of the Regeneration Committee which had agreed the demolition.
- The council's Cabinet Member who oversaw the Heygate project for four years, was hired as a consultant for one of the Heygate Project bidders after they lost their seat.
- In 2011, Land Lease hired the council's Heygate Project Manager to work on the Heygate Project as their Development Manager.
- The Council's communications manager for the Heygate Project was hired by Lend Lease to be their communications manager for the Heygate Project.
- The Council's chief regeneration manager overseeing the Heygate Project left the council to form his own regeneration consultancy company EnterHomes.
- The current leader of the council negotiating with Lend Lease was given £3,200 worth of Olympics Tickets for him and his partner by Lend Lease.

This project is just one example of The Revolving Door at local level. Anna Minton, in a report for Spinwatch on lobbyists and local councils, revealed that almost 20% of *existing* Southwark councillors worked as lobbyists, not even waiting to retire, to sell their political expertise to corporate paymasters.

The Heygate's financial details were shocking. The council had agreed to pay the £44 million tenant-eviction (social-cleansing) and the £15 million demolition costs. A leak revealed that Lend Lease paid the council just £50 million, plus potential profit-share, for these 23 acres of prime central-London land. This meant a potential net loss of £9 million, on the deal for the council if no profits resulted. An immediately adjacent 1.5 acre site with similar planning permission had been sold in 2012 for £40 million. This meant the 23-acre site sold to Lend Lease by Southwark Council for a net loss of £9 million, plus possible profit-share, was then potentially worth £610 million on the open market! But fear of corporate pressure suppresses free speech even in local newspapers. When I wrote my monthly eco-column in our local newspaper on this extraordinary scandal it was spiked. They could not afford the risk of being sued. I reported the scandal to the District Auditor who has yet to respond.

Another strand of government corruption is Regulatory Capture. Governments set up legitimate regulatory bodies to address various aspects of our economy and society. They cover everything from the safety of pharmaceuticals and pesticides to the security of our financial services and healthcare systems. Here the revolving door spins both ways. Corporations not only pluck managers directly from the regulatory body overseeing them, but also have their own employees directly hired by their regulatory body or even worse have them appointed to chair them.

This destroys trust in the impartiality of the regulatory processes. The corporate state simply buys the inside expertise and contacts that the regulatory-body managers have. This is invaluable when lobbying for corporate-friendly regulations. A good example of corporate capture is the UK's Statutory Advisory Committee on Pesticides. It has numerous voting members who were employed by the chemical corporations who produce poisonous pesticides or whose research is funded by them. It repeatedly resists banning pesticides that independent studies indicate are damaging to environmental and human health. A recent infamous example was when they refused to ban the neonicotinoid pesticides associated with catastrophic bee and insect losses across Europe.

The government is similarly neutralising the regulatory powers of the Environment Agency, which will oversee gas-fracking regulations, by outrageously appointing Philip Dilley, a former chair of Arups, to head the agency in 2014. Whilst he was chair of Arups, they carried out significant work for the gas-fracking corporation Cuadrilla and funded the All Party Parliamentary Group on gas-fracking. And in yet another move to place the corporate state in charge of education regulation, Michael Gove's successor as Education Secretary Nicky Morgan, appointed David Hoare, former chair of the private mail corporation DX Group and a trustee of AET, the largest chain of school academies, to be the chair of Ofsted the schools regulator in August 2014. The DX Group's holding company is based in the Cayman Islands.

Another breath-taking example is again the privatisation of the UK's National Health Service. McKinsey's, a major international lobbying corporation lies at the heart of this particular web. Shortly after the new Tory Secretary of State for Health, Andrew Lansley, was appointed, McKinsey Consulting signed a £300,000 "strategy" contract with the NHS competition "regulator" NHS Monitor. The Department of Health also awarded McKinsey a £6 million contract to provide '*services to the NHS Leadership team*' and a company representative would attend meetings of that team. McKinsey (a global corporation worth over £4 billion), despite having a direct conflict of interest by being simultaneously a consultant for

Chapter 10

many global health corporations, had also been hired by the previous Labour government to review the Department of Health. It produced a report recommending the slashing of 10% of the Department of Health's staff.

If governments get rid of their internal civil service expertise, they then have to expensively buy it in from external consultancy corporations like McKinsey, with the crucial difference that the hired consultants are purely in it for profit, not for public service. McKinsey's even designed the structure of the new NHS Commissioning Board. Meanwhile, McKinsey's global health corporation clients have been circling the NHS's £105 billion budget for years like hungry vultures.

So let us look at *The Revolving Door* between McKinsey and the NHS:

- David Bennett, Chief Executive of NHS Monitor is a former McKinsey executive.
- Lord Carter, Chair of the NHS Co-operation and Competition Panel, was simultaneously Chair of McKesson, one of the UK's largest private health firms, which is a client of McKinsey's and has NHS contracts.
- Adrian Masters, NHS Monitor Director of Strategy, is a former McKinsey executive.
- Paul Bate, senior health adviser to Prime Minister David Cameron, is a former McKinsey executive.
- Nicolaus Henke, health adviser to David Cameron, is a director of McKinsey's Health Care Division.
- Ian Dalton, Head of the NHS Commissioning Board, was an after-dinner speaker at McKinsey events.
- Tom Kibasi was a McKinsey executive, then became policy advisor to the NHS Chief Executive and then returned to again work for McKinsey.
- David Cox, London NHS Strategy Manager, is a former McKinsey executive.

McKinsey also operates an "Alumni" scheme which hosts networking events for former employees embedded in government and senior-executive roles, enabling it to maintain personal contacts with some of those overseeing government privatisation and consultancy schemes. The Daily Mail reported that David Bennett, Head of NHS Monitor, enjoyed a £6,000 two-day freebie to New York for a lavish McKinsey banquet.

Despite frequent Freedom of Information requests by the lobbying-monitoring group Spinwatch, they are unable to determine how many former NHS officials now working for McKinsey are employed on NHS privatisation contracts, as the Department of Health insists on redacting all names on the papers released. Many advice papers submitted by McKinsey are treated as confidential by the

Department, thus preventing the public from seeing what they are recommending, despite the fact that our taxes are paying for them.

McKinsey executives regularly attend meetings of the Extraordinary NHS Board, which is overseeing the privatisation of NHS services mandated by the Cameron government's health "reforms". As under Blair, "reform" is the consultancy-speak for moving government services into the corporate for-profit sector. It usually means slashing staff numbers, pay, pensions and conditions and hefty pay increases for senior civil servants who become senior executives in the newly privatised services.

There is now almost no separation between the government's health policy-making and the consultancy firms. The "regulatory" system put in place to oversee the "fair" treatment of public and private NHS contractors has been truly captured, as exemplified by the audacity of NHS Monitor Chair David Bennett's call for the exemption of private health corporations from taxation. In January 2013, the Guardian reported this former McKinsey executive as saying during an earlier consultation that *"tax rules"* were preventing private healthcare companies operating on an equal footing with the NHS. After privatising large parts of the health service against the public's will, they now outrageously want these corporations to not even pay taxes on the huge profits they are making on the NHS, as they cut staff and squeeze pay and conditions for those remaining!

Another example of regulatory capture demonstrates the disastrous consequences it can have for the public. The financial services regulator (the FSA) between 2002 and 2006 repeatedly warned Halifax Bank of Scotland (HBOS) about its corporate governance. Yet, in 2004, its CEO James Crosby was appointed by the Labour government to be a director of the FSA. Later that year, HBOS Director of Risk, Paul Moore, who had reported serious failings in the bank's risk assessment processes to the bank's board, was fired. These failings led to the collapse of the bank and its disastrous takeover by Lloyds, which required £11 billion of taxpayers' bailout money. HBOS commissioned its own auditors (KPMG) to examine the claims by Moore, despite their conflict of interest. They exonerated the bank and said Moore had been fired for *"personality clashes the previous year"*. Moore's successor, Peter Cummings, was banned from banking for life and fined £500,000 for his part in the bank's collapse. In 2006, Gordon Brown then promoted Crosby to be deputy chair of the FSA, which failed to protect the UK from the 2008 economic meltdown, with terrible consequences for ordinary workers and the poor.

Another version of the Revolving Door opened up under Thatcher. This is the practice of placing corporate executives on secondment to civil service departments. In December 2011, Damian Carrington reported in the Guardian that fifty employees of the nuclear corporations were working on secondments within government departments on *"energy issues"*. The nuclear and fossil-fuel industries have been adept at using this route into government policy-making departments. Among those with employees embedded in government departments are EdF, Centrica, npower, Shell, ConocoPhillips, and the UK Petroleum Industry Association, as well as employees of the energy departments of the Big Four accountancy/consulting firms.

The departments infiltrated include the Department of Energy and Climate Change, Department for Environment, Food and Rural Affairs, Department for Business, Innovation and Skills and crucially The Treasury. Many are working in senior civil-service roles. For example, a secondment in the Department of Energy is an executive from ESB, the only corporation in 2013 actually building new UK fossil gas-powered generating stations. He was appointed Head of Capacity Market Design and was in charge of designing the state subsidy scheme for gas-powered stations! Incredibly, they claimed there was no conflict of interest. His salary was jointly paid by ESB and the Department.

Vince Cable's Department for Business, Innovation and Skills (BIS) refused to tell the Guardian which corporations had taxpayer-funded staff working for them. The Treasury refused to reveal the identities of those corporations with fewer than five paid staff working within it. Carrington reported that many secondments were being paid by the departments in which they were embedded rather than by their corporate employers. Britain's sole Green MP, Caroline Lucas, said that these companies do not lend their staff for nothing: *"They expect a certain degree of influence, insider knowledge and preferential treatment in return."* In other words, they are legally buying access to the corridors of power and it is done with the full consent of elected Lib Dem, Tory and Labour ministers.

How deep this *government of the people, by the corporations, for the corporations* has gone, was demonstrated after the catastrophic explosion at the Fukushima nuclear power plant in 2011. Instead of Vince Cable's department issuing independent scientifically-informed statements about what had happened and the potential for it happening in the UK, civil servants from BIS, DECC and the nuclear corporations colluded on a PR campaign to downplay the disaster in the UK media including the BBC. The express purpose was not to impartially inform the public, but to protect proposals for government subsidies for a new fleet of private corporate nuclear power plants, from public disapproval. This version of the Revolving Door also has a reverse mode, whereby civil servants work on secondment in the fossil-fuel and nuclear corporations such as Shell and Horizon Nuclear Power.

Cameron's government is destroying what is left of our previously world-renowned civil service. Tory Ministers such as Michael Gove, the former Education

Secretary, hired advisers directly from the corporate state to oversee the slashing of thousands of civil service posts. In a blood-curdling Guardian article Warwick Mansell reported, in July 2012, that Tory Ministers want to end completely the civil service role in policy-making by outsourcing all of it to corporate think-tanks, private consultancies and even directly to corporations themselves! Future governments may have absolutely no in-house policy expertise left that is independent of the corporate-controlled consultancies and think tanks. One has to admire the ruthless elegance of this final solution to the participation in government policy-making by what remains of the independent civil service.

In the Department of Health, the civil-servant policy-experts made redundant are being replaced with representatives from the fast-food corporations, whose products are helping to create an obesity epidemic. Executives from Pepsi and the Spirit Trade Association are chairing Department of Health Food Policy Groups. Other policy group members include Diageo (Guinness), McDonald's, Compass (Turkey Twizzlers), Mars, Kellogg's and Unilever. The department said it did not want to lead on food policy but would be guided by these policy groups. Unsurprisingly they ruled out regulation or pricing to tackle the obesity crisis but they recommended "*voluntary*" agreements by food corporations. And so the obesity and ill-health of our kids is the price being paid for these corporate profits.

There is another important section of our economy without which this exposition of **The Prostitute State** would be incomplete. Almost everybody experienced the disastrous consequences of its actions including myself. It is, of course, the Banking and Financial Services Industry – the conglomeration of investment banks, private equity firms, ratings agencies, global financial auditors and consultancies. These so-called masters of the universe brought the world's financial systems tumbling down in the Great Recession, leading to massive financial rescues paid for by taxpayers across the planet. It led to terrible job losses and the greatest collapse in our collective wealth since the Great Depression. I myself experienced a nearly 80% drop in my self-employed income from my eco-consultancy work and environmental journalism as a result. Saving the planet had been truly and disastrously kicked off the agenda by the financial meltdown.

If you examine the underlying causes of the financial crisis, you frequently find they lead back to the capture of our democratic systems by the corporate state. The financial-services industry is the example *par excellence* of the use of regulatory capture, political lobbying, hiring of former politicians, corruption of think tanks, hijacking of academia, political donations, media ownership, offshore accounts, revolving doors, tax havens, etc. You name it and they were and are at it.

Barclays Bank was at the heart of the Libor market-fixing scandal. This involved nearly all the major banks in illegal manipulation of global interest rates in major currencies. It was the banking equivalent of match-fixing globally, except that instead of thousands of football fans and gamblers being cheated, literally millions of small businesses and home mortgage-payers were ripped off.

The chief executive of the Financial Services Agency, which was supposed to be regulating the industry, was Hector Sants. He had previously been a senior banker as Vice-President of UBS and managing director at Credit Suisse Boston. UBS was also at the heart of the Libor scandal. Sants admitted to the UK's Treasury Select Committee that he knew Bob Diamond was under investigation in the Libor-fixing scandal at the time of Diamond's appointment as CEO of Barclays! What was his punishment for being at the helm of the FSA when its failure nearly brought down the entire UK economy? A senior executive post with Barclays Bank as their head of compliance and a knighthood in Cameron's 2013 New Year's Honours List! His taxpayer-funded FSA pay package for 2010/11 was £800,000. His salary at his new Barclays post was £3 million a year, whilst society picked up the pieces of the FSA's multi-billion-pound failures.

The financial services industry, through regulatory and government policy capture, were able to engineer a bonfire of government financial regulations, first in the UK and US and then around the world. This deregulation frenzy which led to the 2008 financial Armageddon was supported by both Democrats and Republicans in the US and by Labour and the Tories in the UK. Having used the processes of the corporate state to free themselves from any meaningful oversight, they went on a wild feeding frenzy.

Through the insanity of a basically regulation-free derivatives market they created a system that was effectively a direct tax imposed on the world economy. Instead of being paid to governments for investment in public services, it was creamed off as immense personal wealth for the doyens of the financial markets. Will Hutton neatly summarised it in the Observer in December 2012: *"The business model of modern finance is banks trading on their own account in rigged derivative markets, skimming investment funds and manipulating interbank lending, all to under-lend to innovative enterprise while over-lending on a stunning scale to private equity and property. We now understand that it was capitalism at its most rotten."*

The meltdown would not have happened if the corporate state had not ensured that the regulators did not effectively regulate the derivatives markets or had not ensured that politicians did not intervene as the market went into overheated insanity. The derivatives market was supposed to be an insurance system to protect clients from sudden shock moves in interest rates. One simple statistic reveals the vast global failure of the regulatory bodies. *The world's actual GDP in 2012 was about $70 trillion. Yet the market in interest-rate derivatives was $310 trillion!*

The Brothel's Revolving Door

Once this paper roundabout stopped, all hell was bound to break loose and so it did in 2008, with the global financial collapse from which the world economy struggled to emerge.

A BIJ report in July 2012 revealed that the financial services industry had spent a whopping £93 million lobbying the UK government in 2011 alone. This was a period when the government was trying to get to grips with re-introducing some sensible financial regulation after the horse had bolted. Among the policy victories this lobby achieved according to the BIJ report were:

- The slashing of UK corporation tax and taxes on banks' overseas branches. This reform cost the taxpayer billions.
- The neutering of a national not-for-profit pension scheme launching in October 2012 that was supposed to benefit millions of low-paid and temporary workers.
- Killing off government plans for a corporate super-watchdog to police quoted companies.

The BIJ reported a staggering 129 organisations engaging in some form of lobbying for the UK's finance sector, with over 800 people employed directly. Lobbyists included in-house bank staff, public-affairs consultancies, industry-body representatives, law firms and management consultants. This lobbying onslaught means the government legislates and regulates too often in the banking industry's interest rather than the national interest.

Another BIJ report revealed that the financial services industry's donations to the three main political parties amounted to £6.1 million out of a total of £30 million in 2011 i.e. more than 20% of political donations came from this one industry. This gives them an immense amount of access to political leaders, access that they can use to promote their disastrous deregulation agenda and to protect their offshore tax-avoidance empires. 27% of Tory donations in 2010/11 came from the sector, making them very sensitive to their needs.

Interestingly since the departure of Blair and Labour's loss of government, Labour's donations from rich billionaires has collapsed from being between 30-43% of total income between 2001 and 2010, to less than 6% in 2011. Corporate money as usual follows where the political power is. As mentioned with tax-havens, the Party Treasurers route to political influence also applies to the finance industry, with the two frequently overlapping. Michael Spencer, Tory Party Treasurer from 2006 to 2010 is Chair of ICAP, the industry's major inter-dealer broker at the heart of the dysfunctional derivatives industry. Mark Florian, who is a former Tory Deputy Treasurer, is chief executive of British Private Equity and Venture Capital Association (BVCA).

Chapter 10

TheCityUK and the British Banking Association (whose then chief executive, Angela Knight, was formerly Tory Economic Secretary to the Treasury and an MP) were among those lobbying hardest against the re-introduction of EU and UK banking regulations following the 2008 meltdown. The Deputy Mayor of London, Kit Malthouse, is on the board of premier finance-industry lobbyist TheCityUK, as well as being a director of various hedge-fund and capital investment companies. And whilst the billionaire media shrieked about a non-existent EU invasion of Romanians, they facilitated the finance industry's neutering of government financial regulations by remaining largely silent about it.

The BIJ also reported on the deployment of yet another lobbying tool by the industry - the hijacking of the political party conferences by the financial services industry. This is enabled by paying so called independent "think tanks" such as the Smith Institute or the Policy Network to host events at the Labour and Tory Party Conferences. This gives them a role in selecting platform speakers at fringe meetings and the subjects selected for debate. It also buys them invaluable personal contacts with government or opposition spokespersons.

Private Eye reported that Geoff Cook, the CEO of Jersey Finance and lobbyist for that tax-haven's banking sector, had funded an Adam Smith Institute fringe meeting with Tory MP Kwasi Kwarteng (former financial-services analyst) at the 2012 Tory Party Conference. It reported that Cook was met with 'loud applause' for commenting that British banks were over-regulated and over-taxed! The truth behind the Great Recession obviously had not permeated into this little bubble within the conference security barriers.

These examples are just the tip of how the finance industry uses think-tanks to influence government policy. All of the top 18 think-tanks cover the finance sector. The BIJ quotes an example of a 2011 Demos report urging the downplaying of criticism of senior bankers following the financial meltdown, whilst Demos was being funded by 13 different financial institutions. In addition, the report itself was funded by financial-services lobbyists.

Sam Read from the New Economics Foundation neatly summed it up by saying those *"who don't like a government policy could give millions of pounds to a think-tank to promote their agenda. As well as utilising the think-tank's professed close links to politicians, they can help to create a debate in the media where they will give the impression that certain policies are backed by independent experts."*

Where the finance industry is at its most blatantly effective is in its capture of the House of Lords. In 2012, the BIJ reported that the House of Lords had a staggering 124 of its 775 members in the paid employ of the finance industry. UBS, which was fined £940 million for its part in the Libor rate-fixing scandal, had Lord Brittan as its vice-chair, Lord Garel-Jones as its managing director and Lord Waldegrave as a paid "adviser". The Lords legislative committees overseeing the banking sector are packed with them. It reported that FIVE of the eleven peers on the committee overseeing the Finance Act 2011 (i.e. the Budget), with full voting powers and the right to submit legislative amendments, were in the employ of the finance industry.

This Act unbelievably gave yet more tax advantages to banks and financial institutions' offshore subsidiaries. The committee members included a director of Goldman Sachs, a partner of the private bank GP Bullhound, a paid senior KPMG adviser, a board member of Rabobank International and a soon to be appointed director of the Royal Bank of Scotland. They only needed one more vote from the rest of the committee to have a majority on any votes taken. And remember that about 40% of The House of Lords amendments become law! No wonder the cowboy practices of the private equity, tax-haven and banking industries are allowed to run riot when *The Prostitute State* has so many legislators in its pay.

The embedding of staff in government is yet another of the usual array of effective lobbying tools, employed by the finance industry including the Big Four accountancy firms (KPMG, Deloitte, Ernst & Young and PWC). In 2012, they had fourteen paid employees embedded in the Treasury, with numerous others seconded not only in other government departments but even in the political parties themselves! For example, PWC in 2014 had paid analysts seconded to the Lib Dems to advise on their new health policy. As their spokesperson put it so nicely *"KPMG has a policy of seconding senior members of staff to all three major political parties, to underpin the fact that KPMG has a strong interest in good and practical public policy."* KPMG does have a strong financial *"interest"* in public policy, both in terms of its own multi-billion-pound business and for its billionaire corporate clients also. But what is *"good policy"* for KPMG and its corporate paymasters is not necessarily good for voters or the general public and this conflict of interest means its insider access to our political and governmental policy-making processes is politically corrupt.

An ignominious example of the corporate state being simultaneously gamekeeper and poacher was Ian Barlow who, having worked for KPMG for 37 years, served as one of the four non-executive directors on Her Majesty's Revenue Collection Service (HMRC) board. He was simultaneously serving as director for PA Consulting, whose owners took HMRC to court over its crackdown on its tax-minimisation procedures. The HMRC Board has only eight members. The other non-executive directors were all from large corporations including Tesco, ITV, BT, Travelex and Smith & Nephew. No wonder large corporations successfully avoid paying billions in corporation taxes, when their representatives have captured the democratic regulatory taxation oversight body.

The financial services industry makes full use of the revolving door by recruiting from the government's financial regulatory bodies. The actual head of

Chapter 10

HMRC was hired by another one of the Big Four, Deloitte, in May 2013. Dave Hartnett had resigned after a series of scandals erupted about the behind-door tax-deals he had made with various corporations. He had agreed a deal with Vodafone where they paid only £1.5 billion out of the £6 billion, that tax campaigners UK Uncut claimed was owed. It was under his watch that Starbucks paid zero corporation taxes for three years in a row. Vodafone is also a client of Deloitte. And in another action symbolic of how our senior civil service is merging with the corporate state, Hartnett also joined the serial tax-haven facilitator HSBC as an adviser in January 2013.

KPMG in a spectacular coup even infiltrated the civil-service process for drafting new tax legislation covering multinational corporations, under both Labour and the Tories. Felicity Lawrence in a Guardian article outlined in detail not only how both parties had handed over development of government offshore corporate tax policy to offshore-benefiting corporations, with their consultative committees consisting almost 100% of their representatives. She reported that *"Under the new coalition government, a senior manager in international corporate tax from accountants KPMG, Robert Edwards, was seconded to the Treasury for 20 months to see through developing the policy on Controlled Foreign Companies rules."* Lawrence reported that Edwards' KPMG speciality was in advising corporations on tax-efficient cross-border financing and restructuring! The Treasury itself estimated that the resulting new rules on taxation of offshore subsidiaries of UK corporations will result in losses of about £20 billion to the Treasury. These losses will outrageously have to be made up by the remaining taxpayers or paid for in cuts in public services, especially those that serve the poor.

KPMG has its talons in the Lib Dems also. Neil Sherlock, who was appointed Director of Government Relations for Lib Dem Deputy Prime Minister, Nick Clegg, in November 2011, was still listed on the KPMG website as their Partner in charge of Public and Regulatory Affairs in February 2013. Sherlock, whilst principal lobbyist for KPMG, had for years paid a monthly standing order to Nick Clegg's office when Clegg was an MP and later to his leader's office.

A crucial question for the audit industry is how were so many of the world's banks operating with disastrously dangerous balance sheets prior to the 2008 financial meltdown, due to their exposure to the US sub-prime mortgage market and the insane global derivatives market, without it showing up in their annual financial audits? The answer is quite simple. Financial oversight of banking and corporate accounts is carried out by the private sector and it is the banks and the corporations themselves who hire their own auditors. It is the equivalent of being able to select your own tax inspector. If an auditor makes a disputed ruling on a corporation's accounts that are not in its interests, this endangers the re-hiring of that firm for the following year's audit. Bluntly, the system has a systemic inbuilt direct conflict of interest for the auditors. The oversight of corporate accounts clearly should be a government regulatory activity and a not profit-making industry.

When you add the fact that all major UK banks are audited by the Big Four global auditing corporations, you have a recipe for market corruption and eventually market failure. These four corporations employ over 800,000 staff worldwide and had a turnover of over $108 billion in 2012. In 2011, a report by Parliament's Economic Affairs Committee found them guilty of complacency and dereliction of duty in the lead-up to the 2008 economic meltdown. The report also found that the Big Four's domination of the audit market limited choice. All banks and ninety-nine out of the FTSE 100 accounts are audited by them. They gave a clean bill of health to a plethora of national and global banks and financial institutions, in every year leading up to the financial sub-prime and derivatives meltdown.

In 2013, the UK's competition authorities found that due to the Big Four oligopoly, companies were offered "higher prices and lower quality" than if a genuine market existed. It attacked the cosy relationship that exists between company managers and their auditors and said that they were failing shareholders. Instead of being drummed out of business, the Big Four are still outrageously at the heart of our corrupted government and political parties.

Since the economic collapse they have continued to have:

- Significant involvement in government and regulatory decision making.
- Generous allocations of lucrative government contracts.
- Lucrative share of the profits from government privatisations.

And of course, there has been almost no increase in effective regulatory controls on auditing or any move to address their conflicts of interest. Nobody from the Big Four has been jailed or received significant financial penalties for their contribution to the UK's financial meltdown. Another major problem with the Big Four is the fact that, parallel to the financial-auditing services that they provide, they are also huge providers of corporate and government consultancy services, often simultaneously to the same clients. If you are selling billions of pounds worth of services to the corporations or banks that you are auditing, you have a direct conflict of interest. This is what led to Andersen's catastrophic failures in their auditing of the energy giant Enron, prior to its $64 billion bankruptcy in 2001, which was then the US's largest. It caused the breakup of Andersen's and the consolidation of the global auditing industry from the Big Five to the remaining Big Four.

Chapter 10

The global scandals associated with the banks and financial institutions audited by the Big Four continue unabated. Take for example HSBC, which was found guilty in 2013 by US authorities of massive money-laundering operations at its Mexican subsidiary, resulting in fines of over £1 billion. Standard Chartered were fined $1 billion for similar laundering offences. Or take the mis-selling of payment protection insurance in the UK resulting in £13 billion in compensation payments by the combined big banks. What were the auditors doing and why are they not being held accountable? In yet another direct conflict of interest, the Big Four provide consultancy, tax and policy advice services to governments and regulatory bodies around the globe, whilst *simultaneously* providing consultancy, tax and auditing services to the very corporations those governments are seeking to tax and regulate.

The incestuous relationship between these behemoths and our political system is personified by Lord Freeman who is a former Tory health minister. He is chair of the Advisory Board of PWC, whose consulting arm claims to have "been at the *heart of shaping [healthcare] reforms and working with clients to respond to the opportunities they present"*. In other words, they have the audacity to boast they were helping to form the NHS privatisation policies that their lucrative clients could then profit from! Freeman is also the Chair of Parity Group plc. They won a contract with NHS Direct to develop the Health Information Search Portal for £1.4 million. So he is simultaneously a paid voting member of the legislature overseeing NHS privatisation, a paid advisor for the consultancy advising the government on privatising health-policy and the paid chair of a company hired by our health service!

This brings us to the central role The Big Four and the big banks play in another pillar of *The Prostitute State* – the international tax-haven system. In addition to their auditing and consultancy arms, the Big Four frequently also provide *"tax minimisation services"* to the corporations that they are auditing, whilst simultaneously they are in the heart of the Treasury and HMRC advising on corporate tax policies. Whilst this lucrative triple conflicts of interest existed under the previous Labour government, under George Osborne the fleecing of the UK taxpayer has gone into overdrive. Whilst Osborne and Cameron paid lip service to tackling tax-stealing havens, at home they have allowed the corporate lobbyists full rein in designing the UK's offshore regulatory systems, whilst seeking to increase the UK's role as an international tax-haven in its own right.

The Chancellor slashed funding for the Serious Fraud Office by 40%, reducing it to a puny £30 million. After all, why should they irritate their donors by funding serious-fraud investigations into the corporate state? Uncovering, say, hundreds of millions of pounds of fraudulent credit-default activities in the markets would not be in the interests of *The Prostitute State.*

Michael Rake, who was chair of KPMG when it was fined nearly half a billion dollars by the US government for creating tax shelters that led to the loss of $2.5 billion dollars in US taxes, is now deputy chair of Barclays Bank in the UK, which was as mentioned at the heart of the Libor scandal. During his time at KPMG, it was also found by two tax-tribunal judgements to have set up tax shelters for a group of 60 UK millionaires. He is also chair of BT and easyJet. Instead of being jailed, his *"illustrious"* career earned him a place on the Prime Minister's "business advisory group" and a knighthood.

In a blatant attempt to steal corporate domiciles from other OECD countries, Osborne reduced UK corporation tax to the lowest of any western major economy. This creates an international race to the bottom and encourages global TNCs to buy-up UK corporations in order that they can base their HQ here to benefit from the lower taxes. It also fleeces workers in other countries as their governments react to protect their own corporate tax bases by reducing their own corporate tax rates and either raising rates for workers or cutting services to compensate for the resultant losses in revenues. Osborne calls it a *"competitive corporate tax rate"*. The logical conclusion of such a *"competition"* is a zero corporate tax rate in all countries, with corporations paying no taxes. Osborne's reductions in the corporate tax rates will transfer a mouth-watering extra £60 billion to corporate coffers from ordinary UK workers and welfare recipients over the next ten years. In 2014, Labour also promised to undercut all other OECD countries' corporate taxes.

Embedded corporate "advisors" in the Treasury have managed, despite widespread public protests about corporate tax avoidance, to make it even easier for UK corporations to use offshore tax-minimisation scams. Osborne changed the rules for what the jargon calls "Controlled Foreign Companies" that is, corporate subsidiaries based in tax-havens, so that many of their activities now become literally tax-free and in addition has reduced the headline tax rate for profits based in such locations to a token 5%.

Osborne invited the representatives of 30 large corporations with 3,000 tax-haven subsidiaries to advise him on drawing up the new rules. Action Aid believes the new rules further facilitate the rip-off of third-world countries' corporate tax bases. They estimate another £4 billion pounds in taxes will be lost from these countries via these tax-haven based corporate subsidiaries.

Instead of tackling the conflict of interest at the heart of the Big-Four auditing monopoly, Cameron is extending it into local government where, outrageously, he is abolishing the state supervisor of local government financial probity, The Audit Commission. Local councils will now select their own financial auditors, most of whom will come from the Big Four. This means, in future, that if a local citizen wants to refer a deal like the Heygate land-sale to the local auditor, instead of an independent auditor appointed by the Audit Commission, they will be dealing with the auditor picked by the local council, who will have a vested financial interest in ignoring their complaint.

Polly Toynbee, in the Guardian in February 2013, outlined another nice earner for KPMG. KMPG seconded their tax adviser Jonathan Bridges to the Treasury to help draw up a new tax regime for patents, which was called The Patent Box. The new regime reduced taxes not only on new patents but on the whole product, even if the patent is only for a tiny widget within it. Bridges then returned to KPMG where it used him to promote this new tax loophole to its clients on its website. The Treasury has estimated that this loophole will lose yet another £1.1 billion in UK taxes. Would you not love to be in the Treasury writing the tax rules that potentially benefit your company's lucrative clients?

It is clear that the Revolving Door and Corporate Regulatory Capture are a disaster for UK workers and our democracy. The loss of an independent civil service is equally disastrous. It is crucial for the future protection of the economy that the stranglehold that the banks and financial institutions have over government policy and its regulatory systems needs to be broken. Nothing less than a complete separation of powers between the banking and political systems will protect us from repeated destructive banking collapses. And, finally, the oligopoly represented by the Big Four auditing/consulting corporations needs to be broken up before it consumes what remains of our government's policy-making systems.

Chapter 11

The European & American Bordellos

In a globalised world, actions taken by the US and EU have a profound effect on the UK's environment, taxes, economy and military. For example, let us look at the climate crises and 9/11. Due to intense lobbying, President Obama has failed to get any carbon-reduction legislation through Congress, which placed him in an impossible situation at global climate conferences. The Republican veto on US legislation meant the rest of the world refused to agree any substantive actions at the crucial Copenhagen climate summit. This destroyed one of the last windows of opportunity to avoid the threatened eco-system Armageddon, which in the UK would lead to rising sea levels causing irreversible flooding of vast tracts of land, cities and even coastal nuclear power stations.

The US's response to the 9/11 attacks have also had a profound impact on the UK. It invaded and toppled the government of Afghanistan, where Al Qaeda had a training camp and also invaded Saddam Hussein's dictatorship in Iraq. The Blair government took the UK into both wars. In 2012, the government admitted that the Afghan War had cost the UK over £17 billion since 2001. The Iraq war had cost £9 billion. Over 600 soldiers had been killed. Over 600,000 Iraqis are estimated by The Lancet to have died violently in the war, millions lost their homes or fled as refugees and continue to do so over ten years later, as the resulting horrific civil war continues with the barbaric Islamic State filling the power vacuum left by the destruction of Iraq's army, government and civil service by the US/UK. In addition, large numbers of Iraqi, Afghan and UK soldiers have been killed or maimed physically and psychologically for life.

Let us be clear:

- The Iraqi government had absolutely nothing to do with 9/11.
- The Iraq invasion had absolutely nothing to do with Al Qaeda.
- There were absolutely no weapons of mass destruction in Iraq.

Saddam Hussein's regime was secular and was opposed by Islamic militants. But there was a clear connection between US oil corporations and the US Presidential decision to invade Iraq. Iraq has the world's third largest proven oil reserves. Two

Chapter 11

overlapping groups dominated the George W Bush presidency. They were the oil industry and the Neo-Conservatives, many of whom were members of The Project for a New American Century (PNAC) think-tank. PNAC's funding came from foundations with direct links to US arms-manufacturing and the oil corporations.

The following Bush administration members were PNAC supporters:

- Dick Cheney, US Vice President
- Donald Rumsfeld, Secretary of State for Defence
- Paul Wolfowitz, Deputy Secretary of State for Defence
- Richard Perle, Chair Defence Board Policy Advisory Committee
- Richard Armitage, Deputy Secretary of State
- Robert Zoellick, US Trade Representative
- John Bolton, Under Secretary of State for Arms Control
- Peter Rodham, Assistant Secretary of Defence for International Security
- Paula Dobriansky, Under Secretary of State for Global Affairs
- Elliott Abrams, Assistant to the President for International Operations
- Lewis Libby, Assistant to the Vice President on National Security Affairs

The following Bush administration members had oil industry connections:

- George W Bush, US President, former Chair of Spectrum 7 (oil).
- Dick Cheney, US Vice President, former CEO Halliburton (world's largest oil-services corporation).
- Condoleezza Rice, US National Security Adviser, ex-Chevron Oil board.
- Donald Evans, US Commerce Secretary, ex-CEO Tom Brown Inc (oil and gas)
- George Bush Snr., former US President and father of George W, made millions from the Texas oil corporation Pennzoil.
- Six of the top ten political donations to George W Bush's election campaign came from the oil industry.

Prior to 9/11, PNAC had not made a secret of their desire for regime change in Iraq. In a public letter to President Clinton in 1998, they urged the removal of Saddam, due to the threat they claimed he posed to oil supplies. So when I was personally urging Lib Dem leader Charles Kennedy to address the oil link when he spoke to the millions on the UK Peace March, it was absolutely valid. But the billionaire-media can make rock-solid facts appear extreme, when made by anti-war campaigners. Paul Wolfowitz and Donald Rumsfeld are quoted in John Kampfer's book *"Blair's Wars"* as proposing invading Iraq as well as Afghanistan, at the very first meeting of the US National Security Council on 9/11 itself! Thus the corporate capture of the Bush administration, led to the UK joining the invasion, to advance the interests of American oil corporations.

In 1997, despite the Democratic President Clinton having signed the Kyoto International Treaty on Climate Change, the Democrat controlled Senate, rejected it. This was despite its cumbersome market-based carbon-trading system having been specifically adopted at America's request and a large majority of Americans (68%) believing that global warming posed a serious threat to their way of life within their lifetimes, according to a Gallup Poll. Between 1990 and 2000 the oil industry spent a whopping $122 million on political donations. Millions more were poured into lobbying Congressional by oil corporations such as Exxon and by the American Petroleum Institute (API). Millions more were lavished on the previously mentioned PR campaigns aimed at frightening the public about Kyoto.

If any one person can be characterised to personify *The Prostitute State* it is Lee Raymond, who was CEO of Exxon Mobil, the world's largest oil corporation. During his chairmanship of API, through the 1990's, he masterminded the lobbying campaigns that ensured the US Senate scuppered any hope of an international treaty on climate change. Forbes reported that his retirement package alone was $321 million. If the scientific predictions, made in 2012, are true, that we may have passed the tipping points, making a global rise in temperatures of 6°C almost unstoppable, then this man will be one of those responsible for more human deaths, eco-systems destruction and financial ruin than almost anyone in history.

It is crucial therefore that we also understand how the corporate state manipulates the US government, due to its impacts on the UK. It has infected all the same pillars of their democracy, the political system, the media, the taxation system and academia. Money from the corporate state is drowning American democracy. A staggering $2.3 billion was spent on the 2012 presidential election. The Centre for Public Integrity reported that 149 super-rich donors each gave more than $500,000 each, raising $290 million. A total of $5.8 billion was spent on the combined Presidential, House and Senate elections!

The Massachusetts Senate race saw sitting Republican Senator Scott Brown and his successful Democratic challenger Elizabeth Warren, spend $76million. Brown raised only 16% of his funds from small donors, whereas Warren managed 44%. Brown's large donors came from corporate America and Wall Street including PWC and Goldman Sachs, whilst Warren's were hospitals, universities and the grassroots campaign group Moveon.org (which is funded by small donations).

The money spent influencing US elections has exploded, since the so-called "Citizens United" case was won in the Supreme Court in 2010, to the fury of President Obama. The pseudo-grassroots group, Citizens United, was founded in 1988 with funding from the oil-billionaire Koch brothers. As well as seeking the destruction of campaign-finance reforms, it wants the US to withdraw from the

United Nations and to block the International Criminal Court. The court ruling overturned a century of democratic legislation limiting the influence of big money and opened the floodgates for the ultra-rich to buy even more of American government. In the 2012 election, over 90% of donations came from the richest 1% of Americans. Over a quarter of all political donations came from just 31,385 people. That is less than 1% of 1% of the US population! And those who pay the piper call the tune. Members of congress, instead of being legislators, are now basically full-time fundraisers. This means that the 1% get almost unlimited access to the candidates at endless fundraising dinners, receptions and meetings. And with that access they get to influence their decisions. If a candidate's major donors come from Wall Street, then they are unlikely to curb Wall Street's greed when elected.

Mitt Romney, the losing 2012 Republican candidate, is another classic exemplar of *The US Prostitute State*. All of Romney's top donors came from the banks and Wall Street institutions responsible for the 2008 financial collapse. He is the son of the former Michigan Governor and Chair of American Motors, George Romney. After attending Harvard Business School, he set up Bain Capital which became one of the US's largest private equity firms. It specialised in vulture-capitalism type leveraged buyouts.

This involves private equity firms using a small amount of their own capital to borrow massive amounts from investment banks such as Goldman Sachs, to buy out existing companies. This is done either aggressively against the company's wishes or by ensuring their consent, by promising large bonuses to the company's existing senior executives. The debt incurred in buying the company is then added to the purchased company's balance sheet. This often tips a profitable company into losses due to the interest payments on the private equity firm's debt. To maintain these interest payments the vulture capitalists then provide advice to the victim company on how to slash staff benefits, fire long-serving staff, destroy their trade unions or ship the jobs offshore.

Huge multi-million-dollar management fees are then charged by the vulture capitalists for this "advice" on how to service the debt that *their* takeover had saddled the company with. They often force the victim company to take out huge loans to pay the vulture capitalists massive unearned dividends. This was done to Dunkin Donuts, which was forced to borrow $1.2 billon to fund a cash dividend to the private equity firms which had captured it. This nasty smash and grab on companies is branded as *"dividend recapitalisation"*. The victim companies often go bankrupt and employees regularly get zero severance pay, even though they may have helped build it from scratch for their entire working lives. Meanwhile vulture capitalists make off with up to 1,000% profits on their original investment.

KB Toys provides another horrible example. In 2012, Rolling Stone reported that Bain used just $18 million of their own capital, to borrow $302 million from

Wall Street to buy KB Toys. Under Bain, KB Toys then redeemed $121 million dollars of stock and took out a $66 million bank loan. This funded an $83million dividend payment to Bain, which went to Romney and other Bain Capital owners. KB Toys soon went into bankruptcy but Bain had made a return of 370% on its $18 million "investment". The employees, many of whom had worked over 40 years for the company, got zero severance-pay.

This vulture capitalism is facilitated by the US government, which allows the interest on the capital borrowed to be set against their taxes. Thus the American taxpayer is helping to destroy millions of US jobs and enabling vulture capitalists to make billions of dollars at workers' expense. Even worse, taxes on private-equity profits are charged at half the rate on normal corporate profits. These Wall Street and private-equity barons are major political donors. This ensures that the rapacious preferential tax treatment remains in place. Whilst Obama did try to stop it, the Republicans vetoed his attempt.

Romney's fortune was estimated, in 2012, to be over $240 million but his tax rate was estimated to be 14% or half what middle-class Americans pay on wages that are a fraction of his. He also uses the usual plethora of labyrinthine financial instruments and tax-havens to manage his wealth. There is no evidence that any of these are illegal but their advantages are not available to the average salaried worker.

Some of Mitt Romney's revealed legal shenanigans included:

- An unknown amount of Romney's wealth is invested in his shell company called Sankaty High Yield Asset Investors in Bermuda.
- His wife Anne held $3 million in an offshore Swiss UBS bank account.
- Whilst Romney was CEO of Bain Capital, profits from the $960 million Italian Yellow Pages (of which $50 million was estimated to be Romney's) went through Luxembourg.
- In 2009 whilst Romney was a board member, the Marriott chain funnelled $200 million dollars into Luxembourg, paying a corporate tax rate of 16.9% compared to the US 30%.
- He has nearly $30 million invested in 12 different Bain accounts in the Cayman Islands.
- He has $87 million stashed in his tax-free Individual Retirement Account despite a limit of $30,000 in contributions to such accounts per annum, through a range of complex financial manoeuvres.
- As a partner in Bain Capital, the payments he receives for Bain managing investors' funds (usually a cut of 30% of annual profits generated) are declared as "carried interest" and so taxed as investment (15%) rather than

earned income (35%). There are no Medicare or Social Welfare taxes on this income, unlike salaried workers.

- His wife's blind trust charges a Bain fund in the Cayman Islands "carried interest" for "performing services".
- Romney placed up to $100 million in a family trust fund, which is not included in his declared worth of $240 million. If given directly to his children it would have incurred a gift-tax of up to $29 million but none was paid on the trust fund. It alternatively avoids inheritance taxes of up to $31 million.
- In a gloriously ironic phrase, he uses an "intentionally defective grantor trust" which means he pays the low capital gains taxes due on profits made by the family trust himself personally, which enables more money to accumulate in the fund, free of the higher gift-tax,.

The collapse in corporation taxes due to offshore tax avoidance has contributed to the enormous $16 trillion deficit accumulated by the US government, along with the unfunded wars in Iraq and Afghanistan and the Bush tax cuts for the rich. These corporate-created national debts are now being paid for by cuts to benefit programmes for the less-well-off. The offshore billions could fund a Keynesian stimulus to help get millions back into work and transform the US into a renewable-energy economy.

The following figures demonstrate the size and power of *The US Tax Haven Pillar*:

- **$100 Billion:** Amount the Senate Subcommittee on Investigations, in 2008, estimated that the U.S. loses in taxes due to offshore tax abuse every year.
- **759:** Number of offshore subsidiaries in tax-havens for just the three major US banks, Citigroup, Bank of America and Morgan Stanley combined.
- **83:** Number of the 100 largest U.S. companies that use offshore tax-havens.
- **6.6%:** Corporate share of US taxes in 2009 compared to 30% in the 1950's!
- **$0.00:** Amount of US corporation tax paid by General Electric between 2006 and 2011, despite making US profits of $26 billion. They even demanded a tax refund of $4.1 billion dollars.

In addition to offshore tax-havens, corporate America, through the usual political machinations, has created its own onshore tax-haven in the small Democrat-controlled state of Delaware. A staggering 64% of publicly-traded U.S. parent companies are now incorporated in Delaware. One house on Orange Street, Wilmington, houses over 217,000 company headquarters, demonstrating what a farce the tax-haven scam is.

General Electric (GE) provides a good example of the Revolving Door in the US. It employs nearly a thousand people in its tax department which, the New York Times reported in 2011, devotes half its time to ensuring tax compliance and the rest to seeking means of avoiding taxation. Their head of taxation is John Samuels who is the former Tax Legislative Counsel for the US Treasury Department. GE's tax department is packed with former officials from the Internal Revenue Service and tax-setting Congressional committees.

The NY Times reported that GE alone had spent a staggering $200 million dollars on US political lobbying in the past decade, which it credits with getting it billions of dollars' worth of tax credits. GE moved vast swathes of its former US profits into offshore low-tax jurisdictions. They moved thousands of jobs out of America also. When one of their most lucrative tax credits was under threat from the congressional Ways and Means Committee, its chair, Rep Charlie Rangel's, school district received an $11 million donation from GE, just a month after he abandoned his opposition to the tax break.

I had a small run-in with GE's lobbyists in the UK myself. One of them rang and asked if, as an environmental writer, I would endorse one of their energy-efficient products. I declined, as I did not have the technical tools to judge whether their claims were correct or not. He contacted me a number of times and in the end got quite aggressive, as if offended that anyone could have the cheek to turn down his corporate dollar. In an echo of UK Prime-Minister David Cameron's appointment of arch tax-avoider Philip Green, to advise him on UK government spending, unbelievably Jeffrey Immelt, Chair of GE, was appointed by President Obama, in 2009, to be chair of The President's Council on Jobs and US Competitiveness.

In the US, senior civil-service posts are political and so generally change with each election. This disastrously legitimises their Revolving Door in a way that is only just beginning in the UK and brings many opportunities for regulatory capture. The GM corporate giant Monsanto hires numerous former government officials as lobbyists and also has former employees embedded right across the top of the US Government, including even a former Monsanto lawyer on the Supreme Court. The following list of Obama Administration officials with links to Monsanto gives an idea of the power the pro-GM Foods lobby has at the heart of the US government, whose embassies promote their interests all over the world, as was revealed by Wikileaks:

Michael Taylor: Formerly Monsanto's Vice President for Policy, he was appointed Deputy Commissioner for Foods of the Federal Drugs Agency. This includes responsibility for food labelling. Monsanto opposes the labelling of GM Foods which would allow consumers to know that they were eating GM products.

Chapter 11

Hillary Clinton: The former Secretary of State's Election Campaign Head was Mark Penn, CEO of one of Monsanto's main lobbying firms, Burson-Marsteller. Her former employer, the Rose Law Firm, was Monsanto's law firm.

Lidia Watrud: Formerly Monsanto's Director for New Technologies, she was appointed to the Environment Protection Agency and US Department of Agriculture.

Roger Beachey: Formerly Director of Monsanto's Danforth Centre, he was appointed Director US Department of Agriculture.

Islam Siddiqi: Formerly a Monsanto lobbyist, he was appointed Obama's Agricultural Negotiations Trade Representative.

A similar Monsanto cohort was present in both the George W Bush and Clinton administrations. So there is not much chance of the US joining the EU in banning Monsanto's GM-contaminated foods during the remaining Obama Presidency or indeed under a possible Hillary Clinton Presidency. The system of political appointments to head government departments also operates at State level where the corporate state often has a field day. In 2013, the Portland Press Herald ran a report detailing how the lobbyist Patricia Aho had been appointed to head the State of Maine's Department of Environmental Protection by the Tea Party Republican Governor Paul LePage. The newspaper listed a slew of government programmes and legislation that corporations had previously hired her to lobby against, which she proceeded to block once appointed. These included lifting ban on toxic chemicals in children's toys, scrapping recycling programmes and slashing enforcement actions on big developers. As the paper put it, the fox again had truly been put in charge of the henhouse.

Like in the UK, the US media market is fast being concentrated in the hands of a small number of vast media corporations, including Rupert Murdoch's News Corporation. In 1983, fifty companies owned 90% of the American media. By 2012, that 90% was controlled by just six corporations: GE, News Corp., Disney, Viacom, Time Warner and CBS. Note GE's domination of yet another pillar of the corporate state. In 2014, Murdoch's News Corps attempted to take over Time Warner.

Despite this overwhelming concentration of media power, in 2013 the corporations sought a similar further concentration of power, to that nearly acquired by Rupert Murdoch in the UK with his BSkyB bid. They lobbied the Federal Communications Committee (FCC) to abolish rules preventing TV corporations from owning all the newspapers in specific regions of the US. The Obama-appointed chair of the FCC Julius Genachowski announced his support for the abolition of such limits and wanted to abolish public consultation on any proposed relaxation of the regulations. Genachowski is another US example of the Revolving Door. He is credited with the founding of Fox Television. This brazen grab for what is left of a free press in the US, by a handful of extremely rich US media barons, has been strongly criticised by the courageous independent Senator from Vermont, Bernie Sanders.

The US political-lobbying industry is the largest in the world. A CBS report in 2012 estimated that it spent $9 billion dollars per annum and employed over 100,000 people. That works out at about 186 lobbyists working full-time to influence each of the 535 US Senators and Representatives! Lobbying is the third largest industry in Washington DC. An Elect Democracy survey in 2012 reported that the Finance Sector alone has spent $4.2 billion on lobbying since 2006 and employed 18,000 full-time lobbyists on the task! The same links between ex-politicians and corporate lobbying exist in the US as they do in the UK. Think Progress reported in 2006 that there were 248 former senators, congress members and heads of federal agencies working as professional lobbyists, as well as over 2,000 ex-senior government officials.

A study by Public Citizen found that an astonishing 43% of Members of Congress, who left between 1998 and 2005, had registered as lobbyists.

Former members of congress are allowed continued access to Congressional gyms, dining rooms and floors of the chambers. They are only barred from direct lobbying of existing elected members for two years. That does not block them from lucrative lobbying posts immediately after they leave Congress, as all the ban means is that they themselves are not allowed to talk directly to congress members. The hiring also extends to the Senators' staff. Jailed US political lobbyist, Jack Abramoff, explained how he captured entire congressional members' offices for his lobbying interests, by simply mentioning that they could come and work for him when they were finished in Congress.

Former Governor and Republican presidential candidate, Tim Pawlenty, is now a senior financial lobbyist as head of the Financial Services Roundtable. This lobbies on behalf of financial institutions such as JP Morgan, which manages $780 billion worth of assets and has revenues of over $26 billion. Senator Bob Bennett (R), who was a member of the Senate Banking Committee until 2010, set up a lobbying company immediately after leaving Congress, which was paid to lobby against the banking reforms proposed after the 2008 banking meltdown.

Another recent Republican Presidential candidate and House Speaker, Newt Gingrich, was reported by Bloomberg in 2011 to have been paid over $1.8 million for consulting services by the financial services giant Freddie Mac. And former House Majority Leader Dick Armey (R) worked for DLA Piper (the same transatlantic lobbying firm as Lib Dem Treasurer Tim Clement-Jones). Armey later helped found the right-wing "think tank" Freedom Works, which was a successor to the Koch brothers-funded, Citizens for a Sound Economy (CSE), by whom he was paid an annual fee of $500,000. He hit the headlines in 2012 for a reported $8 million dollar payoff from Freedom Works. CSE was infamous for its opposition to US government action on acid raid ("*largely non-existent*") and the climate crisis ("*a verdict in search of evidence*").

In 2013, Dr Robert Brulle, a sociologist at Drexel University in Philadelphia, estimated that over the past decade, about $500m has been given to US organisations and think tanks devoted to undermining the science of climate change, most of it anonymously. This is just a tiny taste of the US political/lobbying industrial complex, which just as it has in the UK, has sunk its tentacles deep into the US government, to the detriment not only of the US but of the wider world including the UK.

In one aspect however, the US *Prostitute State* currently differs markedly from the UK. It is the extraordinary conspiracy by the two oil multi-billionaire Koch brothers, to hijack the US democratic state for their extreme right-wing libertarian nightmare vision for America. Through a plethora of think tanks, pseudo-grassroots front-groups and millions poured into lobbying, political donations and special-interest groups over decades, they have set out to usurp US democracy and replace it with their own far-right oligarchy.

The Koch conspiracy involves three clear tactics:

- **Establish the freedom to pour unlimited money from corporations like theirs into political campaigning.**
  To do this they needed to destroy the state and federal campaign laws seeking to prevent elections being bought by the ultra-rich. As mentioned, this was achieved by the Citizens United Supreme Court victory, which ruled corporations could spend unlimited amounts advocating the election or defeat of specific candidates.

- **Destroy the Democrats' main source of political funding.**
  Whilst traditionally Republicans have been funded by corporations and billionaires, the Democrats' largest donors have been the public-service trade unions. If a trade union has no negotiating rights, its members will leave. The Koch's have already destroyed public-sector trade union negotiating rights in numerous Republican-controlled states. When membership falls, political donations to the Democrats collapse also.

- **Block the Democrats' natural supporters from voting.**
   This is being done through a plethora of voter suppression laws being passed in Republican-held states which block the ability of students, poor people and ethnic-minority voters to vote.

In 2013, the Koch brothers were reported to be attempting to buy a string of major newspapers across the US. These included the LA Times, Chicago Tribune, Baltimore Sun and the Orlando Sentinel. Thus, their conspiracy is widening to include the domination of the press.

Parallel and entwined in the Koch conspiracy, has been a wider plot by corporate America to hijack the US democratic state. In July 2011, the Campaign for Media & Democracy launched a spectacular report about the American Legislative Exchange Council (ALEC), which is an alliance of a wide range of American (and UK) Corporations with over 2,000 right-wing Republican state legislators. They were drawing up literally hundreds of bills which promoted their corporate interests at state level. Significant numbers of bills had already been passed by state legislatures across the US, without the public having any idea that these laws were drawn up by corporate lobbyists in tandem with Republican politicians. The information released by an ALEC whistle-blower included the details of over 800 laws secretively submitted to state legislatures that had been drafted by ALEC, which was inspired, frequently chaired and significantly funded by the Koch brothers.

Nine ALEC working parties secretly drew up and voted on draft right-wing legislation that affected every aspect of voters' lives, from maximising profits for private health-care corporations to the destruction of local pollution protections. Once drafted and passed by ALEC, the legislators according to its membership rules then had a "duty" to seek to have the legislation passed in their state legislatures. Particularly pernicious examples of ALEC-drafted legislation are the so called Ag-Gag laws. These have already been passed in eight states and "*prohibit a person from entering onto a farm or photographing or video recording a farm without the owner's written consent*". They therefore criminalise animal-rights activists exposing industrial farm cruelty. ALEC is also working to get anti-renewable energy legislation passed across the states, in order to protect the oil and coal corporations' profits.

In addition to maximising corporate greed, the conspiracy included a cold-blooded determination to undermine US democracy. Legislation drawn up by the ALEC working party on "*democracy and voters rights*", (i.e. the suppression of democracy and voters rights!) and passed by numerous states, is successfully suppressing the ability of millions of Democrat voters to vote. These laws cut polling hours and days, cut access to postal ballots, eliminated weekend and reduced evening voting, when black churches and those in full-time employment traditionally voted and introduced requirements for voter IDs, that the poor, elderly and many minorities do not hold or are expensive to acquire such as gun licences, driving licences and passports, whilst banning student IDs.

The whistle-blower revealed the list of global consumer brands involved in this corruption. Almost every time a US citizen bought their groceries or filled their gas tanks, they were directly funding ALEC's attacks on their own voting rights. Their shopping pays for the lobbyists drafting legislation maximising corporate wealth at the expense of their family's health, government services and environment!

Corporations supporting ALEC at the time the scandal was exposed included Coca Cola, Wal-Mart (owners of ASDA in the UK), Pfizer Pharmaceuticals, Koch Industries, Kraft Foods (owners of Cadbury's in UK) , Amazon, Johnson & Johnson, General Motors, AT&T, Bayer, United Parcel Services, American Express, AOL, Astra Zeneca, BP, Chrysler, Dell, eBay, ExxonMobil, Ford Motors, Fruit of the Loom, General Electric, Hewlett Packard, Mars (Inc.), Microsoft, Monsanto, Nestlé, Pepsi-Cola, Philip Morris Tobacco, Procter & Gamble, T-Mobile, Time Warner, Visa, Yahoo and Zurich Insurance. The UK-based multinationals who were members of ALEC included Shell, BP, Diageo (owner of Guinness etc.) and GlaxoSmithKline. UK consumers would be horrified to know their shopping was funding attacks on black voting rights and destroying environmental legislation in the US.

Having described how *The Prostitute State* operates in the US, let us look at the European Union. The EU has been one of the most successful democratic experiments in peaceful supra-national co-operation in humanity's history. Its contribution to peace was marked by the Nobel Peace Prize in 2012. Its 500 million citizens elect the European Parliament and its other two democratic pillars consist of the European Council, made up of the elected prime-ministers from all of the member states and the executive, which is called the European Commission. Commissioners are appointed by their country's elected Prime Ministers. EU legislation is the second largest source of democratic law and regulations in the UK after Westminster. For example, many environmental issues have to be tackled at EU level, due to the cross-border effects of air and water pollution and the export of goods to other EU members.

A letter to the Guardian in 2013 summed up nicely some of the EU's achievements to date:

"What did the EEC/EU ever do for us? Not much, apart from: providing 57% of our trade; structural funding to areas hit by industrial decline; clean beaches and rivers; cleaner air; lead free petrol; restrictions on landfill dumping; a recycling

culture; cheaper mobile charges; cheaper air travel; improved consumer protection and food labelling; a ban on growth hormones and other harmful food additives; better product safety; single market competition bringing quality improvements and better industrial performance; break up of monopolies; Europe-wide patent and copyright protection; no paperwork or customs for exports throughout the single market; price transparency and removal of commission on currency exchanges across the Eurozone; freedom to travel, live and work across Europe; funded opportunities for young people to undertake study or work placements abroad; access to European health services; labour protection and enhanced social welfare; smoke-free workplaces; equal pay legislation; holiday entitlement; the right not to work more than a 48-hour week without overtime; strongest wildlife protection in the world; improved animal welfare in food production; EU-funded research and industrial collaboration; EU representation in international forums; bloc EEA negotiation at the WTO; EU diplomatic efforts to uphold the nuclear non-proliferation treaty; European arrest warrant; cross border policing to combat human trafficking, arms and drug smuggling; counter terrorism intelligence; European civil and military co-operation in post-conflict zones in Europe and Africa; support for democracy and human rights across Europe and beyond; investment across Europe contributing to better living standards and educational, social and cultural capital.

All of this is nothing compared with its greatest achievements: the EU has for 60 years been the foundation of peace between European neighbours after centuries of bloodshed. It furthermore assisted the extraordinary political, social and economic transformation of 13 former dictatorships, now EU members, since 1980. Now the union faces major challenges brought on by neoliberal economic globalisation and worsened by its own systemic weaknesses. It is taking measures to overcome these. We in the UK should reflect on whether our net contribution of £7bn out of total government expenditure of £695bn is good value. We must play a full part in enabling the union to be a force for good in a multi-polar global future.

Simon Sweeney,
Lecturer in international political economy, University of York"

My only personal experience of the EU institutions came from running some EU programmes, which were crucial to the funding of many local support agencies, when I was the manager of the Islington Chamber of Commerce. Although I was elected to be a Liberal Democrat European Parliamentary candidate for London for the 2004 elections, I withdrew to concentrate on other campaigns. I personally knew quite a few of the Lib Dem MEPs, nearly all of whom were decent hard-working democrats.

Chapter 11

To a certain extent, the corporate state has captured the EU's institutions, but not to the same degree as in the UK and US. One of the main reasons for this is that there is not the equivalent yet of a Europe-wide popular media for it to capture. It has however an iron grip on many EU individual states' media. Italy is in an even worse state than Britain, with just one multi-billionaire, Silvio Berlusconi (net worth $9 billion), who dominated Italy's media landscape and used that power to be elected Prime Minister repeatedly. Although, very worryingly, the Murdoch dominated BSkyB started putting together a $10 billion pan-European pay-tv network in 2014.

However, the corporate state has managed to infiltrate the specialist Europe-wide trade magazines which depend for content on corporate PR and lobbying machines. As these specialist EU journals are read by key EU decision-makers, this enables undue corporate influence on decision-making.

The European Union of Journalists passed a motion at their Annual Delegate Meeting stating:

"This ADM is concerned that some industry lobbyists target EU specialist-media with financial sponsorship in order to shape the presentation of policy debate in their interests. This ADM is concerned that some of these specialist media are so financially over-dependent on lobby groups that there is a lack of transparency on lobbyists' relations with media and that journalists are unduly pressured to serve lobby interests."

Whilst the EU has many large global corporations, due to the varying national political cultures, they have been unable to capture yet the European political classes to the same extent as they have in the UK or US. This means the EU can sometimes be a positive brake on the corporate bullying of the individual EU states. Indeed, the EU is one of the few global democratic institutions large enough to take on the corporations and occasionally win victories on behalf of the interests of the EU's citizens. This ability however is now being put at risk by the truly dangerous Transatlantic Trade and Investment Partnership (TTIP) proposals to give corporations the power to sue governments over legislative impacts on their profits.

To counteract this European democracy, in addition to seeking the passage of TTIP, corporations fund a massive political-lobbying operation in Brussels, the EU's capital. This lobbying industry is the largest in the world after the US. Corporate Europe Observatory (CEO) estimated in 2011, that there were between 15,000 and 30,000 professionals lobbying the EU institutions. This means there are up to 40 lobbyists for each elected MEP or nearly the same number of lobbyists as bureaucrats working for the EU's small bureaucracy, which despite its immense pan-continental responsibilities, employs only 31,000 staff. To put this in perspective, the city of Birmingham in the UK employed 35,000 staff in 2010 and there are about 2.9 million federal civil servants in the US. EU corporate lobbyists outnumber civil-society lobbyists by a factor of over 5:1 and civil-society lobbyists have only a tiny fraction of the almost unlimited financial resources that corporations are throwing at EU lobbying.

The corporate state has also not been able to capture the pan-European parliamentary electoral process, by funding campaigns or political parties in the same way as it has in the UK or US. It has however been more successful at capturing ex-politicians to work as lucratively paid EU lobbyists. It is estimated that former MEPs can get paid about €500 per hour, putting their expertise, knowledge and contacts gained as our elected representatives at the service of the corporate state.

Some infamous examples include John Bruton, the former Irish Prime-Minister and member of the EU Council of Ministers, who became head of the financial lobbying firm International Financial Services Centre and also joined EU lobbying firm Cabinet DN. EU Commissioners, like former US Secretaries of State and UK Ministers, are prime targets for the lobbying firms. A staggering thirteen out of the last Commission of twenty-seven became lobbyists. The Enterprise Commissioner Gunter Verheugen set up his own lobbying company immediately upon retirement. The commissioner who was responsible for overseeing single-market financial regulation, Charlie McCreevy, now earns a lucrative income providing political expertise to corporations including Bank of New York Mellon, Ryanair and Sports Direct.

Former MEP Pat Cox was the first Irishman to be elected President of the European Parliament, from 2004 to 2006. After his retirement, Cox sadly sold out by working for the lobbying conglomerate APCO, whose clients included Microsoft, Michelin and Pfizer. In a study of three Brussels lobbying corporations, The Alliance for Lobbying Transparency and Ethics Regulation in the EU (ALTER) found that 73% percent of their staff had previously worked for EU institutions, including 6 former MEPs.

As in the UK, the corporate state does not always wait until politicians leave their EU elected posts to sink its tentacles in. In a notorious case, the Tory MEP Giles Chichester, in 2013, whilst serving as Vice President of the European Parliament and leader of the Tory MEPs, was also President of the European Energy Forum, the pan-European lobby for the nuclear, gas and oil industries. Unsurprisingly, he is a climate sceptic and has no compunction about serving fossil-fuel corporations rather than protecting his constituents from the devastating effects of the climate crises.

Chapter 11

Another example was the Chair of the Committee responsible for oversight of the financial services industry, French Socialist MEP Pervenche Berès, who was simultaneously a member of the Financial Services Forum, the industry body responsible for lobbying his own committee. The right-wing Finnish MEP Piia-Noora Kauppi served on the Economic Affairs Committee from 1999 to 2009 with responsibility for regulating the financial services industry, but also served as President of the EU financial lobby group EPFSF. For this she won the Worst Conflict of Interest Award at the 2008 Worst EU Lobbying Awards.

Peter Mandelson was rewarded by Tony Blair, with the appointment to be the powerful EU Trade Commissioner, after he had to resign in disgrace from the UK cabinet for the second time following a second financial scandal. Mandelson, famous for his friendships with the world's mega-rich, signed the decision to lift import tariffs for Rusal, the aluminium giant owned by his friend and Russian oligarch Oleg Deripaska. In 2007, Mandelson was nominated for the Worst EU Lobbying Award for Privileged Access. In 2010, he set up his own political lobbying firm advising corporate European clients on EU regulatory and legislative processes. Mandelson is famous for saying Labour was *"intensely relaxed about people getting filthy rich, as long as they pay their taxes"* but that caveat does not seem to preclude accepting the backing of Martin Sorrell's tax-avoiding WPP for his lobbying operation.

His extensive contact list and knowledge of both EU and UK legislative processes makes him a very attractive servant for the corporate state. We do not know what clients Mandelson advised, as he avoided House of Lords transparency rules by describing what he does as *"strategic-advice"* rather than lobbying. The Lords has changed the rules to try to close this loophole. In addition to setting up his lobbying company, he is also now Chair of Lazard International (a financial advice corporation).

Unlike MPs, Members of the Lords, bizarrely, do not have to declare the amounts that they are paid by outside interests. However the Telegraph in 2012 estimated that he had earned £1 million from his role at Lazard, his lobbying consultancy had earned £600,000 in its first year and his speaking and writing engagements had earned another £375,000. Mandelson's cashing in on his EU and UK government expertise has enabled him to move into a luxury £8 million home.

The EU's Revolving Door is as well-oiled as its counterparts in the UK and US. In 2011, ALTER published this summary of senior European Union civil servants and regulators who had moved directly from their EU posts into lucrative EU corporate lobbying posts:

Name/EU Role	Corporate Role
Peter Carl Mogens Director General, Environment	Adviser: Kreab Gaving Anderson (Lobbying Corporation)
Jean de Froidville Adviser, Competition Commissioner	Associate Director Competition: Interel (Lobbying Corporation)
John Richardson Top Executive, Maritime Directorate	Adviser Maritime Policy: FIPRA (Lobbying Corporation)
Derek Taylor Energy Adviser, EU Commission	Energy Adviser: Burson-Marsteller (Lobbying Corporation)
Suzy Renckens Head, GMO Panel European Food Safety Authority	Head of Biotechnology (GM) Regulatory Affairs Syngenta (GMO Seed Corporation)
Thomas Lonngren Director: European Medicines Agency	Founded: Pharma Executive Consulting (Medicine lobbying company) Also Senior Adviser: NDA Group (Pharmaceutical Lobbying Corporation)
Jean-Paul Mingasson Director-General, Enterprise & Industry	Adviser: Business Europe (Pan-Europe Business Federation)
Diana Banati Chair, European Food Standards Agency	Chief Executive International Life Sciences Institute (Biotech Lobbyists)

Thus, the EU Revolving Door provides a steady supply of gamekeepers turned poachers. Their insider knowledge of the systems that they themselves set up, enables their new corporate employers, whether GM, food, pharmaceutical, nuclear, fossil fuel or chemical corporations to get past them. Only rarely do these senior former Eurocrats go to work for civil society, as it does not have the mega-euros that the corporate sector has to pay them.

Take the example of Suzy Renckens: she was in charge of protecting the EU's food supply from the dangers of GMO foods but was then hired by the GM corporation Syngenta, to lobby her own former department to permit Syngenta's GM food products! This hijacking of the democratic process makes people angry against the EU itself, when their real anger needs to be against the hijacking of EU civil servants by the corporate world. However, in the EU, the corporate state thankfully does not always win. The EU states voted to reject the appointment of Mella Frewen, an ex-Monsanto employee, to the Board of the European Food Standards Agency (The EU equivalent of the US FDA) when she was nominated in 2012. A real but invisible danger of the Revolving Door is the temptation for regulators still in EU employment, to adjust policies, in the light of the lucrative work they can obtain when they leave the EU civil service. It is crucial therefore in the interests of public faith in its institutions that the practice is halted.

The corruption of academia is also alive and well in Brussels. Corporations have sponsored a plethora of "think tanks", which just as they do in the UK and US, pose as serious sources of academic analysis, when often they are simply highly paid corporate lobbying fronts. A study by Notre Europe found that there were 149 think tanks operating on EU issues with 3,000 people employed.

I had a personal experience of EU lobbying, when I ended up in an online debate with a lobbyist from BASF, a pesticide corporation. We were discussing Neonicotinoids, the pesticides which scientists have identified as one of the causes of the disastrous rise in honey bee deaths and linked to an equally disastrous fall in a whole range of insects and through them bird-populations. The lobbyist claimed that there was no clear scientific evidence for this and a ban would be disastrous for farmers. I had read press reports that an *"independent report commissioned from the EU's Humboldt Forum for Food and Agriculture"* had warned of 20% losses in yields and costs in billions of euros for farmers if they were banned.

Smelling a rat, I had delved into the story. I discovered that the Forum was *not* an "EU" institution but a corporate think-tank with funding from the pesticide industry including BASF. Secondly, the report was not *"independent"*. It was funded by the Neonicotinoid manufacturers Syngenta and Bayer. And thirdly, the claimed losses were based on no pesticides being used, rather than alternatives used in Italy where an already existing ban had resulted in no massive losses for farmers. The lobbyist was a bit surprised at the speed at which I was able to demolish his case. But had I not been aware of how the media is manipulated, I would have been unable to refute his corporate arguments. Alan Day's study of European think tanks estimated that 45% are merely advocacy or lobbying fronts for specific ideologies or corporate interests, 38% carry out worthwhile academic studies, 10% are affiliated to political parties and 7% actually do genuine research.

The deceitful practice of naming right-wing think-tanks that block action on the climate crisis and other environmental emergencies, with deliberately pro-environment-sounding names has also crossed the Atlantic to the EU. The corporate think-tank International Policy Network's (IPN) associated Sustainable Development Network spends heavily on anti-environmental lobbying in Europe.

Their recent reports include attacks on green-jobs and EU GM food regulations. Brussels think-tanks were also used by fossil-fuel corporations such as ExxonMobil to funnel cash into promoting EU climate scepticism, as uncovered by a CEO report in 2006.

Fiona Hall, then UK Liberal Democrat MEP for the North-East, kindly agreed to be interviewed for this book. She had devoted a lot of time in the EU Parliament to tackling environmental issues, such as improving HGV safety regulations to help protect Europe's cyclists. She confirmed that former MEPs who had become corporate lobbyists do try to influence her. She gives them one meeting out of courtesy and then discounts the input if it appears inaccurate or biased. But it was her reply to my question about banning the Revolving Door, that is should it be illegal for former EU legislators to be hired as lucrative corporate lobbyists, which revealed the depth of the challenge to close it down.

She was opposed to a ban, as she herself hoped to work as a lobbyist, after she retired as an MEP, for environmental groups advocating greater environmental action by the EU. She understandably felt her expertise garnered as an MEP of long standing, would be invaluable to that effort. In other words, as she put it, if you ban former MEPS working for *"the bad guys"*, you also end up hurting *"the good guys"*. The problem with this is that the odds are nowhere near even. The funding available from *"the bad guys"* to hire EU politicians dwarfs that available to civil society and drowns out their voices. Hall is right to point out the difficulties in tackling lobbying corruption. One potential way round this objection would be to ban former EU officials from lobbying directly for corporations or for organisations largely funded by corporations.

Europe is likewise plagued to a certain extent by *The Thieving Tax-Haven Pillar*. In 2012, the EU Commission estimated that over €1 trillion were lost each year through criminal tax evasion and legal avoidance in the EU states. Like the UK's colonial tax-stealing havens, Europe has an additional handful of tiny feudal jurisdictions, which are exploited by ultra-rich Europeans for tax avoidance. These include Andorra, Lichtenstein, Monaco and San Marino. In addition, some EU governments have started passing corporate-inspired competitive taxation loopholes that are transforming these EU members themselves into *de facto* tax-havens. These include the UK, Ireland, Malta, Luxembourg and Austria.

The use by Europe's rich elites of these tax-havens significantly contributed to the economic crises in a number of Eurozone countries including Greece, Italy and Spain. Italy lost 12% and Spain 8% of their GDP in unpaid taxes in 2010. If the rich refuse to pay their taxes, you cannot fund a liberal democracy without going bankrupt. Switzerland's notorious bank secrecy laws facilitate the robbing of taxes from countries across the EU, even though Switzerland itself is not an EU member.

Chapter 11

The grip *The Tax Haven Pillar* had on the political classes in Greece, burst into the open with the Lagarde List scandal in 2010. This list was provided by then French Minister and now Managing Director of the IMF Christine Lagarde to the Greek government. It contained a list of rich Greek citizens using Swiss banks for tax evasion. The list included a number of relatives of senior Greek politicians. Its suppression by them, led to an explosion of outrage in Greece. Of course Greece would not lose over 5% of its GDP in evaded taxes, if it had Scandinavian tax transparency laws where tax returns are publicly available. The EU should have demanded tax-return transparency in return for providing the bailouts in these countries. It would have helped to avoid many of the devastating austerity measures imposed on the poor, to pay for the crisis.

In a display of how the EU's collective pooling of democratic sovereignty can occasionally take on the corporate state, where individual nations like the UK cannot, the EU recently developed and passed the European Savings Tax Directive which seeks to tackle tax avoidance. The corporate state, through its grip on a number of EU national governments, sought to undermine its closure of some significant tax loopholes.

In particular Germany and Britain sought to undermine the EU directive, by doing direct deals with Switzerland, which would have allowed cover to Luxembourg and Austria to veto the EU legislation. Some commentators said that wealthy Germans who had been using secret Swiss bank accounts had been exerting influence at the top of the German government. However, the dual deal was defeated in the German Parliament. The Social Democrats said the German deal would have made *"honest taxpayers feel like fools"*. However, the UK's deal with the Swiss banks and government became law in 2013 and unsurprisingly has again failed miserably to deliver the billions of recovered unpaid taxes promised by the UK government. The UK's political class has repeatedly sought to undermine democratic efforts to crack down on tax evasion across the EU, despite the best efforts of the elected officials of its 503 million citizens.

The fact that the EU's pooled democracy is one of the few brakes on corporate power in the UK, is a major unstated reason why the UK's media barons have waged an all-out propaganda war against it for over thirty years. This relentless propaganda is finally paying dividends, as the lies about Europe are now deeply embedded in the minds of many UK voters, leading to a frightening surge in support for the far-right UKIP party in the 2014 EU and local elections.

Whilst it is essential for the protection of workers' rights and environmental regulations in the UK that we defend the institutions of the EU and block TTIP, it is also crucial that the EU's institutions are made a no-go area for *The Prostitute State* and that it be cleaned out of the areas of the EU that it has already infected.

Chapter 12

The 21st Century Great Democratic Reform Act

So on a positive note what can we do to reclaim our democracy from *The Prostitute State* and get it working for the greater good rather than for the greater wealth of a tiny elite? How do we recover democratic control of our government, establish a fair taxation system, restore freedom to our media and liberate our academic systems from corporate capture and restore their rightful place as the proud pillars of our democratic state? How do we stop the apocalyptic destruction of our planet and ensure our common wealth benefits all of us and not just a tiny group of billionaires?

When I got asked to give that talk at the Tent City University, based on the steps of St Paul's Cathedral during the 2011 Occupy Demonstrations, I suddenly realised that having become more eco-responsible in how I lived my own life, I had almost by accident moved most of my own personal spending away from corporations.

Over 99% of my food is now corporate supermarket free, coming from local farmers markets, a local organic community shop and an independent health food store. I bank with the eco-bank Triodos and the mutual Nationwide Building Society. I buy the Guardian and do not have Sky. I produce most of my own electricity and provide nearly all my own water. My heat comes from local untreated waste wood and logs. I buy and sell my green electricity from the small independent company Good Energy and nearly all my clothes come from a gay charity shop in Pimlico. My furniture was all pre-loved and my main modes of transport are bicycle and public transport. If out and about, I try and eat at independent cafes or restaurants. My plants for the garden come from a local community garden-farm or the charity Garden Organic. I have not become totally free of corporations but have managed to move a very significant chunk of my spending away from them.

So, instead of all my money going to the corporate state for it to fund lobbying for legislation that goes against my interests or beliefs or to enrich tax-dodging billionaires, more of my money is used to support the kind of world I want to live in – ecologically and socially just and community friendly.

Chapter 12

Leading by example is essential, because we cannot be effective advocates for ending the corporate state, if we ourselves are not free from its tentacles. Otherwise we will end up like the Lib Dems, who failed to deliver so many promises in government because they failed, in many ways, to run themselves in line with their principles prior to being in government. Just as greening our own lives is the first step in saving our ecosystems from destruction, so too freeing ourselves from the manacles of the corporate state is the first step to liberating our democracy from its enslavement by the super-rich. And then we have to take those processes out into our communities and political lives at a local, regional or national level.

Supporting organisations campaigning for the cleaning up of our politics like UK Uncut, Unlock Democracy, Corporate Europe Observatory, Transparency International, the Alliance for Lobbying Transparency, The Transition Movement and Spinwatch is another constructive action. As is joining whatever political or environmental movement your intuition draws you to, whether that is FOE, Greenpeace, The Green Party, the Occupy Movement, The Women's Institute, RSPB and so on. The positive solutions that society needs to make the corporate state history will be myriad and creative once people know and understand the urgent need for it. Regulation, transparency and accountability are key requirements. But it is worth examining some potential solutions.

Lobbying is actually a valuable pillar of a democratic state and a constructive legal framework has to be developed for it. The same types of separation of powers, transparency and regulation need to be put in place as exist for the other pillars of our democracy. For lobbying to work effectively and fairly for the common good, the roles of lobbyist and politician must be legally separated. Members of the legislature should not work for, own or be paid directly or indirectly by any professional lobbying companies. Neither should they become paid parliamentary advisers or corporate directors after election. Prime Ministers, MEPs, MPs, Members of the Lords, civil servants, army and police officers should be banned for life from working as professional corporate lobbyists. Professional political lobbyists or in-house corporate lobbyists should be barred from active participation in policy decisions or the holding of office in our political parties. Just as senior council officers and civil servants are politically restricted in the interests of transparency, so must political lobbyists.

An independent Office of Fair Access should be established by parliament, to oversee and ensure fair access for civil society, to openly lobby government ministers and civil servants for any potential ministerial, regulatory, civil service or legislative actions proposed. Never again should a major government decision such as the purchase of BSkyB by Rupert Murdoch be subject to such a skewed level of access between the two sides of that debate, with thousands of contacts between the government and News International and almost none with the media coalition opposing the deal.

Lobbying also needs to be made fully transparent. Notes of all government meetings with lobbyists should be placed on the web. A statutory code of conduct for lobbyists should be passed by Parliament. Any casual meetings/phone calls/emails between Ministers and corporate lobbyists need to be a matter of public record. It should become an offence for ministers or their employees to have any unrecorded/unreported meetings or communications with corporate lobbyists. Juries and judges are not allowed to meet secretly with defendants outside the courtroom; the same standards should apply to politicians making far bigger decisions on society's behalf. Political lobbying is too important a part of our democracy to be tainted with even the perception of secret or publicly known conflicts of interests.

In addition to lobbying reform, the role of government minister needs radical reform. Current practice is very similar to that of a senior administrator in a monarchical system, who just so happens to have been appointed by an elected Prime Minister rather than a monarch. Ministers have too much unaccountable power, unlike the judiciary which is carefully regulated by statute on how its decisions are reached. This is insane, as the decisions made by a minister can affect millions more people and involve billions more pounds than a simple car-theft trial, which has carefully set out procedures with proper checks and balances to ensure a fair trial.

A greater amount of major ministerial decision-making needs to be quasi-judicial, with formalised requirements set out for fairness, transparency and the rights of the different players to have their say. The evidence base for major decisions should be exposed to equal public scrutiny and questioning as it is for a trial, prior to a ministerial decision being made. This judicialisation of major decision-making in government will help establish a fairer democracy.

It is essential for MPs and Peers to be banned from voting on legislation that they personally directly or indirectly have a significant vested financial interest in, just as currently rightly applies to local councillors. The Commissioner for Parliamentary Standards should no longer be appointed or fired by the MPs whom they are supposed to oversee but rather by an independent appointment system via a trusted outside body such as the Supreme Court.

The iron grip that the corporate state exerts on political parties through political donations has to be broken. Political parties are essential for a healthy democracy. They are the means by which sets of values and policies can be democratically agreed so that people can vote with some idea of which direction the country could take after the elections. But, as long as they are funded by the corporate state, they will be hijacked by it and voters will sense no matter whom they vote for, their interests will be frequently ignored.

Three simple steps could free our political parties from their paymasters. Despite the propaganda waged against it by the tabloids, the modest amount required for the state funding of political parties is essential for a fair playing field. The media barons want to persuade voters that it is an appalling idea because they know such funding will free political parties from billionaire control. A simple system of allocating for example £10 from the Treasury per vote (equivalent of £2 per year) in a general election to the party or independent candidate could be introduced, which would move the power for party funding from the billionaires to the voters. Making such a small investment (about £92 million per year based on 46 million voters in UK) in our political parties is a no-brainer, as it could literally help save billions spent on corporate welfare or lost to tax-havens.

Secondly, an annual limit on maximum donations of £1,000 should be introduced. Finally, the parties themselves should introduce an elected official tithe of 10%, whereby any individual elected to paid public office on behalf of the party would sign a promise prior to the election, to allocate 10% of their elected office salaries to their political party.

Trade unions would still be legally entitled to collect a political levy on behalf of political parties but would have to allow members to tick a box as to which party they wanted the political levy to be paid to. These reforms would eliminate the corrupt funding of parties by the tax-haven nexus, destroy the ability of the ultra-rich to buy seats in the Lords and reduce considerably the corrupt "cash for access" to our political leaders, through the various leadership fundraising events. The nepotistic process of appointments to the Lords by the three main party leaders needs to be ended. Whilst waiting for democratic reform to the Lords, the parties should immediately introduce internal elections for the posts. It is intolerable that such a medieval system of patronage still exists in our 21st-century parliament. Parliament should represent the democratic state and not the corporate state.

A free press is one of the most fundamental pillars of a democracy. It is not known as The Fourth Estate for nothing and as such needs to be protected from corruption and monopolisation by any one section of society. Ending the media-billionaire domination by Murdoch, Desmond, the Barclay brothers and Lord Rothermere is the single most urgent action required to reclaim our democracy. Satish Kumar, editor of Resurgence/Ecologist Magazine believes the ideal media ownership model would be various forms of not-for-profit or employee-ownership models, such as the John Lewis Partnership. For-profit corporations and individual billionaires should not be allowed to own significant percentages of any media market. Any corporation or individual with bank accounts or trusts in tax-havens should be banned from UK media ownership. As the media serves a crucial role and has enormous power in our democracy, the media companies are not normal businesses and so their owners must be domiciled in the UK.

Experience has shown that self-regulation almost never works. Some form of independent oversight is always needed. This is also absolutely true of the press. In the UK, press self-regulation consisted basically of self-regulation by the clutch of media-billionaire-appointed editors. This supposed self-regulation resulted in the type of blackmailing and corrupt practices evidenced in the News of the World phone-hacking scandal and in the far more serious treasonous abuse of political power by the media barons, as evidenced in the Leveson Inquiry. We have to put an end to foreign-based media billionaires dictating UK government policy on war, fossil fuel subsidies, the welfare state, environmental regulations, membership of the European Union and so on.

But press regulation backed by statute runs the opposite risk of putting the power to abuse in the hands of the politicians, whom a free press is required to hold to account. Due to this obvious conflict of interest, politicians cannot be in charge of press regulation. The creation and protection of a genuinely free press undoubtedly is a complex challenge. But the fact that it is challenging to develop regulatory structures that maintain genuine press freedoms, but which still hold them to account for abuses of the enormous power that they wield, does not mean that it is impossible. Indeed, that is exactly the situation that society has constructively solved for an independent judiciary.

Finland's press, which is rated as being the freest in the world according to the 2013 Press Freedom Index, has an independent statutory-based press-regulatory system. Despite the propaganda by the tabloids about such regulation being a threat to our democracy, independent regulation is essential for the press to carry out its core function as a pillar of our democracy.

The European Initiative for Media Pluralism already has the backing of many EU trade unions and civil society groups but you will not read about it in the Daily Mail or The Sun. It calls on the EU Commission to pass legislation containing:

- Effective barriers to prevent concentration of ownership in the media and advertisement sectors.
- Guaranteed independence of media regulatory bodies, with a politically, culturally and socially diverse membership.
- A definition of conflict of interests with media ownership.
- Requirements for broadcast, print and online media to submit to a national media authority and sufficient ownership information to allow identification of the beneficial and ultimate owners of media outlets.

Chapter 12

Of course, such a definition of unacceptable conflicts of interests would need an independent regulator with the power to enforce the code of practice. Likewise the rights of journalists to join a trade union should be upheld in European law. It is no accident that News International and The Daily Mail Group's journalists are denied the right by their owners to be represented by the National Union of Journalists.

In addition, the corporate state has to be stopped from using the UK's libel laws to suppress free speech and restrict the freedom of journalists to expose its corruption and cover up its wealth grab. Throughout my political career, I was constantly being threatened with libel suits for standing up for my political beliefs. These included the various legal threats I received from Charles Kennedy over individuals connected with party funding, political lobbying and tax-havens and the party's censorship of my election address over its mention of RTZ. As a councillor I was even threatened by Southwark Council with a £32 million lawsuit for writing an article criticising the council for proposing to incinerate all the council's waste instead of recycling it. As I was not wealthy, every time I stood up to such threats, I had to acknowledge that they could destroy me financially if they took me to court. Even if I won, the legal fees would have bankrupted me.

Every time I was threatened, I felt confident enough in the truth and legality of what I had written that I did not back down and thankfully no action was ever taken. It was, however, a bit stressful to deal with. Many people simply will not take such risks and thus so much wrongdoing never gets reported, to the detriment of us all. The libel laws should protect genuine journalism and the newspapers from unfair punitive damages, whilst still ensuring individual reputations can be fairly protected. A right to correction, removal of offending articles or reply of equal prominence to articles found to be libellous, could be overseen by an independent regulator and would be more beneficial to society than recourse to expensive legal proceedings and punitive fines, which currently are a major suppressor of press freedom.

The link between tax-havens and our political parties need to be broken. The malign financial tax-haven colonial empire which replaced Britain's former geographical empire, now needs to have the sun set on it also. Britain's rightful place in the world is as a beacon for liberal democracy not as a tax-thieving oligarchy. Nobody who is a director of a tax-haven based company or who has or benefits from offshore bank accounts or trusts should be allowed to hold office in a political party or government. Donations from such individuals should be banned. A ban on being a director or shareholder of a tax-haven based corporation needs to be introduced for MPs and the Lords.

Cutting the umbilical cord between our politicians and the tax-haven robbers will enable parliament to tackle the wholesale theft of public taxation via tax-havens. Britain must urgently close down its global network of tax-haven jurisdictions. All of these obscure legal hangover oddities from our days of empire, such as the Cayman Islands, Gibraltar, the Channel Islands, the British Virgin Islands, The Isle of Man and so on, need to have their relationships with the UK legislatively reformed and regularised. There really needs to be zero tolerance for this wholesale theft of legitimately due taxes by the rich, in all such British jurisdictions.

Whilst it may provoke outrage from millions of the self-employed, one key to ending the tax-haven culture for the rich would be the introduction of full transparency into individual and corporate tax returns. It is no accident that some of the countries with the best quality of life and the most equal societies such as Finland, Denmark and Sweden, also require the publishing of all tax returns. It is only when the rich have to reveal their full earnings and taxes that they will stop the secretive funnelling offshore of their wealth. It will encourage a greater climate of social justice and responsibility. As Polly Toynbee put it in the Guardian: "*The boss of Nokia, pop stars and politicians face annual embarrassment as the press explores their returns. Transparency underpins a culture of social justice and civic duty*".

If getting rid of the media barons is the most important step required to reclaim our democracy, closing the tax-havens is the most important step to halt the hijacking of our communal wealth by the ultra-rich. The UK must stop being a leading facilitator of the pillaging of developing countries' wealth by their dictators and corrupt politicians. We need a bonfire of offshore trust funds, blind trusts, secret accounts and all the rest of the elite's tax-stealing architecture. It is time to protect decent tax-paying businesses from the predatory private-equity sharks and vulture-capitalists. Bringing the offshore funds back to Britain will restore the finances needed to provide essential public services for the vulnerable and eliminate many unnecessary austerity measures.

We need to absolutely guarantee that the education and research upon which our democracy is built is free from corporate manipulation. A liberal well-educated critically-trained citizenry is an essential ingredient for a thriving democracy. We need to clear the lobbyists and money men out of our halls of learning. Universities, colleges and schools must not be run for profit or controlled by corporate interests. Published research must be free from even the suspicion of corruption. It should be accompanied by a declaration of who directly or indirectly funded the research and the researcher's university department. Professors must not be dependent on corporate funding. Additional independent pharmaceutical research for example could be funded by a levy on pharmaceutical corporation turnover. This would help address the current distortion in research which is biased towards those medicines which will be most profitable, such as for obesity and heart disease rather than for antibiotics and third-world diseases.

Chapter 12

Standards of academic transparency and independence need to be overseen by an independent standards board, to which whistle-blowers or critics of potentially biased published research can take their concerns. Ideally, journalists would report whether any research quoted in the press had the stamp of independence from this standards board. No longer should corporations be able to invisibly use biased academics to confuse the public as to the veracity of the science on issues such as genetically modified foods, pesticides, climate science or smoking.

Whilst smaller in scale, the growing number of think tanks is another important pillar of our democracy, valuable hotbeds of democratic debate and a cauldron of ideas. Their research and proposals are widely covered in the press and read by government policy-makers. Therefore they need to be subject to the same standards of fairness, accountability and transparency as all the other pillars. All funding of think-tanks should by law be published on their websites. The end-donors must be made clear and if not, then such donations must be impermissible.

It should be standard journalistic practice for news coverage of think-tank reports funded by corporations, to include that information, so that the public can make up its mind about the independence of the information being fed to it. Our influential think-tanks should not be anonymous propaganda fronts for various corporations. Never again should an industry such as the fossil-fuel or tobacco industry be allowed to use our think-tanks as a smokescreen for destructive propaganda. Let's reclaim them for their true purpose of developing public policy that serves the democratic state rather than the corporate state.

The wildly spinning door, where public servants working in regulatory bodies are cherry picked by the corporations that they regulate, must be stopped. No more should GM food lobbyists swim back and forth between their global chemical corporations and the bodies supposed to oversee their products safety standards. The auditing and consultancy arms of the corporate auditing firms need to be separated, with the consultancy arms remaining in the for-profit sector. The costs of corporate financial audits could continue to be covered by auditing fees but the service would be provided by a new governmental National Corporate Financial Auditing Authority and not by compromised private monopolies. Judges do not and should not sell services to defendants and so it should be with auditors. As the Enron collapse demonstrated, the inherent conflict of interest in allowing a company's auditors to be also selling them consultancy services is unacceptable.

The core issue of how money is created needs to be addressed if we are to rebalance the distorted distribution of wealth that has become a stark reality in our society. Until recently the printing and production of money in the UK was primarily the role of the state via the UK's central bank, The Bank of England. This system worked reasonably well until financial deregulation and the arrival of computing. Suddenly the private banks which, are still unable to create paper money, were able to create electronic money and the state gave up its monopoly over the money supply. The New Economics Foundation explains that new money is now almost totally created by the commercial banks when they extend or create credit. This electronic money dwarfs the paper and coin money produced by the state which now makes up only 3% of the total money supply.

Control over all the ways that money is created must be returned to the democratic state via the Bank of England. It could then lend such money at zero interest to the state to fund the positive investments the country needs. The handing over of the State's money supply to the private banks to fund whatever they think best is nonsensical. It has resulted in the funding of not only the disastrous property bubble and the ruthless private equity sharks, but hundreds of billions of pounds continue to be lent for fossil-fuel developments which are lethal for the planet's ecosystems and so implicitly are destroying the future health of the economy. Meanwhile small businesses are being unfairly starved of loans. If the Bank of England channelled these billions via the Green Bank, for example, to the renewable energy and sustainable transport industries, that money would create employment and would circulate in the real economy.

The feudal monopolisation of UK land ownership needs tackling. The Scottish government is taking some tentative steps towards this with their land reform bills, aimed at the legacy of the brutal clearances. They are allowing communities to bid for control over the enormous private estates that were created. Land reform in England is centuries overdue. Local parish and borough councils could be required to buy open land in their communities for the purpose of community orchards/allotments. Likewise community groups could be given the right to buy land for the creation of genuine eco-villages on England's vast aristocratic and oligarchic country estates, with the permission of their local county councils. In addition a version of Henry George's proposed Land Valuation Tax would ensure developers contributed more towards the taxpayer-funded infrastructure investments that they make huge profits from. Commercial property cannot hide in the Cayman Islands.

An end to the corporate takeover of politics would allow legislation that would end the various multi-billion-pound corporate welfare schemes. The state must stop picking up the massive welfare bill resulting from corporations making huge profits on the backs of poverty wages to their staff. They must be forced to pay a living wage. The Big Four Supermarkets make over £2.4 billion extra profits per year, due to local governments paying for the disposal of the packaging waste they pour into local communities. They should be required to pay a Supermarket Waste Reduction Tax based on the amount of packaging they create and the costs to councils for its disposal. Very quickly market forces would slash the amount of wasteful packaging and returnable packaging would become economic. The council tax wasted on subsidising the disposal of supermarket-generated waste is desperately needed to fund local social services at a time of savage council cuts. The multi-billion-pound existing and proposed subsidies for the oil and gas-fracking industries should also be brought to an immediate end and invested in making poor people's homes zero carbon, simultaneously ending fuel poverty.

The right-wing press and politicians frequently talk about freedom when they are seeking to abolish state regulation, taxes and the welfare state. But surely the greatest freedom is to have choice over how we spend our lives and freedom from economic enslavement and poverty? In the 1950s, prior to women's liberation, the average married middle-class couple, between them, worked five days a week, for forty hours, for the money to provide for themselves. However, when women rightly won the right to be a normal part of the workforce, something inadvertently happened which suited *The Prostitute State* enormously. There were now two wages available to get a mortgage. Combined with the collapse in the building of council housing and the failure of the private sector to substantially increase the building of new homes other than profitable executive homes, the price of housing soared through the roof. So it was the banks, through increased mortgage costs, who grabbed most of a couple's second income, an income that women had fought so hard to gain.

So now we have the ludicrous situation where the vast majority of married couples have to work ten days per week between them to pay their way, despite the average family size now being far lower. That is a staggering 100% increase in the hours worked by many couples in just fifty years. Of course, this happened gradually and almost invisibly over time but can you imagine the uproar that quite rightly would have happened in the 1960s, if the government had announced a doubling of the family working week?

To add insult to injury, the bankers laughed all the way from their banks to their retirement palaces and yachts, with literally billions of pounds in hijacked bonuses. Ideally and on a voluntary basis, what we need to aim for are people working an average three-day week. Even then, it would represent a 20% rise in the combined average working week for many couples, compared to the 1950s. Like bankers' bonuses, house prices in the UK are artificially inflated. We need to find ways for the property market to go through a correction like it did in Ireland but without placing undue hardship on those affected.

Land ownership, land taxation and the production of electronic money all need to be reformed to ensure home ownership is again affordable and not subject to repeated bank-created property bubbles. Otherwise another generation will be enslaved against their will to the banks or become permanent asset-less renters chained to private landlords. We need to reclaim those four days per couple per week back from the corporate state. Working an average of three days a week for money per person, would allow us to contribute a day a week of voluntary work for our local communities and the remaining three days for quality time for ourselves, our families and our friends. Politics should not be about that depressing meme *"hard-working families"* but rather about how we can ensure they do not have to be *"hard-working"* in the first place but rather have a healthy work/life balance and how can we create a positive quality of life for everybody, not just the 1%.

But to achieve all of the above will require an urgent UK democratic constitutional revolution. Civic Society, from the National Trust to Trade Unions, from churches to credit unions, from universities to community associations, need to call for a *21st Century Great Democratic Reform Act*, just as it did in the 19th century, when popular pressure from the people overcame the bloated aristocracy through the Reform Acts. Its core provisions would ban politicians from becoming lobbyists and free political funding from billionaires and corporate domination. It would reform The Fourth Estate's ownership structures, to ensure our media represents the interests of all of society, academia would be liberated from corporate manipulation and the tax-havens closed. It would introduce a proportional voting system that returned real power to the voters from the billionaire tabloid owners.

Once that is in place our newly liberated democratic government would need to tackle urgently the environmental catastrophes that the corporate machine is creating. It would immediately make all investments in new fossil fuel exploration and development illegal and would abolish all the massive state fossil-fuel subsidies. A new Energy Efficiency Bill would make it a civil offence for businesses to negligently waste energy. Inefficient electrical goods and heating products would be banned. A moratorium would be placed on road-network and airport expansion and the construction of a segregated National Cycling Network would be made the top national transport priority instead. A national programme to bring all housing up to zero carbon standards would be launched as quickly as possible.

We have no time to lose. The global environmental catastrophes and the destruction of social justice are in danger of overwhelming us if we do not act immediately. And when we do act, make no mistake, the billionaire media, the primary pillar of the corporate state, may seek to destroy such a movement. This is why, above all others, this should be our first and most important target. With unity we can and we must cleanse the soiled temples of our democracy and restore them to their true purpose of safeguarding our social and environmental justice.

There is one final tool that will definitely need to be employed, if we are to effect the changes needed at the speed required. This is non-violent direct action.

Gandhi seized the moment by using civil disobedience to symbolically challenge the British Empire's Salt Tax and employed the powerful force of peaceful direct action across India, which helped defeat an empire. The Balcombe anti-fracking protests of the summer of 2013 were an inspiring example of how a determined brave group of peaceful non-violent direct-action activists, in the face of significant police brutality on behalf of the corporate interests at stake, can force the corruption of *The Prostitute State* into the open and force the national media to pay attention.

Similarly the peaceful protests by the non-violent direct-action group Stop Killing Cyclists, which began after a horrific series of six cyclists being killed in London in November 2013, have started to change the media treatment of such deaths and the responses from the traffic planners for the better. Having been the co-organiser of them with Steve Routley, has brought home to me how powerfully positive a tool direct action can be, when all other legitimate avenues have been exhausted. The first targets for such direct-actions ideally would be the media billionaires and their empires.

Having related some of the challenging personal battles that I experienced whilst in the Liberal Democrats, I would like to finish with a positive example of how, working with others, we managed a victory over *The Prostitute State*. Whilst acknowledging its immense power and reach, it is crucial that we realise that despite the odds, it has been frequently beaten by ordinary people working together persistently. It is powerful but not all-powerful.

Two months prior to the 2003 historic anti-war march in London, when nearly two million people thronged London's streets protesting against the impending war, James Graham and Susan Kramer had successfully proposed at the Lib Dems Federal Executive meeting that the party should officially participate in the Peace March. As the party's Deputy Chair, I contacted Hugh Rickard, the party's then chief executive, the following day to organise the decision's implementation, only to be told the instructions could not be implemented because the leadership had changed their minds.

Constitutionally, Charles Kennedy could only overrule an FE decision by requesting an emergency meeting to rescind it. He called no such meeting, so I decided as a senior officer to implement the decision. Along with other volunteers we set about organising the party's presence on the march, despite access to the party machinery being denied to us by the leadership. As the party's newspaper and email lists were barred to us, we asked the Euro-candidates to allow us to include details about the party's participation in the Peace March in their candidate-mailings to members. We set up a special website, as we could not get any coverage on the party's own website. Liberal Democrat Youth & Students produced thousands of placards saying *"Lib Dems Say No"*. We raised donations independently. For two months my back bedroom became the de-facto Liberal Democrat campaigns HQ, as a flood of emails from members across the country poured into my PC.

Ten days before the march, as Deputy Chair, I wrote a letter to the Guardian stating the party's support for the march and where the party was officially meeting on the day of the march. The next day, the Guardian picked up the substance of my letter in its editorial and demanded to know if Kennedy was going. Then David Frost, in a live TV interview the following day, confronted Kennedy with the editorial and demanded to know if he was going. He finally caved in and said yes. He then allowed the campaigns director Chris Rennard to meet me on the last Tuesday before the march. They demanded that the placard slogan be changed from "*Lib Dems Say No*" to "*Give Peace a Chance*". I said it was too late as the placards had already been printed but they printed half a dozen with their weaker slogan anyway.

On the morning of the march, an extraordinary sight unfolded in front of us at the Southbank Plaza assembly point. Thousands of party members from all over Britain had responded to the call and the Southbank was a sea of yellow. Young and old, pregnant and disabled, they all turned up. It was the largest meeting ever of the party's membership. They were excited that, alone of the major parties, they were standing up against Blair and Murdoch's march to war. The sea of "*Lib Dems Say No*" placards drowned the tiny number of "*Give Peace a Chance*" placards that the leadership had printed to prevent Kennedy being photographed with our slogan. However, he could not avoid being photographed again and again with it and he was not happy about it. I will never forget the look of fury on Kennedy's Chair of Campaigns Lord Razzall's face when he saw what we had done, despite the campaign's department having been banned from helping us up to the last moment.

Whilst Kennedy had reaped wall to wall media coverage for his presence on the march, the unpalatable truth was that Kennedy did not want to campaign against the war. He hoped to sit on the fence and let the UN decide, hence the insistence on the change of slogan for the banners to "*Give Peace a Chance*". He wanted the wiggle room to be able to say if the UN approved the war, that we had given peace a chance but were now backing the war. But I was determined to brand him as being anti-war that day, so that he would have no option but to vote no when parliament eventually voted. And I wanted him to lead a campaign in the country to oppose the race to war. But that too, tragically for the potential success of the anti-Iraq War Movement, was something he categorically did not want to do and refused to do.

At the first meeting of the FE immediately following the march, instead of celebrating one of the most successful events in the party's history, the leadership finally announced the setting up of a committee to oversee the members' opposition to the war but I was to be specifically excluded from it. They also announced that nothing could be organised without the permission of this committee. The FE agreed to my exclusion but baulked at banning all party actions against the war. That committee subsequently did not organise a single event to oppose the war. But, independently, we successfully organised media event after media event with party members, relentlessly getting across the message that the party opposed the war.

Kennedy was furious and over the following year made my life impossible. He repeatedly tabled motions of personal censure against me at the Federal Executive. He repeatedly sabre-rattled about libel actions due to my efforts to introduce equal opportunity procedures, clean up the corruption of Lib Dem peers working as corporate lobbyists and dealing with the stench that existed around party's funding and Lords appointments. The FE, to its credit, rejected all of Kennedy's motions of censure against me.

But seeing the party's MPs subsequently vote unanimously against the Iraq war at the crucial parliamentary vote, made all we had gone through worthwhile, even if we had failed to help with the wider objective of actually winning the vote. The end of my minor political career was a small price to pay. But, the real tragedy was the refusal of Kennedy to lead, even after we had engineered a leading role in the leadership of the anti-war movement for him, thanks to the generosity of the Stop the War Coalition. He point blank refused to help build on the massive momentum built up by the Peace March. This meant that this momentum was crucially unable to build to such an extent as to enable Clare Short to follow Robin Cook in defecting from Blair's cabinet of yes-men and with her, the Labour MPs needed to defeat the war motion in Parliament.

However, our successful bottom-up organisation of the party's participation in the Peace March showed what an empowered party membership could achieve, despite the corporate machine's grip on the party leadership and the billionaire media's support for the war. It is my view that the precedent set by the Lib Dems in voting against the Iraq War and the extraordinary movement built by the heroes in the Stop the War Coalition, whilst unsuccessful then, were crucial in laying the groundwork for the unprecedented historic defeat for the government in 2013, when the establishment were again seeking to start another war against Syria.

Ordinary people can and frequently do defeat *The Prostitute State*. With knowledge, commitment and unified collective action it can be defeated. Indeed it must be defeated if the twin goals of a fairer economy and a future for humanity is to be achieved. The alternative is of an increasingly small global oligarchy presiding over the vast majority of humanity's wealth and the wholesale destruction of our planet's eco-systems, jeopardising a decent future for our grandchildren and their successors.

The catastrophic summer Arctic Ice melt that occurred whilst this book was being written indicates that we are fast running out of time, if it is not already too late, with NASA scientists announcing in May 2014 that the entire Western Antarctic Ice-cap was now in irreversible meltdown!

Each and every one of us can take direct action in our own lives and in the lives of our wider communities to wrest control back from The Prostitute State. Please don't just read this book. Let us heed the simple exhortation from Mahatma Gandhi calling on us *"to be the change we wish to see in the world"*. Stop supporting the media barons. Change your bank account. Wean yourself off your destructive consumer and fossil-fuel addictions. Spend your money with local and planet-friendly companies. Avoid funding corporations and their lobbyists. Eat organic and locally produced food. Taking steps in this direction may be easier than you first imagined. And then urge your friends, work colleagues and community to do the same and finally gird your courage for the historic mass peaceful non-violent direct actions that will inevitably be needed for our democratic counter-corporate revolution to succeed in time.

All corporate power comes from us, the consumers and voters. By taking back our own power, we can put in place the building stones for a genuine democracy, a fairer economy, healthier communities and a beautiful, protected and loved environment.

Yes We Can! And Yes We Must!

Bibliography:

The Prostitute State

Climate Cover-Up - James Hoggan/Richard Littlemore, Greystone Books 2009

Lobbying: The Art of Political Persuasion – Lionel Zetter, Harriman House 2008

Private Empire: Exxon Mobile and American Power – Steve Coll, Allen Lane 2012

People, Politics and Pressure Groups - Arthur Butler, Picnic Publishing 2010

Treasure Islands – Nicholas Shaxson, The Bodley Head 2011

Outsider in the House – Bernie Sanders, Verso 1997

Twilight of the Elites – Christopher Hayes, Crown 2012

Universities in the Marketplace – Derek Bok, Princeton University Press 2003

Dial M for Murdoch – Tom Watson & Martin Hickman, Allen Lane 2012

Deadly Spin – Wendell Potter, Bloomsbury Press 2010

Blair's Wars - John Kampfner, Free Press 2003

Where Power Lies - Lance Price, Simon & Schuster 2010

The Burden of Power – Alastair Campbell, Hutchinson 2012

A Blueprint for a Safer Planet - Nicholas Stern, The Bodley Head 2009

Boiling Point – Ross Gelbspan, Basic Books 2004

Ground Control – Anna Minton, Penguin 2012